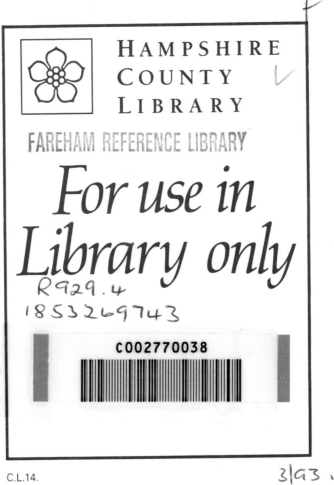

A Dictionary
of

TRADITIONAL FIRST NAMES

A Dictionary
—of—

TRADITIONAL FIRST NAMES

by
Eric Partridge

Wordsworth Editions

This edition published 1992 by Wordsworth Editions Ltd,
8b East Street, Ware, Hertfordshire.

ISBN 1-85326-974-3

Printed and bound in Great Britain by Mackays of Chatham.

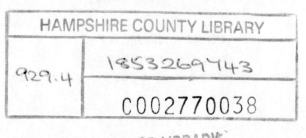

TO

CARLILE NORRIS

WITH DEEP RESPECT

AND, IF ANYTHING, DEEPER AFFECTION

AUTHOR'S NOTE

FIRST published in 1936, on the invitation of the late E. V. Lucas, this book bears the title he suggested; he resisted my counter-proposal that it should be called *The Nameless Child.*

Not unfittingly, most of the work in this field – dictionaries and studies of given or Christian names – has been done by women, beginning with Charlotte Yonge's great piece of pioneering, *A History of Christian Names*, 1863, revised and enlarged in 1884; Helena Swan's *Christian Names*, 1905; Flora Loughead's *Given Names*, an American publication (full though terse) of the middle 1930's; and E. G. Withycombe's excellent *The Oxford Dictionary of English Christian Names*, in the middle 1940's. The most readable account – fundamentally a very scholarly account—of given names is Professor Ernest Weekley's *Jack and Jill: A Study of Our Christian Names*, 1939, revised edition in 1948; and this might be supplemented by the introductory essay in Miss Withycombe's book.

My own aim has been less serious, hence – ostensibly – less scholarly, than Miss Loughead's and Miss Withycombe's: as the title-page fairly and honestly states, my aim is to present to the general, rather than to the learned, public 'a dictionary of given names'. This little book is admittedly based upon the erudite Charlotte Yonge's; I have been much less eager than a certain scholar to upset all her etymologies. Her Classical and Romance etymologies are mostly correct. In the Teutonic etymologies, she sometimes said 'German' when 'Scandinavian' (especially 'Norse') would have been more accurate, or 'Gothic' for 'Frisian', and so forth, but she did at least keep the fault within the family – the Common Teutonic sub-family of languages. (*Odium scholasticum* can be a very unkindly, disproportionate business!)

My attitude towards given or Christian names, the reader may have gathered, is not wholly academic; it is, moreover, tolerably up to date; the reader or consulter will find *Hank* no less than *Henry*, *Washington* no less than *William*, *Avril* no less than *Alicia.*

CONTENTS

INTRODUCTION

A NOTE ON GIVEN OR CHRISTIAN[1] NAMES

'A Rose by any other name would sound less sweet.'

ANON. 20TH CENTURY SCHOLIAST

I. Introductory

THERE are two reasons why this should be a mere note, brief and perhaps rambling; not a full-blown introduction.

The first is that the general reader does not need, nor does he desire, an introduction that, if it is to be adequate, must necessarily be lengthy. For him, the name's the thing.

The second: that the learned, still more the alarmingly erudite, man and woman desiderate no such introduction, for he or she has only to consult (if, by some odd chance, he does not already know) Charlotte Yonge's wholly admirable *History of Christian Names,* fascinating in text and texture and very comprehensive in the terse glossary preceding the history proper. Moreover, both for the learned and the general reader, there is much interesting, informative and witty matter in Professor Ernest Weekley's *Jack and Jill* and in his other essays on the English language, especially in *The Romance of Names* and in *Words and Names.*

Therefore, being sincere in my protestations and not, I believe, enslaved by laziness (one of the few faults of which I have not, so far, been accused), I shall content myself with setting down, very briefly, a few casual remarks on a few selected aspects of a subject of almost innumerable, almost limitless ramifications: such remarks as, though eminently unsatisfactory, are yet (I trust) tolerably clear and commendably devoid of profundity.

* * * * *

[1] In 'Christian name', *Christian* is probably folk etymology for *christened*; i.e., used at a christening.

2. *General*

It has been suggested that names exercise a great influence on those who bear them. That this was true in primitive times cannot be denied: for, to strangers, many surnames and font-names conveyed a description or a useful hint. As then, so now, the influence is mainly adverse, and, which is worse, infelicitous names affect the sensitive, who should be spared these unnecessary handicaps, far more than they do the insensitive.

Names like *Christopher* and *Julian* should induce the most enviable qualities. But do they? To strain for what is beyond us generally results in leaving us inferior to what we should have been without that effort. But names that, by their length or their sound (or both), excite derision; names that, intrinsically, invite puns; names that are too ambitious in their associations; names that, whether pronounced in full or as initials, are, in combination, sheer cruelty to their bearers: such names as *Algernon* and *Ermentrude* – *Sally* – *Caesar* and *Virgil* and *Napoleon* – and those forming the initials *W.C.*[1]: – all these should be avoided by parents loving, or having the slightest regard for, their children. For in such names and collocations, we are reminded of the old Roman tag, *numen et nomen,*[2] which may, in this particular connexion, be rendered, 'the divinity that, by the majesty of its name, rough-hews our ends'. Moreover, the proper reference of

[1] Especially if the surname be *Bowles* or *Drane.* Also, note such initials of font-names as *E.D.* or of font-names plus surname as *E.L.C.*—when the victim is a boy.

[2] *Numen et nomen,* 'essence and name,' may, philosophically, be translated as 'essence and manifestation'. An early Egyptian text (see E. A. Wallis Budge, *From Fetish to God in Ancient Egypt,* p. 266) shows the origin of the idea: there, 'heart-thought' is our *numen,* whereas the 'tongue-utterance' thereof is *nomen.* In the Scriptural 'the Word is God', the Latin for 'Word' is *verbum,* the Greek is *Λόγος* (Logos). The tabu mentioned springs from the primitive notion of the name equalling the potence or reality of the God, person, or thing. (Thanks to my friend Mr Jack Lindsay, whose knowledge of the Classics renders me almost envious.)

that tag is to the tabu imposed against attaching divine names to mortals, for, precisely as the God is sacred, so is his name; hence *Jehovah*, an evasion of *Jahweh*, has not become a Christian name, and only in the Near East and in Spanish South America has *Jesus* been made one. True; those are extreme cases; but at the present day we go further – we fight shy of *Caesar*, *Augustus*, and the like.

3. *Origins*

Charlotte Yonge's dictum that 'the history, the religion, and the character of a nation [are] stamped upon the individuals in the names which they bear' is, in essence, true, but we must remember that it is true only for the educated. She kept that fact in mind when she wrote her *History of Christian Names*. (So has the present writer in this dictionary.) With that purpose in view, she gave considerable space to the etymology of Christian names, and her remarks on their origin can hardly be bettered. These names arose –

'First, from some circumstance connected with the birth, such as Esau, hairy; Jacob, taken by the heel. . . .

'Secondly, from the complexion, *e.g.* . . . Don, brown; . . . Blanche, fair.

'Thirdly, from the qualities desired for the child, such as David, meaning beloved; the Persian Aspamitas and Greek Philippos, both lovers of horses; . . . the Teutonic Eadgifu, happy gift [cf. our Edith] . . .

'Fourthly, from an animal, Deborah, the bee; Jonah . . .

'Fifthly, from a weapon, as the Teuton Gar, a spear. [Cf. our Garth, Gerald, Gertrude.]

'Sixthly, from a jewel . . . ; the Greek, Margarite, a pearl . . .

'Seventhly, religious names, dedicating the child to the Divinity, such as Ishmael, heard of God; Elijah, God the Lord; and among idolaters, . . . Brighid, the Irish goddess of smiths and poets . . .

'To these we may add a few names of flowers,[1] chiefly borne by women, . . . such as Susanna, Lilias, Rhoda, Rose . . .

'Also a few indicating a time of deep sorrow and distress when the child was born, such as . . . Jabez, sorrow, . . . Una, famine . . . and Dolores . . .

'Natural defects have likewise furnished names, such as . . . the Irish Dorenn, the sullen.'[2]

At this point, however, it is well to note that, for the most part, Christian names have, in all countries and at all times except the earliest, been bestowed with no reference to the meaning of those names; and even in the earliest times, a name was often adopted blindly from another language. When *Alfred* became an Anglo-Saxon name, it probably did so without conscious allusion to its dithematic meaning. Moreover, we must remember that Teutonic dithematic (or compound) names, as occasionally monothematic (or single-element) names whether Teutonic or other, were frequently apprehended as mere counters, and that, in the former, the early bearers thought of two distinct elements (e.g., in *Alfred*, 'elf' and 'counsel'), not of one idea (e.g., 'crafty counsellor'). This psychological factor should be kept in mind by such scholars as may persuade themselves that I have, unconsciously, been guilty of over-simplification in my etymologies of dithematic names: it is merely that I have consistently used the convention implicit in explaining *Alfred* as 'elf-counsel' in preference to that implicit in 'elf' + 'counsel': the determination and distinction of names according to the latter convention is not only arbitrary and personal

[1] Cf. the so-called harvest-names and such names as *Sylvanus*.

[2] This classification is tolerably complete, yet it admits of several gaps, of which the most important consists in such names as, originally endearments or pet-names formed from already recognized Christian names, have, from being derivative and considered derivative, become independent font-names. Moreover, Mats Redin has remarked, 'It often happens that the hypocoristic [i.e., pet] name supersedes the real name, and also that later on it passes over to other individuals as a proper (Christian) name': e.g., *Essie* (from *Esther*) and *May* (from *Mary*).

but somewhat too erudite[1] for so unambitious a dictionary as this.

To speak of sources as distinct from origins, and of influences and fashions as distinct from both origins and sources, is perhaps to split hairs. Sources, origins, influences or fashions are so inextricably mingled that to be logical is, sometimes, to be absurd. And yet I shall ask the reader to tolerate the ensuing dichotomy of sources and influences.

4. *Sources*

The operation of the sources on Christian names is more fundamental and, in general, more extensive than is that of the influences and fashions.

The old Anglo-Saxon names have survived, especially in the rural districts; many are ultimately of Common Teutonic origin. So, too, the old Celtic, notably in Ireland (Erse), in Scotland (Gaelic), in Wales (Cymric). But Anglo-Saxon[2] and Celtic were soon to receive a considerable admixture of Latin: many Roman names derived from Greek, many Greek names were nothing but transliterations of Persian and, far more importantly, Hebrew: the influence of Latin was reinforced by that of the principal Romance languages (Italian, Spanish, French) – chiefly French, though 'French names are nearly all of German origin, the Celtic names and the Latin names which encroached on them having been swept away by the Frankish invasion, a parallel to the wholesale adoption of Norman names in England'.[3] In short, one source merges with another; parallels converge; doublets arise. The English language has been a melting pot, and in it Christian names have either seethed and solidified, or bubbled and vanished.

[1] Some of these questions are admirably treated in the Introduction to Mats Redin, *Uncompounded Personal Names in Old English*, 1919 at Upsala – whence come so many able and learned theses and treatises on the English language.

[2] Now usually called Old English.

[3] Weekley, *The Romance of Names*.

Take Hebrew. When the Jews returned from captivity in Babylon, they spoke Aramaic. 'They still called their children by mangled and contracted Hebraisms . . . but were in general not aware of their meaning, and were willing to give them Greek terminations to suit the literary taste of the East. . . . Yet it is these corrupted Hebrew names, marred by Aramean pronunciation, by Greek writing, and by the speech of every country, that are the most universally loved and honoured in every land. . . . Religion has . . . been the primary guide to individual nomenclature, and next in order must be ranked the family feeling that renders Christian names almost hereditary' (Yonge).

Religion has been thus instrumental largely because Christianity was filtered through Greek. More than that, 'Greek may be said to have never died, and it has, from first to last, been the most vigorous of all languages in creating and spreading names . . . Hellas, though frequently conquered, has by its glorious literature, both pagan and Christian, gained wide dominion for its language.' As for Latin, the same authority continues to say that, all in all, it is not 'so much the names actually borne by ancient Romans, as appellations formed out of the Latin language, that have been the Latin contribution to Christian nomenclature'. The Latin nomenclature was of the most prosaic kind, but the richness, the attractiveness and the vigour of the Greek found a parallel in Old German and therefore in Old English.

In addition to Hebrew, to Latin and Greek, to the Teutonic and the Roman languages, there is Russian – a curious blend of East and West. From this source, a few names have been adopted. Such as *Ivan* and *Olga*.

5. *Influences and Fashions*

These may be incidental and fortuitous, at least in their beginnings; or general and inevitable, although not necessarily more enduring – except in the mass. When I amplify *fashions* as fashions sponsored or unwittingly caused by great persons (saints and kings, mostly) or occasioned by great events (principally wars), and *influences* as influences springing from a widespread movement, religious or cultural, or from a *Zeitgeist*, a 'spirit of the age', a prevalent national atmosphere, I feel – although I know I can cite valid examples – that Ambrose Bierce uttered two profound thoughts when he defined an accident as 'an inevitable occurrence due to the action of immutable natural laws' and logic as 'the art of thinking and reasoning in strict accordance with the limitations and incapacities of the human misunderstanding'.

Wars have given a brief popularity to the names of admirals and generals (see *Arthur*, *Horace*, *Nelson*) and have even originated *Alma* and *Maida* and the happily obsolete *Inkermann*. Important scientific discoveries have resulted in a very few inventors' surnames becoming 'Christians' – but only among the scientifically inclined. Saints, princes, kings and queens have exercised a much wider influence, although often (as with *Albert*) it has been merely a fashion. The saints, as Saints, are revered mostly by Catholics: it is among them that the Saints' names are mainly to be found, though we must except the Apostles' names as being co-extensive with Christianity and therefore hasten to differentiate between religion as such and, on the other hand, creed and theology and hagiolatry, for 'religious' names such as *James*, *John* and *Mark* may fairly be described as 'general and inevitable', whereas *Aloysius* and *Xavier* cannot justifiably be included in that class. Queens and princesses have received due honour, the three best English examples being *Elizabeth*, *Anne*, *Victoria*. A very modern instance is *Marina* (q.v. in the dictionary proper). But then, as Professor Ernest Weekley[1] notes, 'female names are curiously subject to fashion and are apt to "date" their bearers. Just now [1932] nearly all babies of the more important sex are being christened *Jane* or *Ann*, which were decidedly out of fashion a few generations ago. A decade or two earlier *Joan* had a great vogue, a name which, in Shakespeare's time, was equivalent to a kitchen-wench. [*Susan*, to me, is a domestic servant; so also to the poet Gray.]

[1] *Words and Names*, pp. 83–4.

It is symptomatic of the game of general post now being played by the classes and masses that *Susan* is taking refuge, with *Betty*, *Peggy*, *Jane* and *Ann*, among the aristocracy, while *Gladys* and *Muriel* reign below stairs. . . . A modern Quarles [early C17] would be inclined to reverse the names in the line – "Courtly Mildred dies, while country Madge survives".' If princes (Edward the Black Prince, dashing Rupert, brilliant Eugene) have left a lesser mark than kings, they are yet not to be despised. Among kings, we may select, first of all, Arthur and Alfred, both encrusted with legend and patina'd with romance. William the Conqueror's name set a fashion among the aristocracy; as a general name, it belongs to the more permanent class. The kings Edward have added their prestige to that of the princes. The various Henrys,[1] but especially Henry V (mostly as *Harry*), have so determined fashion that it has become an influence. Charles the Martyr King. The Georges, none more than the two latest of the name: much-loved, quietly effective.

Many of these royal names might, therefore, have fallen into the category of 'general and inevitable', a description that we, in our folly, have reserved for names arising from, or, more accurately, favoured by the time-spirit or by religious[2] and cultural movements.

The embryonic Anglo-Saxon culture was quickened and broadened by the Normans. From 1066 to *circa* 1300, England was bi-lingual; the Normans impinged on Wales, Scotland and even Ireland.[3] Anglo-Saxon and Celtic names were softened or re-shaped by French names, mostly Norman at first but soon Angevin and Provençal as well. The knights and ladies of the Round Table mingled with the paladins and sparse royalties of Charlemagne to introduce a few of their names into the nomenclature of aristocrat and 'learnèd

[1] See, e.g., Weekley, *Romance of Names*, p. 61.

[2] I have already noted the difficulty of distinguishing between 'religious' names and the names of the Apostolic Saints.

[3] Ireland, by the way, exported certain of her Christian names through those Norwegians who, after settling in Ireland, returned to England. (See especially an article by Dr A. H. Smith in *La Revue Celtique*, vol. XLIV, 1927.)

clerk'. Chaucer combined the two cultures as no one before him – and none after.

Chaucer dead, England passed through a very dull period until the 16th century, when, for the English, ecclesiastical and legal Latin yielded to Classical Latin; when, in significant addition, the literature of Greece swam, meteor-wise, into the ken of eager Scot and Welshman and Irishman and Englishman. Lydias and Corinnas and Phyllises, Sacharissas and Cecilias and Celias, Chloes and Chlorises sported from the lyric page into the lyric heart; though the Classic males fared badly. Literary influence upon nomenclature has, in C19–20, been more marked in England, France and the United States than in Germany and even Italy and Spain, but Classical names have thrived less in England than in France and America.

Late in the 16th century, there began the Puritan influence, mainly religious – for Milton is half-Classical, half-Puritanical. Biblical names had entered in the wake of the Reformation. The Puritans, however, were not content with *Habbakuk*, *Adam*, *Deborah*, *Sarah*, and other Biblical names: they wanted, and got, such abstractions as *Patience*, *Prudence*, *Faith*, *Charity* and *Mercy*. 'The prominence of a fresh doctrine,' says Charlotte Yonge, 'is shown in . . . the outburst of Scripture names in all Calvinist countries; so that in French pedigrees, Huguenotism may be traced by the Isaacs and other patriarchal apparitions in the genealogy, and Puritanism has in England produced the quaint Old Testament appellations to be found in every parish register.' Whereas the more obscure prophets, judges and kings – and their wives, if any – have fallen into comparative disuse, the abstract virtues have lasted tolerably well.

This usually sober influence was succeeded by a glorified fashion in ambitious names, some of them not a little pretentious. In the 18th century and until the late 19th, men's names were occasionally portentous (*Adolphus* and other *-us*'es), but it was, as ever, women's names that suffered most, some of them being the C16 literary prettinesses kept alive beyond their time, others indicating the ravages of such a plague of *-a*'s as went far beyond Classic bounds. *Amelia* and *Augusta* ran riot with others of the same termination.

But, somewhere about 1890, there began a natural reaction towards simplicity, a reaction that became very marked during the war of 1914–18, a reaction that represents something much more deep-rooted than a fashion. We have already seen the reinstatement of *Ann(e)*, *Jane*, *Joan*, *Susan*, *Betty*, *Peggy*, and *Madge*. In men's names, the 20th century shows a marked preference for 'simple *John*, *Henry*, etc., or [for] good old names which were long out of fashion, such as *Roger*, *Michael*, *Peter* and *Anthony*. The hero of the modern novel is usually *Dick*, *Bill*, or *Jim*, the last being almost *de rigueur* in . . . the "thick ear" school of romance. . . . The more ornamental type [of male name] has become derisive' (Weekley, *Words and Names*). *Algernon* and *Archibald*; *Vere* and *Percy*; *Clarence*, *Claud(e)* and *Cuthbert*; *Harold* and *Horace* and *Howard*: these gallant or those stately men, twirling their Regency or Victorian cane, have lost their popularity. But perhaps they have gone to console *Claribella* and *Clarimond*; *Dulcibella*, *Augusta*, *Walburga* and *Wilhelmina*; *Jacintha* and *Josephine*; *Chloris* and *Sacharissa* and *Aminta*; *Malvina* and *Marcellina*; *Euphemia*; *Phyllida* and *Priscilla*; *Robinette*, *Rosalia* and *Rowena*, those fair ladies and beauteous damsels a-languishing that they are ogled no longer, no longer cynosured.

NOTE. – Many surnames are used as 'Christians'; virtually all of these are bestowed on the masculine sex, mostly for family reasons – to keep a fine old name alive (most of the ensuing names are both old and very distinguished), to flatter a wealthy relative, to show aesthetic appreciation of a euphonious or an etymologically interesting name, and so forth. A few of these have been noted in the course of the preceding pages. Here are a few more surnames that have been, and still are, bestowed as font-names, given names, Christian names: –

Arlington, *Arnott*, *Athol*, *Beresford*, *Bolton*, *Carey* or *Cary*, *Chester*, *Clifton*, *Compton*, *Courtenay*, *Coventry*, *Dawson*, *Delano*,

Digby, *Dudley*, *Duke*, *Dwight*, *Earl*, *Egerton*, *El(l)smore*, *Filson*, *Fitzroy*, *Gladstone*, *Gower*, *Graham*, *Grant*, *Groves*, *Hamilton*, *Harris*, *Hedley*, *Hesketh*, *Holman*, *Irving*, *Jefferson*, *Johnson*, *Kynaston*, *Lascelles*, *Lennox*, *Lincoln*, *Madison*, *Maitland*, *Manley*, *Maxwell*, *Melville*, *Mor(r)ison*, *Morton*, *Nugent*, *Ormond(e)*, *Paget*, *Pelham*, *Pitman*, *Prince*, *Quincy*, *Reay*, *Ross*, *Russell*, *St. Clare*, *St. George*, *St. John*, *Selwyn*, *Seymour*, *Sherard*, *Sinclair*, *Somerset*, *Stewart*, *Studley*, *Talbot*, *Tarver*, *Topham*, *Tyrone*, *Vesey*, *Waldorf*, *Wallace* (*Wallis*), *Warwick*, *Washington*, *Webster*, *Whitney*, *Willoughby*, *Winston*, *Winthrop*.

For the origins, see Ernest Weekley's *Surnames*: as 'Christians', these names are incidental and therefore do not merit further treatment here. To mention them at all is more than a certain noted authority would do; to me, that procedure seems to be just a little too severe.

MODERN ENGLISH GIVEN OR CHRISTIAN NAMES

LIST OF ABBREVIATIONS

A.-S. Anglo-Saxon. The same as O.E.; some writers prefer the one, some the other.

Apperson. G. L. Apperson, *English Proverbs and Proverbial Phrases*, 1929.

Benedictines. *The Book of Saints*, by the Benedictine Monks of St Augustine's Abbey, Ramsgate, 1921.

Blakeney. E. H. Blakeney, *A Smaller Classical Dictionary*, 1910.

C. Century; e.g., C19, the 19th century; C14–20, during the 14th–20th centuries.

ca. About (in dates).

cf. Compare.

'Christian'. A Christian or given name.

d. Died (in).

Dawson. *A Book of the Saints*, by Lawrence Dawson, 1908.

e.g. For example.

f. Feminine.

Fr. French.

Ger. German; Germanic.

Gr. Greek.

Grose. The present writer's annotated edition of Francis Grose's *Dictionary of the Vulgar Tongue*.

Harvey. Sir Paul Harvey, *The Oxford Companion to English Literature*.

Heb. Hebrew.

ibid. In the same 'authority'.

i.e. That is.

It. Italian.

Jack and Jill. Ernest Weekley, *Jack and Jill*, 1939.

L. Latin.

lit. Literally; literal.

Loughead. Flora Loughead, *Given Names*, 1934.

m. Masculine.

M.E. Middle English.

O.E. Old English.

O.E.D. *The Oxford English Dictionary*.

q.v. Which see. Plural; qq.v.

S. and S. *Songs and Slang of the British Soldier*, by John Brophy and Eric Partridge, 3rd edition, 1931.

Searle. W. G. Searle, *Onomasticon Anglo-Saxonicum*, 1897.

Slang. The present writer's *Slang To-day and Yesterday*, 3rd edition, 1949.

Sp. Spanish.

Swan. Helena Swan, *Christian Names*, 1905.

Webster. *Webster's New International Dictionary*, 2nd edition, 1934:

Weekley. Ernest Weekley, *An Etymological Dictionary of Modern English*, 1921.

Weekley's *Romance of Names*, *Surnames*, *W. & N.* Respectively his *The Romance of Names*, 1914; *Surnames*, 1916; and *Words and Names*, 1932.

Underworld. The present writer's *A Dictionary of the Underworld*, 1950.

Withycombe. E. G. Withycombe, *The Oxford Dictionary of English Christian Names*, 1945.

Words. The present writer's *Words, Words, Words!*, 1933.

Yonge. Charlotte Yonge, *History of Christian Names*, revised ed., 1884 (1st ed., 1863).

A

A A R O N. Perhaps from the Heb. for '(a) light', but probably of Egyptian origin (Withycombe), this Biblical patriarch's name, though still fairly common in the U.S.A., is now, in England, used mainly by the Jews. Contrast *Abel.*

A B B E Y. A diminutive of *Abigail.*

A B E. A mainly American diminutive of *Abraham.* The Americans tend naturally to this kind of contraction: cf. *Rube* for *Reuben.* See also *Aby.*

A B E L. This pleasantly manly name is, like *Aaron,* derived from the Heb. (literally, vanity), but, unlike Aaron, it is still bestowed on Jew and Gentile alike – to the advantage of both – though it is now given less frequently than in C18–19.

A B E L A R D. Now extremely rare, *Abelard* was originally Teutonic ('noble firmness') but is most famous as the surname of that Gallic priest and scholar (1079–1142) whose love-affair has been so arrestingly commemorated by Pope in his not so Classical poem, 'Eloisa to Abelard', 1717, by George Moore in 'Héloïse and Abélard', 1921, and by Helen Waddell in her novel, *Peter Abelard,* 1933.

A B I G A I L. Likewise rare, this Biblical name ('father of joy,' says Charlotte Yonge; 'a father's joy,' says Helena Swan; 'My father is joy', says Ernest Weekley) occurred in English registers from ca. 1570 and was for many years a frequent one for girls, perhaps because of the original's prompt courtesy to David. Since ca. 1615, it has been much used as a colloquialism for a waiting-maid: probably because of the frequency of the phrase 'thine handmaid' self-applied in chapter 25 of the First Book of Samuel. See also my *Dictionary of Slang and Unconventional English.* Diminutives: *Abbey* and *Gail.*

ABIE. See *Aby*.

ABNER. Lit. 'father of light' or 'my father is light', this *m.* name, like so many names in *A*, derives from the Hebrew. Now rare except in parts of the English provinces and in certain American backwashes – for one can no longer speak of backwoods.

ABRAHAM. The greatest of the Biblical patriarchs was originally called 'Abram (father of height or elevation), which was changed by Divine appointment into Abraham (father of a multitude), foretelling the numerous and enduring offspring that have descended from him, and even to the present hour revere his name,' Yonge. Made safe for American democracy by its most distinguished non-Semitic tenant, Abraham Lincoln.

ABRAM. See *Abraham*, of which it is, in England and Holland, also a contraction. It is doubtful whether the word has ever, in its lit. sense, been used in England.

ABSALOM. From the Heb. ('my father is peace'), the name has, in C19–20, fallen rather into disuse. How any boy now so named would be teased by his fellows, to whom the story of the hair-hanged prince is much less tragic than comic!

ABY or ABIE. An American pet-form of *Abraham*. Cf. *Abe*, q.v.

ACHILLES. Rare in England but hardly rare though now rather uncommon in the United States, this name of the Greek hero – vanquisher of Hector – signifies, lit., '(he who is) without lips', and, actually – or so I conjecture – 'the courageous one (who compresses his lips)'. Known in post-War England mostly in its French form: the French rather affect these Classical names: cf. Mrs Agatha Christie's delightful detective, Hercule Poirot.

ADA. This *f.* name is obscure in origin, for whereas Charlotte Yonge derives it from a Teutonic word meaning 'happy', Helena Swan declares that, lit., it signifies 'rich gift' and is 'an early English contraction of Edith': both, however, are agreed that it is distinct from *Adah.* What two more recent authorities have to say is more important, especially as they agree: 'I conjecture that Ada is short for Adela' (Weekley in *Jack and Jill*); '*Ada* is probably a hypocoristic [= affectionate] form of some name in *Adal*' (Withycombe) – compare, here, the names in *Adel.*

ADAH, which, in Heb., denotes an ornament. More frequent in the U.S.A. (dashing Adah Mencken, for instance) than, except among Jews, in Britain, 'this was the reputed name of one of the daughters of Adam and Eve', Swan.

ADAM. This fine old name – apparently one of the earliest of all Names whatsoever, as Carlyle did not say – meaneth, in Heb., 'man', itself from Heb. *adamah,* red earth. It lost, centuries ago, its Semitic connotations: like *John,* it is a frank and sturdy name, sitting ill on milksops and effeminates: but, unlike *John* and *Jack,* it has made little impression on the proverb, for in English there are only two, 'When Adam delved and Eve span, who was then the gentleman?' (Eve), and the C17–18 'We are all Adam's children, but silk makes the difference', with which contrast 'All God's chillun got wings'. (Apperson.) Diminutive : *Ade.*

ADAMINA, which is, mainly (though decreasingly) in Scotland, the *f.* companion of *Adam.*

ADDIE, ADDY. Pet-name forms, in Devon of *Audrey,* elsewhere of *Adelina, Adeline,* and:

ADELA. Of Teutonic origin ('noble'), this is now regarded, especially by the girls who occasionally bear it, as a name 'quite too Victorian, my dear!' The Ger. *Adal,* Ger. and Eng. *Adel,* derive from Old Ger. *athal.*

ADELAIDE. Likewise of Teutonic origin ('nobility', lit. 'noble sort'), this is going the same way as *Adela*, with the proviso that it is still reputed to be suitable for princesses and duchesses. A flippant scholar, unimpressed with even his own erudition, might be tempted to exclaim, 'What's wrong with it, anyway?'

ADELBERT, *m.* Now obsolescent, this Teutonic name ('nobly bright') has never been so common in Britain as in Germany. Of the numerous *m.* and *f.* names in *Adel-*, this is the only one that has survived for males; for females, *Adela*, *Adelaide*, *Adelina*, and *Adeline* have withstood (but will they long withstand?) the ruthless wear and tear of time. See also *Albert.*

ADELINA or ADELINE. Of Teutonic origin: 'noble'. It lengthens *Adela.* See also *Aline.*

ADOLF, ADOLPH, *m.* The anglicized forms of *Adolphus*, or, from another angle, the German forms of *Athaulf* (Swan). Owing to the notoriety of Adolf Hitler, *Adolf* is now very rarely bestowed; but then, a bogy-man hardly expects that dear Mamma will confer his front-name upon her little darling.

ADOLPHUS. From the Teutonic for 'noble wolf'. Charlotte Yonge, 'Athaulf . . . stands in our own roll of English kings as the father of Alfred, namely, Aethelwulf; but this good old name was dropped in England, while its German cousin, in honour of a sainted bishop of Metz . . . became very common in [Germany], and was imported with the house of Hanover in the barbarous Latin form of Adolphus.' Now to be avoided, for it ranks with *Algernon* and *Cuthbert* as comically pompous.

ADRIAN. This attractive *m.* name comes from the L. *Adrianus* or *Hadrianus* (cf. the Roman emperor Hadrian), from the city of *Adria* (whence the Adriatic Sea), itself from L. *ater*, black. (Yonge.) Cf.:

ADRIANA, the *f.* form of *Adrian.* Now rare in the British Empire, it survives mainly in its Fr. form:

ADRIENNE, which has been adopted, though not yet whole-heartedly, in England, where, despite a romantic tinge (not taint), it deserves to become as distinctively popular as *Adrian*, q.v.

AEMILIA. Now usually *Amelia,* q.v. For etymology, see *Emily.*

AENEAS. Now rare in England and almost obsolescent in the U.S.A., it was 'adopted in Scotland under the impression that it was a variant of Angus', Swan. 'Pious Aeneas,' as Virgil calls him, 'owes his modern fame' to that poet, who takes it from Homer. A Greek name, it 'probably comes from *αἰνέω* (aineo), [I] praise', Yonge; the Greeks themselves derived it from *αἰνός*, aweful: see the Homeric hymn to Aphrodite (vv. 198–199). For its ending, cf. *Phineas.*

AFFRICA, *f.* A Manx and Irish name that has nothing to do with Africa; it derives from the Celtic for 'pleasant'.

AFRA, APHRA. Probably from the name, or the nickname, of a queen, for it means 'peaceful ruler'; Charlotte Yonge, however, implies that it was the Heb. *Aphrah,* 'house of dust', adopted by the Puritans ('with their love of piteous names'); it may possibly represent a shortening of *Aphrodite,* as Dr Randolph Hughes has suggested to me. Now somewhat obsolescent, it adorned that earliest of women dramatists, the far from puritanical Afra or Aphra or even Aphara or Ayfara Behn (1640–89), who was also a novelist (*Oroonoko,* or the History of the Royal Slave, published ca. 1678).

AGATHA. A responsible name, for in Gr. it means 'good'. It is, however, an incitement to virtue: perhaps this is why, in C20, the name is regarded as rather Victorian. Its diminutive, *Aggie* (q.v.), is certainly to be avoided. Cf. *Agnes* and:

AGATHIAS, which is its *m.* companion. Now rare.

AGGIE. The pet name given to those who are called *Agatha* (q.v.) or:

AGNES, *f.* The L. *agnus*, a lamb, should connote gentle domesticity. *Agnus* may have been 'derived from a Greek word signifying "sacred" or "pure", and the emblem of purity and innocence is the lamb. In the Roman Catholic Church St Agnes' – one of the four great virgin saints, the others being Barbara, Katherine, and Margaret – 'shares with the Virgin Mary and St Thecla the honour of being the special patroness of purity. The name in this form is current in [the English-speaking countries,] Germany, France, Denmark and Greece', Swan. It is, however, questionable whether L. *agnus* is akin to Greek *ἁγνός* (pronounced *hagnos*), 'pure, holy'. To lovers of poetry it has been endeared by Keats, but by the 'bright young things' (themselves somewhat *démodées*) it is considered *démodé*. Cf. *Aggie* and *Agneta*; and see also *Ines*. See also *Annys*, at end.

AGNETA, an English (obsolescent) and Swiss variant of the preceding.

AILEEN; occasionally AILLEEN. An Irish 'shape' of *Helen* (q.v.).

AILIE. A Scottish contraction of *Alison*, q.v.

AILSA. A Scottish form of *Elsa* (Ger. *Else*), q.v.

AL. A mainly American diminutive of *Albert*. Apotheosized in Ring Lardner's remarkable collection of baseball stories, *You Know Me Al* (1916). – Also of *Alfred* and *Alexander*.

ALAN, ALLAN, ALLEN; Welsh *Alun*. In Wales, 'the three primary bards . . . were Plenydd, Alawn, and Gwron . . . [respectively] light, harmony, and virtue . . . Alawn is erected by ardent Cymrians into the mythic Greek Olen, who is said to have been the first writer of hymns in hexameter . . . ; this name is said to mean the flute-player. . . . This must be the real origin of the Breton Alan' (Yonge), 'introduced into England at about the time of the Norman Conquest. . . . It was first spelt with only one "l"; later variants are Allan and Allen', Helena Swan.

ALARIC, *m.* This English form derives from L. *Alaricus*, itself from a Visigothic name that presumably signified 'all-ruler'. Popular in C19 but now held to be 'literary' if not, indeed, affected. Those pacifist fathers who christen thus their sons might remember that the most distinguished Alaric of all is that King of the Western Goths who, in 410 A.D., sacked Rome as ruthlessly as thoroughly. 'Tis a fighting word. (For the second element, cf. *Ulric.*)

ALASTAIR, ALASTER, ALISTAIR, ALISTEIR, ALISTER. Of this Scottish contraction of *Alexander* – though few persons, using *Alastair*, think of its kingly original – the first is the commonest form, the fourth the uncommonest; *Alistair* is a mere variation of *Alastair*, and *Alaster* presumably the earliest. For its etymology, see *Alexander*.

ALBAN. As an English Christian name, *Alban* comes from St Alban, that Roman soldier who, the first British martyr, suffered – probably in 303 A.D. – martyrdom at Verulam, 'a town which received the name of St Albans after the erection there of the famous Abbey of that name, the work of King Offa of Mercia in the eighth century' (Benedictines). From L. *albus*, white, whence perhaps the Alps, the Elbe, and Albion (Yonge). Becoming rare. Cf.:

ALBANY. A Scottish and Irish name. From *St Albanus* (or Abban), an Irish bishop, but ultimately, like *Alban* (q.v.), from L. *albus*.

ALBERGA, *f.* A somewhat rare name that, perhaps connected with L. *albus* (white), more probably derives from the Teutonic word for 'noble'.

ALBERT. Either directly from, or intimately cognate with A.-S. *Aethelbeorht*, nobly bright; compare those Ger. saints whose name was *Adelbert* (Old Ger. *Adalberaht*) and the modern *Albrecht.* 'Albrecht, and the feminines Alberta and Albertine' – shades of Proust! – 'were . . . almost entirely German, until the late Prince Consort brought the name to England, where it bids fair to become one of the most frequent of national names,' Yonge, 1884. (Its diminutives are *Al* and *Bert*, qq.v.). Now regarded by 'high-brows' as vulgar and by the upper and upper-middle classes as not very aristocratic, despite Continental royalty's fondness for it.

ALBERTA, ALBERTINA, ALBERTINE. See *Albert.*

ALBIN. A variant of *Alban*, q.v.; rather rare outside of Germany. Cf.:

ALBINA, ALBINIA. A mainly C19 *f.* name, which, like the preceding, derives from *Albanus* in its variant *Albinus* (see *Alban*).

ALDA, *f.* A very old German name, meaning 'old'. In 1905, Helena Swan declared it to be obsolete: though a little unusual, it is not even obsolescent. Cf. *Aldous* and:

ALDGITHA, *f.*; also ALDITH. Somewhat moribund, this name of Teutonic origin ('old strife') seems old-fashioned beside the preferable *Alda.*

ALDIS or ALDUS or, most often, ALDOUS, is the *m.* counterpart of *Alda*: the Old Ger. form of the *m.* name is Aldo. (Withycombe.)

ALETHEA. Another responsible name (cf. *Agatha*), for it signifies 'truth' in Greek. Cf., therefore, *Alice.*

ALEC; ALICK. Scottish diminutives of *Alexander*. Cf.:

ALEX. Properly an English contraction (cf. *Alec*) of, but in these days occasionally used as a substitute for, *Alexander*. Also a diminutive of *Alexandra*, *Alexandrina*, *Alexia* and feminine *Alexis*: for an example of the first, see Beatrice Kean Seymour's novel, *Daughter to Philip*, 1933.

ALEXANDER. Originally that complimentary by-name (not a nickname in the modern sense of that word), 'helper, or defender, of men,' which was given to Greek Paris 'for his courage in repelling robbers from the flocks. It was afterwards a regular family name of the kings of Macedon, he who gave it fame being the third who bore it. So much revered as well as feared was this mighty conqueror, that his name still lives in proverb and song throughout the East', Yonge: see especially W. W. Tarn, *Alexander the Great*, 1948. Whence *Alaster*, *Sandy*, *Sawney*. Cf., etymologically, *Cassandra*, and:

ALEXANDRA. The *f.* form of the preceding. A royal name, its original diminutive being:

ALEXANDRINA. See *Alexandra* and cf. *Alexia*. Becoming rare.

ALEXIA. Sometimes a contraction of *Alexandra*; sometimes a variant of *Alicia*. More Ger. than English. Cf.:

ALEXIS. An English contraction of *Alexander*. Now somewhat rare as a *m.* name; but occasionally *f.* in C20.

ALF; ALFIE. Pet-forms of:

ALFRED. From a Teutonic word meaning 'elf-counsel', hence a 'crafty counsellor', which is the motto on King Alfred's Jewel preserved at Oxford. (Whereas *elf* is probably cognate with L. *albus*, white, elves being white sprites, *red* is the *rede* of archaic English.) It was the fame of King Alfred which popularized the name in England: though it is to be noted that after the Anglo-Saxon period it virtually lapsed until the 18th century, when it experienced a remarkable revival. A derivative is the obsolete *Alured,* from *Aluredus,* the Latinized form (? from misreading of *Alvred,* a variant) of *Aelfred,* the A.-S. form of *Alfred.* – Cf. *Aubrey.*

ALFREDA. The *f.* of *Alfred;* surviving only in rural districts of England. E.g. in Horace Annesley Vachell's excellent novel, *The Disappearance of Martha Penny,* 1934.

ALGERNON. This aristocratic, by the vulgar ridiculed, name has a slightly comic origin, for it means 'whiskered': from the Norman *als gernons,* the whiskered (man). The widow of Henry I of England 'married Alex of Louvaine, who wore moustachios. He became the ancestor of the Howard and Percy families, and transmitted his nickname as a baptismal name to both branches of his descendant', Swan. Cf.:

ALGY. The endearment-form of the preceding. Glorified in: 'Algy met a bear. The bear was bulgy. The bulge was Algy.' In the du Maurier period, *Algy* was to be seen 'flitting through Punch . . . as a contrast to *'Arry,* the irrepressible Cockney vulgarian, who first appears (in 1874) "on 'orseback",' Weekley, *W. & N.*

ALICE, ALICIA. The former is an English, the latter a Latin handling of Gr. *alētheia,* truth. *Alicia* has become old-fashioned, and, among the facetious, the other form evokes a guffawed 'Alice, where art thou?', much as *Maud* evokes 'Come into the garden, Maud' – how very rude Tennyson would have been to the perpetrator of the latter desecration! Cf. *Alys.*

ALICK. See *Alec.*

ALINE. This *f.* name, like the next, is from a Teutonic word for 'noble'. In other words, it contracts *Adeline*.

ALISA. A variant of *Alicia*, q.v. at *Alice*.

ALISON. A Scottish diminutive of *Alice*; *-on* is a French suffix, present also in *Marion*.

ALISTAIR, ALISTEIR, ALISTER. See *Alastair*.

ALIX, *f.* From *Alicia*.

ALLAN, ALLEN. Variations of *Alan*, q.v.

ALLIE, ALLY. The usual diminutive of *Aileen* and *Alice*.

ALMA, *f.* This now slightly unfashionable name is really four names, according to its various origins: of which the latest is the Russian place-name, popularized by the Battle of Alma (September 20, 1854); L. *alma* (fair or kindly girl: cf. one's *alma mater*); a Celtic term for 'all good'; and a Hebrew term for 'maiden'.

ALMEIRA, ALMERIA. Mere variations of *Almira*.

ALMERIC, ALMERICK. In Teutonic, lit. a 'work-ruler': *Amalric*, whence – by transposition – our word, which is, basically, the same as *America*, itself from the navigator and adventurer *Amerigo* Vespucci. 'A very common name amongst the English nobility during the Middle Ages,' remarks Helena Swan; it is not unknown among the hard-working English middle-classes.

ALMIRA. An import, now tariff-walled, from Spain, the word simply meaning 'a woman of Almeira' or Almeria, a town and province on the Bay of Almeria.

ALOISIA, *f.* From a Teutonic word for 'famous war'. Only occasionally used in Britain and now extremely rare. Cf.:

ALOYSIUS, *m.* either of the same etymology as *Aloisia* or merely a Latinized elaboration of *Louis*. It is virtually confined to Catholics, who greatly reverence Aloysius Gonzaga (late C16), the patron saint of the young.

ALPHONSO, *m.* A discredited name of which the It. and Sp. form is *Alfonso*. 'Nobly eager for battle' (might one murmur, 'Stout fellow'?) being its signification, it is linked with the *Adel*-names.

ALTHEA. This pretty femininity derives from the Gr., where its meaning is 'healing' or 'healthy' or 'wholesome'. Not to be confused with *Alethea*.

ALWYN is a variant of *Aylwin*.

ALYCIA. See *Alysia*.

ALYS. A rather fanciful spelling of *Alice*, as

ALYSIA is of *Alicia*, of which another variant is *Alycia*.

AMABEL, AMABELLA. A mostly American variant of *Amy*, probably on the analogy of *Annabel*, *Annabella*; or else an Anglicization of Fr. *aimable* or a derivative from L. *amabilis*, lovable.

AMARANTHA. 'Unfading' is her charm, be she Greek, as originally, or English, as now but rarely.

AMARYLLIS. 'Refreshing stream' in the Gr.; in English, a name now seldom heard, but in C17–18 a convention of pastoral and lyric verse, for 'sporting with Amaryllis in the shade' was a favourite rural occupation. In literature, *Amaryllis*, like *Aminta* (q.v.), is on a par with *Celia*, *Chloe*, and *Clorinda*, 'the three lovable Disgraces'.

AMBER, *f.* With this mainly U.S. name, not general before C20, cf. *Coral* and *Pearl*.

AMBROSE, *m.* Another 'Christian' of Gr. origin; its sense, 'immortal', makes him a fit companion for Amarantha, and renders both of them worthy to eat of ambrosia and sip of nectar. Ambrose, moreover, is a famous name in the history of Christianity: Ambrose, Archbishop of Milan in C4, is a Saint and 'one of the four great Fathers and Doctors of the Western Church' (Benedictines). Becoming rather less general than it was in C16–19. See also *Augustin*.

AMECIA. See *Amice*.

AMELIA. An English offshoot from *Emily*, q.v. In the C20, it is, by the upper-middle and upper classes – whatever they may be – avoided as unfashionable. Many a heroine was named Amelia and was none the worse for it.

AMIAS, AMYAS, can hardly derive from *Amadeus*; perhaps from the surname *Amias*, '(man of) Amiens'. The *Amias* form has fallen into almost complete, *Amyas* into considerable, disuse: many people, in fact, remember the name only in connexion with Amyas Leigh, the hero of Charles Kingsley's *Westward Ho*, itself not much read in these days. (*Jack and Jill*.)

AMICE; occasionally AMECIA or AMICIA. Now rare variants of *Amy*.

AMILIA. A Scottish derivative of *Emily*. Cf. *Amelia*.

AMINTA or AMYNTA. (The *m.* form, *Amyntas*, has long been obsolete.) Seldom heard in late C19–20, *Aminta* was, in C17–18, a favourite name of pastoral and lyric poets; one of Sir Charles Sedley's best and neatest poems has this arresting first stanza,

'Fair Aminta, art thou mad,
To let the world in me
Envy joys I never had,
And censure them in thee?'

which is as effective as the opening sentence in any O. Henry story. Apparently it derives from a Greek word meaning 'to protect'.

AMOS, *m.* From Heb. for 'borne (by God)', it is a friendly sort of name.

AMY. Although somewhat under a cloud, *Amy* is 'not to be sneezed at': if one remembers its origin—Fr. *Aimée,* from L. *amata* (a woman beloved)—it assumes a vesture of beauty or, at the least, of charm. (Sometimes it forms a diminutive of *Amabel.*) *Amanda* and *Amoret,* fanciful cognates harlot-bedizened, have gone the rapid way of the meretricious; simple *Amy* remains.

AMYAS. See *Amias.*

AMYNTA. Another form of *Aminta.*

AMYOT. An English derivative, unhappily rare in C20, of Romance *Amadeus, Amadée, Amadeo.*

ANAIS. An English deviation from *Anne.* Never very general and now unwept, unhonoured, and unsung.

ANASTASIA; occasionally ANSTACE or ANSTICE. This, with its now, except in Ireland, equally rather disused male, *Anastasius,* is one of the two notable names based on the idea of immortality: the other is *Ambrose*; cf. the less permanent *Amarantha.* 'A name of good hope for a Christian, . . . it became dear to the Church at large, through the great Alexandrian patriarch, the bulwark of the faith,' Charlotte Yonge, who adds: 'So again the new Christians took the old word *ἀνάστασις* (. . . an awakening or rising) . . . ; then formed from it *'Αναστάσιος* (Anastasios) . . . having the elements of the Resurrection within him or her, for the feminine Anastasia was as early and as frequent as the masculine.'

ANASTASIUS. See the preceding. (Four popes bore this name.)

ANCELOT, *f.* in England (though now rare), *m.* in France, where the *f.* is *Ancelote.* It was a name in medieval Chivalry; from it came *Lancelot,* q.v. The original is a presumed L. *ancillus* corresponding with *ancilla,* a handmaiden.

ANDREA, ANDREANA, the *f.* of Andrew, were originally It.; the Fr. is *Andrée.* See:

ANDREW. From *'Ανδρέας* (Andreas) in Syriac Gr., it derives from Gr. *ἀνήρ,* genitive *ἀνδρός* (andros), a man. Andreas, that Galilean fisherman who is one of the foremost of the Apostles, was martyred at Achaian Patras, whence, in C4, some of his relics went to Scotland and thus made of St Andrew's the Metropolitan see. St Andrew, patron saint of Scotland, was also its 'knightly champion': hence *Andrew,* as a Christian name, became extremely popular, as did *Anderson,* 'Andrew's son', as a surname. (See especially Yonge, pp. 85–86, and Benedictines.) Cf.:

ANDY. A contraction, more general in Ireland than in England, of *Andrew.* The best-known holder of the name is Andy Rooney, that whimsical character who, in Samuel Lover's humorous novel *Handy Andy,* 1842, has a 'genius' for doing things the wrong way.

ANEURIN, *m.* This name, common in Wales, appears to mean 'truly (*a'n*) golden' (*eurin*).

ANGELA. An English contraction of, and much more frequent than:

ANGELICA, which, however, on the Continent, was obviously a derivative of Continental (especially Romance) *Angela.* It means 'the angelic girl or woman': cf. 'my angel' as a term of affectionate (? doting) address. *Angela* originated as the *f.* of *Angelos* (Gr. ἄγγελος, an angel; in Classical Gr. a messenger, an announcer), first used as an epithetic name in the Byzantine Empire, where it soon became a surname; in C13, *Angelo*, because of saintly associations, it developed into a very popular Christian name, as, with little delay, did also *Angela*. (Yonge.)

ANGELINA. Like the next, a variant of *Angelica*; more precisely, these two names were diminutives of the Continental *Angela*. Becoming unfashionable.

ANGELOT. See the preceding.

ANGIE (pronounced *Anjee*). A diminutive of *Angela*, *Angelica*, *Angelina*, *Angelot*.

ANGUS. Originally *Ōengus*, it was popular in Ireland and then, by migration, in Scotland, where it is 'especially at home'; there, however, it is often 'translated into Aeneas, the christened name of many a Scot who ought to be Angus; and the Irish are too apt to change it in the same way'. 'It comes from the numeral *aon*, one; it also conveys the sense of pre-eminence . . . and it is generally pronounced Haoonish in Gaelic.' Lit., it means 'unique choice'. In Scotland it was, in the old days, often changed to 'Hungus and Ungus, likewise Enos'. (Yonge.) *Angus*, *Andrew*, *Donald*, and *Ian* are perhaps the most popular of Scottish *m.* Christian names.

ANITA. A diminutive of *Ann(a)*.

ANN. See *Anne*.

ANNA. A Latinized, but also original Greek, form of *Anne*; it is the more common form on the Continent.

ANNABEL, ANNABELLA. The latter is probably a lengthening of the former. Like *Annaple*, *Annabella* is too early to derive from (*St*) *Anne*; they are, it seems, from *Amabel*, influenced by *Anna*. Cf. *Arabella*.

ANNAPLE. A Scottish form of *Annabel*: see the preceding.

ANNAS. An English contraction of the obsolete *Ananias*: which, in its Heb. form (*Hananiah*), signifieth 'grace of the Lord'.

ANNE; ANN. The latter is the distinctively English form of *Anne*, from Gr. *Anna*, from Heb. *Chaanah* (our *Hannah*), *Hannāh* (grace). Not from L. *annus* (a year), as was assumed by the Carthaginians, 'confusing it with their Italian goddess, Anna Perenna, the presiding deity of the circling year' (Yonge). The popularity of *Anne* in Britain, drawing on Europe, is largely caused by its Biblical and saintly connexions. 'The Bohemian princess Anne of Prague brought it to England, and gave it to her name-child, Anne Mortimer, by whom it was carried to the house of York, then to the Howards, from them to Anne Boleyn, and thereby became an almost party word in England,' Yonge. It has, in C20, had a revival of popularity.

ANNETTE is, originally, a Fr. diminutive of *Anne*. Cf.:

ANNIE. The pleasantly familiar form of *Ann*(*e*).

ANNIS. See *Annys*.

ANNORA, ANORA, *f.* Now rather uncommon and always confined to Northern England, it derives from either the Gr. for 'light' or the Hebrew for 'grace': it is therefore a variant of *Hannah* and *Anne*, and of *Eleanora* and *Helen*. (Yonge.)

ANNOT, *f.* Mainly Scottish. From the Heb. for 'light'; cf., therefore, *Annora* and *Helen*(*a*), the latter its ultimate original. Often, however, it derives, as a diminutive, from *Agnes* or:

ANNYS, *f.* An occasional English name, now rare, having been virtually absorbed by *Anne.* Perhaps from the Gr. for 'complete', for this seems to be the origin of Anysia, a Thessalonican girl put to death in 304 A.D.,—'in the reign of the persecuting Emperor Maximilian Galerius, Diocletian's colleague' (Benedictines). But its variant *Annis* is often of a different origin, for in the Middle Ages it constituted the pronunciation of *Agnes.* Cf., therefore, *Annot.*

ANORA. See *Annora.*

ANSELM. From the Teutonic for 'divine helmet', it is much more frequently met with on the Continent, impressed with the courage and constancy shown by that great theologian Archbishop Anselm (1033–1109) in his quarrel (no; that is too strong a word to be applied to any contention into which this mild-natured Saint-to-be was reluctantly drawn) with irascible Rufus and diplomatic Beauclerc. (Yonge.)

ANSTACE, *f.* ANSTICE, *f.* See *Anastasia.*

ANSTY. A mostly English contraction of, and in the late 19th–20th century an occasional substitute for *Anastasius.*

ANSTYS, *m.* Yet another variant of *Anastasius.* Cf. *Anstace* and *Anstice.*

ANTHEA. In Gr., '(a lady of) flowers' (ἄνθεια). Now somewhat rare, this name – cf. *Aminta* and *Clorinda, Chloris* and *Phyllis* – was a favourite with C17 pastoral and lyrical poets. It is interesting to note that whereas *Anthea* has become rare, *Rose* and *Myrtle* have remained popular, though less aristocratic.

ANTHONY; ANTONY. The superfluous *h* seems to have been introduced by the frugal Dutch. *Antony* comes from L. *Antonius,* which some authorities explain as 'inestimable' and others as 'strength': the latter, presumably, from the mighty triumvir Mark Antony's derivation of his name from *Antius*, a son of Hercules. Part of the name's later popularity arose from the fame of Antonius (St Antony the Great), the C4 hermit, and from that of St Antony of Padua (1195–1231), a notable preacher, peacemaker, and converter of heretics (Dawson). Diminutive: *Tony*.

ANTONIA. The *f.* of *Antonius*, hence of *Antony*. In England, it has always been a patrician's name. See *Anthony*.

ANTONY. See *Anthony*.

ANTY. An Irish diminutive of *Anastasia*. Cf. *Ansty*, q.v.

APHRA. See *Afra*.

APRIL. See *Averil*.

ARABELLA. Now more frequent in Scotland than in England, it is in the latter regarded as somewhat Victorian. 'I conjecture that Arabella was an amalgamation of this name [*Annabel* or *Annabella*] with Orable' or Orabella, surviving in the surname Orbell and deriving from L. *Orabilis*, 'yielding to prayer' (*Jack and Jill*).

ARCHIBALD. From the Teutonic ('nobly bold'), its earliest form being *Ercanbald*. As *Aeneas* for *Angus*, so, among the Scots, *Archibald* was adopted as the Lowland equivalent of the *Gillespie* of the houses of Campbell and Douglas. In the present century, it is apt to be used derisively: a deterioration both indicated and hastened by the catch-phrase, 'Archibald! Certainly not!'

ARCHIE. The diminutive of the preceding and, unlike it, immune from ridicule. During the 1914–18 War, anti-aircraft guns were affectionately dubbed *Archies*; see, further, S. and S. and my *Dictionary of Slang and Unconventional English*.

ARIANWEN, *f.* A Welsh name from a Celtic word meaning 'silver'; perhaps it was, in early days, applied to what we now call 'platinum blondes'.

ARISTIDES. In Gr., 'son of the best', so that the famous statesman (nicknamed 'The Just') was more aptly named than most. Virtually obsolete in England, it survives in the U.S.A. – and flourishes in France as *Aristide*; cf. the survival in France of *Hercule*. In its etymology, cf. *Agatha*.

ARNOLD. From the Teutonic *Arnwald* (eagle-strong), into which, apparently, the obsolete *Arnulf* (eagle-wolf) and its derivatives have been absorbed, despite the powerful religious associations of the latter; 'the Arnolds and Arnoldines' – *Arnoldine* is a Ger. *f.* name – 'keep their feast upon St Arnulf's day, thus confessing that they have no patron of their own'. (Yonge.)

['ARRY. Note at *Algy*. The *f.* is 'Arriet. See also my *Dictionary of Slang and Unconventional English.*]

ART. A diminutive, in England reputed to be vulgar, of:

ARTHUR. (For its literary associations, see especially Sir E. K. Chambers's pleasantly erudite *Arthur of Britain.*) Searle refers *Arthur*, as an A.-S. name, to *Arnthor* or *Earnthor*, which (I surmise) may mean either 'eagle of Thor' or 'eagle like Thor'; both Yonge and Swan simply define *Arthur* as 'high', but, even if we abandon the picturesque *earn* origin, this explains only the first syllable (*Arth*) as from *ard* (*arth*), high or noble in many Celtic tongues, though not in Welsh. Professor Weekley (*Jack and Jill*) quietly supports my supposition; Miss Withycombe, however, proposes the little-known Roman clan, the gens *Artoria*, the masculine being *Artorius*. To leave etymology for fashion, 'Arthur is a rare medieval font-name, a fact no doubt due to the sad fate of King John's nephew. Its modern popularity dates from the Duke of Wellington' (Weekley's *Romance of Names*). The occasional derisive use of *Arthur* may have, in part, been occasioned by *Little Arthur's History of England* falling into disrepute; in greater part, by the jocular contempt meted out, in C20, by certain classes to *Algernon, Cuthbert, Clarence* and *Percy*, qq.v.

ARTHURINE. This *f.* derivative from the preceding is falling into disuse.

ARTIE. A diminutive of *Arthur* and *Arthurine*.

ASA. Rare in Britain but common in America, *Asa* comes from the Hebrew and signifies 'God healeth', hence 'physician'. (A man's name.)

ASPASIA. Gr. 'welcome', it is now rare. Yonge, 1884, notes that 'it has even been heard as a Christian name in a cottage. "Her name's Aspasia, but us calls her Spash." ' Adopted in England in C17 from the literary fame of Aspasia, the mistress of Pericles. C20 avoidance arises from the fact that *Aspasia* has become generic for a statesman's cultured mistress. (For a witty 'portrait' of the Greek Aspasia, see Richard Ince's 'Lipstick' in *The Window*, October, 1930.)

ASTA, *f.* Somewhat rare in England, though fairly common in Germany, it may derive from the Gr. for 'a star' or, more probably, be a contraction of *Augusta*, which, in L., means 'venerable (one)'.

ASTRID, *f.* This Norwegian name ('divine strength') has, since ca. 1920, gained a footing in England.

ATHANASIUS. Gr. *Athanasios*, 'undying, immortal'. Like *Anastasius*, it has, except as a traditional name in certain families, become rare in England. The most remarkable Athanasius was that C4 champion of the Christian faith who, among Roman Catholics, ranks as one of the Doctors and great 'pillars' of the Church. (Benedictines.)

ATHELSTAN, *m.* This almost obsolescent A.-S. 'Christian' ('noble stone') is an example of the 28 pages of names recorded by Searle as beginning with *aethel*, noble: cf. *Ethelred.*

ATTY, *m.* An Irish name from the Celtic for 'high' (cf. *Arthur*) or, perhaps, 'horseman'. (Yonge.)

AUBREY has come to England, via France (diminutive *Auberon*; or *Oberon*, 'king of the fairies'), from Old German *Albirich*, lit. 'elf-rule', hence 'elf ruler'. Cf. *Alfred.* Not so frequently heard as it used to be, it is, nevertheless, a pleasant name.

AUDA, *f.* Now rare and never very general, it derives from a Teutonic word meaning 'rich'.

AUDREY; occasionally AUDRY. A contraction of *Etheldreda* ('noble might'). 'St Aethelfryth,' remarks Charlotte Yonge, 'was a queen who must have been a most uncomfortable wife, and who, finally, retired into a monastery, getting canonized as St Etheldreda, and revered as St Audrey. From the gewgaws sold at her fairs some derive the term tawdry.' In C16–17 (witness Shakespeare's Audrey), it was mainly a peasant girl's name; in C18–20, it has improved its social status. (The suggestion that *Audry* is connected with Fr. *Andrée* is a mistaken one: quite apart from the evidence stated above, such a theory presupposes a scribal error of an untenable magnitude.)

AUGUSTA. The *f.* of *Augustus.* It has retained its regal associations and its aristocratic status. Diminutive: *Gussy.*

AUGUSTIN, AUGUSTINE. In England, both forms are *m.*; on the Continent, the latter is *f.* It is a diminutive of *Augustus*, and the prevalency of the longer form may be accounted for by the fame of St Augustine of Hippo and of St Augustine the first Archbishop of Canterbury; he of Hippo is one of the four great Fathers of the Roman Catholic Church, the others being Ambrose, Jerome, and Gregory the Great.

AUGUSTUS. Though now, in the British Empire, held somewhat pompous, it is an imperial name of considerable sonority: it appears pretentious only when it is set in juxtaposition to *Bill* and *Jack* and *Tom*. This was the agnomen conferred on Caius Julius Caesar Octavianus, – who (63 B.C.–14 A.D.) was the nephew of Julius Caesar and the first Roman emperor (27 B.C.–14 A.D.), – by a Senate anxious to avoid offending the citizens with *rex*. Its etymology is problematic, but probably it derives from L. *augēre* ('to increase') or from the Teutonic *aege*, awe: *Augustus* may be interpreted as 'hedged with majesty'. (Harvey; Yonge.)

AURELIA, *f.* 'Golden', i.e. goldilocks, from L. *aurum*, gold. It is seldom heard in C20 England: very few L. trisyllabic or quadrisyllabic Christian names are at all popular nowadays.

AURORA. Likewise falling into disuse. From L. for 'dawn', Aurora was originally the Roman goddess of dawn and she corresponded to the Gr. Eos.

AUS (pronounced *ŏs* or *ŏz*). A diminutive of:

AUSTIN. An English contraction of *Augustin*, q.v. Its popularity may have arisen from the Augustin or Austin Friars, 'instituted in honour of the first St Augustin[e], and once the greatest sheep owners in England' (Yonge).

AVERIL, AVERYL, AVRIL, AVERILLA. 'Wild-boar battle-maid,' it has a male companion in *Everard*, q.v.; or it may be 'wild-boar favour'. Thus we cannot relate it to Fr. *avril*, April, tempting though such an etymology be; except, of course, *Avril* when it is being consciously used as a translation of the English 'month'-name *April* (cf. *June*).

AVICE; occasionally AVICIA; erroneously, by confusion with the next entry, AVIS. At one time a very common *f.* name, it began in England as *Havoise* or *Hawoise*, a transformation of Fr. *Hedvige*, from Ger. *Hedwig* (earlier *Haduvig* or *Haduwig*), 'war-refuge'; Helena Swan proposes an alternative origin, a Teutonic word meaning 'lady of defence', but this has less historical justification.

AVIS, *f.* From L. *avis*, a bird. (See also *Avice*.)

AVRIL. See *Averil*.

AVVY. The 'endearment' of the four preceding names. E.g., Avvy Paxton in J. B. Priestley's novel, *Faraway*, 1932.

AWDRY or AWDREY. A variant of *Audrey*.

AWLAY, *m.* A Scottish name from a Celtic word for 'work'. It is thus of the same family as the obsolete *Aymar*, 'a work-ruler,' and as *Almeric*, q.v. It may, however, derive from *Olaf* (q.v. at *Oliver*).

AYLMER, *m.* Perhaps a contraction of the *Egelmar* in Domesday Book. The *egel* part, thus or as *egil*, is a frequent prefix and would seem to be from the dative case of *ege*, awe or fear, and the complete word apparently signifies 'formidable fame'. More probably, however, *Aylmer* derives from the A.-S. *Aethelmaer*, 'nobly famous'. It is a melodious name (seldom heard in these days), sometimes shortened to *Aymar*, not (or is it?) to be confused with the *Aymar* mentioned in the preceding entry. Cf. *Elmer*, q.v.

AYLSA is a rare variant of *Ailsa*.

AYLWIN, *m.* In the Teutonic, 'noble friend'. Regarded as rather poetical, it is seldom used in C20. Compare *Aylmer*.

B

Bab; **Babs**. Diminutives of *Barbara*, the second being the more affectionate form. Cf.:

Babie, which is a Scottish diminutive of the same name.

Babs. See *Bab*.

Baldie, *m.* 'Sacred prince' (Teutonic): a Scottish name perhaps cognate with *Baldur* the Beautiful.

Baldwin; rarely **Baldwine**. Lit. 'a bold friend' (Teutonic): for the *-win*, cf. *Alywin.* It is now seldom used as a 'Christian'. But formerly it was notable as 'the name of four of the Christian kings of Jerusalem (and a nominal Baldwin V, an infant), including the successor of Godfrey de Bouillon, who figures in Tasso's "Jerusalem Delivered" as one of the leaders of the Christian host, and also in Scott's "Count Robert of Paris"' (Harvey).

Baldy. A diminutive of *Baldwin.*

Balthasar, *m.* Now rare in the British Empire, and in Britain never so common as in Italy, Spain, and the Slavonic countries. Proposed origins are four: Chaldean *Belteshazzar* ('may Bel guard the prince'); Persian *Beltshazzar* ('prince of splendour'); Slavonic *Beli-tzar* ('white prince'); or 'a fancy name invented at a period when bad Latin and rude Teutonic were being mixed up to make modern languages, and the Lingua Franca of the East was ringing in the ears of pilgrims', Yonge. Factually, *Balthasar* is a Gr. form of the Biblical *Beltsazzar*, one of the Three Holy Kings.

Bar. An intimate diminutive of:

Barbara. (See also *Bab*, *Babie*, *Bar*, and *Barbary*.) One of the four great virgin saints of the Roman Catholic Church (see also *Agnes*), she came, 'in the floating allegories of the Church', to be the representative of artistic devotion. She is supposed to have been beheaded by her father (*in propria persona*, as they say) for a somewhat florid manifestation of her Christianity. The word is the *f.* of *βάρβαρος* (barbaros), a stranger – a term scornfully applied by the Greeks to all who did not speak their mellifluous tongue; probably it was used in mimicry of the incomprehensible speech of strangers (Yonge). Its popularity was revived in C19 'after a long period of obscurity' (Swan).

BARBARY. A very English form, now obsolescent (even in its stronghold, the rural districts), of the preceding.

BARNABY. Like the obsolete *Barnabas*, it derives from the Hebrew and means 'son of exhortation'; it is now rather old-fashioned. Barnabas was an apostle, but Barnabo Visconti, a medieval Milanese noble, had an unpleasant reputation.

BARNARD; BARNETT. English variants of *Bernard* (Italian and Spanish *Bernardo*), they connote 'the resolution, firmness, of a bear'. The name is much commoner in Ireland than in England. Cf.:

BARNEY, BARNY. A diminutive of *Barnaby* and *Barnard*. The Irish confuse it (when from *Barnaby*) with *Brian* (Yonge).

BARRY. This Irish *m.* name, from the Celtic, either for 'good spearsman' (?) or for 'looking straight at the mark' as applied to a marksman, is a pleasant one – and apparently of literary associations (Barry Cornwall, fluent C19 poet; Barry Pain, neat writer of short stories).

BART. A diminutive of *Bartholomew*. Cf. *Bart's*, St Bartholomew's Hospital.

BARTLE. A diminutive of *Bartlemy*.

BARTHOLOMEW. Heb., 'son of *Talmai* (abounding in furrows)', so presumably the name was given first to a ploughman. Its religious associations are that Bartholomew was 'one of the Twelve [Apostles], by many thought to be Nathanael, the "Israelite without guile" of St John's Gospel' (Benedictines); there was in C11 Italy a notable abbot so named; and in C12 England a monk 'missioning' to Norway.

BARTHRAM. See *Bartram.*

BARTIE. A diminutive of *Bartholomew*; more familiar than *Bart.* Also of *Bartram.*

BARTLEMY. An Englishing of *Bartholomew.*

BARTLET. An English contraction of *Bartholomew.* Cf.:

BARTLEY. An Irish contraction of *Bartholomew.*

BARTRAM, English; BARTHRAM, Scottish. Lit., 'bright raven' (Teutonic), it makes a group with German *Bertram* and French *Bertrand.* The raven (*hrabn*) is prominent in 'the nomenclature of Teutonic Europe, though it is not always easy to distinguish its progeny from those of *ragn*, judgment, and *rand*, a house' (Yonge). Other birds notable for their linguistic offspring are the eagle and the swan. Diminutive: *Bertie.*

BASIL. In Gr., it means 'a King' (βασιλεύς, basileus), or perhaps it may derive from the adjective 'kingly' (βασίλειος, basileios); this is not a majestic but a dignified, though friendly, name. It is famous in Church history: especially on account of Basil the Great, noted bishop (C14), acute commentator on the Bible, and marvellous orator: all his activities, all his virtues and abilities have been worthily described by John Henry Newman.

BASTY is the usual diminutive of *Sebastian.*

Bat. An English contraction, now little used, of *Bartholomew.* Cf. *Bartie, Bartlet* and *Bartley.*

Bathsheba. From Heb., it means either 'daughter of plenty' or 'daughter of the oath'. Like many other Biblical names, especially those for girls, it has lingered latest in the rural districts of England; but, as a 'Christian' of charm and merit, it might easily become popular again.

Bea, pronounced *Bee,* is the most familiar and perhaps also the most affectionate diminutive of *Beatrice*; cf. *Beatie.*

Beata, *f.* 'Blessed' (in the L.), this has modestly survived in rural after having died away in urban England. Cf. the more active *Beatrice.*

Beatie. An English diminutive, like *Trix, Trissy, Trixy,* of:

Beatrice, Beatrix. The latter is the original, as it is also the correct form of the word; although *Beatrice* is now the usual form in England and even in Italy, only Beatrix is heard in the other European countries. In L., it is 'blessed', or, more poetically and more practically, 'joy-giver'. The three most famous Beatrices in literature are perhaps Dante's (*Beatrice, loda di Dio vera*), Shakespeare's, and Thackeray's in *Henry Esmond.*

Beattie. A diminutive of *Beatrice.* A mere variant of *Beatie.*

Becky. A pet-form of *Rebecca.* Its etymology makes it particularly piquant as the 'Christian' of Becky Sharp, a double-damning name.

Bede. A Teutonic name, either 'one who compels' or 'prayer', it is now rarely heard, except among Catholics. Its Welsh form is *Bedaws.* Its greatest tenant is the Venerable

Bede, who has, with an accuracy unusual in most such *clichés*, been called 'the father of English history'.

BELINDA, 'originally the property of the wife of Orlando, was chosen by Pope for his heroine of *Rape of the Lock*' (Yonge); the titular heroine of a novel by Maria Edgeworth; and that niece to whom, on her marriage, Mr John Jorrocks promised £1,000 every time she should give birth to twins. In It., she is a serpent.

BELL, BELLA, BELLE. Contractions of *Isabel* or *Isabella*, the Fr. *Isabelle* obviously being party to the act; *Bella* is also a diminutive of *Arabella*. *Belle*, however, is also an independent name in its own right and derives from Phoenician, where it means 'oath of Baal'.

BEN. The usual, more manly, diminutive of *Benjamin*, not of:

BENEDICT. From L. *benedictus* (blessèd). In various forms, it is general throughout Europe. This prevalence is in part the result of the fame earned by St Benedict, that early C6 abbot who was 'the Patriarch of the Western monks, born at Norcia in Central Italy . . . of the noble family of the Anicii' (Benedictines). The most worthy of the worldly Benedicts is the gay and witty bachelor of Shakespeare's *Much Ado About Nothing*; so heavy was his 'fall' that his name became generic for a married, especially a young married man.

BENJAMIN. Heb. 'son of the right hand'. It owes much of its popularity to the lovable nature of the youngest of Joseph's brethren.

BENJIE, BENJY. A diminutive of the preceding. Cf. *Ben*, q.v., and *Bennie*.

BENNET. A pet-name form of *Benedict*, of which it is a typically English contraction.

BENNIE, BENNY. A diminutive of *Benjamin*. Cf. *Ben* and *Benjie*.

BERENICE. Originally *Pherenice*, a Macedonian name, it derives from Gr. and, there, it means 'victory-bringing'. Daughter of Agrippa I, the greatest Berenice of history figures in literature as the heroine in two plays, Racine's *Bérénice* and Otway's *Titus and Berenice*. (Harvey.)

BERNARD. (Cf. *Barnard*.) Not from *bairn-heart*, 'heart of a child,' as some have poetically and improbably maintained, but from *biornhard*, 'having the resolution, or courage, of a bear'. The first Bernard was an uncle of Charlemagne; the second notable one, the Cistercian monk revered by all in C13, his becoming 'a universal name throughout Europe; in Ireland absorbing the native Brian' (Yonge).

BERNARDA. A contracting of the originally and mainly It. *Bernardina*, the *f.* of *Bernard*; in Ger., more prettily *Bernardine*. Now somewhat rare.

BERNARDINA; occasionally BERNARDINE (mostly Ger.). See *Bernarda*.

BERNIE. Pet-form of *Bernard*, q.v.

BERT. A diminutive of *Albert*; only very rarely of *Bertram* or *Bertrand*. Cf. *Al*, q.v., and *Bertie*.

BERTHA. In Teutonic languages, 'the bright one,' 'the shining one': cf. the first element in *Bertram*. 'This name . . . has the same meaning as Epiphany night, which commemorates the visit of the Magi to Christ, on the twelfth day after that of his birth. The name was first Perchtan . . . contracted into Perchta, thence . . . Berchta, and thence . . . Bertha, or [in Fr.] *Berthe*.' Medievalists have extracted a little innocent fun from a naïve poem entitled *Berthe aux Grands Pieds* (Big-Feet Bertha). Among Catholics, it is a favourite name for girls born on January 6; but in England it is somewhat *démodé*.

BERTIE. A diminutive of *Albert*; also of *Bertha*, *Bertrand* and:

BERTRAM. Like the next, it is equivalent to – and in C20 much more general than – *Bartram*. Teutonic, it means 'bright raven'. The patron saint of all three is Bertichramnus, bishop of Mans until 623. (Yonge.)

BERTRAND. See the preceding. Originally and mainly the Fr. form: and its heroic associations spring largely from the fame of Bertrand du Guesclin, that C14 champion of France whose knightly deeds and character have been nowhere so adequately, so stirringly recorded and depicted as in *Black Mastiff*, by M. Coryn, 1933.

BERYL. By etymology 'a soothsayer', according to Helena Swan, *Beryl* soon came to be considered a 'jewel-name': cf. *Pearl* and *Ruby*. It is, however, possible that the 'precious stone' etymology is the correct one, for the Gr. *βήϱυλλος* (bērullos) is of Eastern origin: cf. Persian and Arabic *ballur*, crystal: hence, *Beryl*, 'the crystal-clear' or 'the crystal-pure'. (Weekley.)

BESS; BESSIE. The usual English diminutives of *Elizabeth*; cf. *Beth*, *Betsy*, *Betty*. Much used in unconventional English: *to hug brown Bess* formerly meant 'to be an infantryman'; nowadays, it would mean exactly what you might expect it to mean. Apotheosized in *Good Queen Bess*.

BETH. A diminutive of both *Elizabeth* and:

BETHIA, BETHIAH, *f*. From Heb. *bith-jah*, 'daughter, i.e. servant, of Jehovah'. It is American and rural English, the former spelling being the more usual; originally, however, it was an Irish name, imported, about 620, 'by some of the Keltic missionaries of the North of England, and St Aidan consecrated her at Whitby as the first nun in Northumbria' (Yonge). It is a Biblical name: see 1 *Chronicles*, iv, 18.

BETSY; occasionally BETSEY. An English diminutive of *Elizabeth*. Cf. *Bess*, *Beth*, *Betty*, and:

BETTA. Originally and mainly a German contraction and diminutive of *Elizabeth*: cf. *Betty*. The C20 prefers *Bette*.

BETTRYS. The Welsh form of *Beatrice*.

BETTY. A diminutive of, and in the 20th century often a substitute for, *Elizabeth*. Cf. *Bess* (q.v.), *Beth*, *Betsy*.

BEVIS; occasionally *Bevys*. 'It appears to be simply the "bull", Old Fr. Bueves being a common name in epic' (*Jack and Jill*). 'Its English fame rests upon a champion called Bogo, . . . supposed to have been Earl of Southampton at the time of the Norman Conquest,' Yonge. Its place in literature is that established by Bevis of Hampton – i.e., Bogo – an early C14 romance in verse, and by Richard Jefferies's delightful *Bevis*, 1882.

BIANCA, *f.* Originally and mainly the It. form of *Blanche*: the British occasionally prefer the Italian, rather rarely a modern Gr., 'shape' to the apparently more English, though in fact French, name; cf. *Andrée* and *Betta*. See *Blanche* and *Blanco*.

BIDDULPH. In A.-S., 'commanding wolf'. Bodvulf founded the monastery of Ikano, died in 655, and by his canonization, and the dispersion of his relics, gave his name to four churches in London, to St Botolf's bridge (Bottlebridge) in Lincolnshire, and to St Botolf's town (Boston) in Lincolnshire. (Yonge.) See also *Botolf*.

BIDDY. This Irish contraction of *Bridget* is generally used as the endearment thereof. 'BIDDY, or CHICK-A-BIDDY.

A chicken, and figuratively a young wench. [Cf. the modern *Irish biddy*, an Irish girl, often specifically an Irish servant girl . . .', Grose.

BILL. A contraction of *William* and by most men preferred to *Willie* and, greatly, to *Billie*; by only a few to *Will*. A member of that manly trio: *Bill*, *Jack*, and *Tom*. Often, like *Jack* and *Tom*, used as a nickname by girls.

BILLIE, BILLY. A familiar form of *Bill* on the analogy of *Willie*.

BLAISE. Properly the Fr. original of *Blase* or *Blaze*. 'Some consider Blasius' – whence, obviously, *Blaise* – 'to be a mere contraction of Greek *basileios* (Royal); but long before that name prevailed, at least among historical personages, we hear of Blatius, Blattius' – in both of which the *ti* is soft – 'or Blasius, as a man of Salapia, in Apulia, whose name seems to have signified a babbler', Yonge. Miss Withycombe convincingly relates it to L. *blaesus*, 'splay-footed; deformed; stuttering', the third sense manifestly linking with that adduced by Miss Yonge. St Blasius was iron-combed to death, hence he became the Patron Saint of English woolstaplers (Swan); in C17 the name was rendered still more illustrious by being attached to Pascal, the great Fr. moralist, mathematician and physicist. See also *Blaze*.

BLANCH. See *Blanche*.

BLANCHARDINE. A diminutive, now rare, of:

BLANCHE; occasionally BLANCH. Lit., 'white'. This is one of the few Teutonic (not certainly Teutonic) names – though the form of *Blanche* is Romance, especially Fr. (*blanc*, *f. blanche*) – suggested by the complexion: perhaps because all Teutons were fair, or, less probably, because they deemed such casual nicknames unworthy of perpetuity as Christian names. In A.-S., *blac* is 'black', but *blaecan* is 'to bleach', i.e.

'to whiten'; *blaec*, 'colourless' (the white of water) was perhaps adopted by the Romance languages to mean 'white'; perhaps the Fr. form was influenced by It. *bianco*, *f. bianca*. (Hence the ease with which a philological dialectician can 'prove that black is white'.) Cf. *Bianca* and:

BLANCO. A Sp. name (cf. Italian *Bianca* and French *Blanche*) seldom heard in England. Lit., 'the white, i.e. fair man'. Its best-known English tenant is Joseph Blanco White (!), who (1775–1841) wrote on religion and composed what Coleridge held to be the finest sonnet in the English language, even though several of Shakespeare's, at least one of Milton's, and one or two of Wordsworth's are manifestly superior.

BLASE. An occasional variant of:

BLAZE. The English form of *Blaise*: cf. *Bogue* and *Bevis*, where the process is in reverse.

BLENDA. Seldom used in the British Empire – or in America – this was originally the name of a Swedish heroine. From a Teutonic word meaning 'dazzling', presumably in her fairness and therefore to be linked with *Bianca*, *Blanche*, and *Blanco*, qq.v.

BOB. A diminutive of *Robert*: cf. the obsolete *Hob* and the obsolescent *Rob*; also *Bobbie* and *Robin*: qq.v. From ca. 1700, though in this sense now obsolescent, it has been a colloquial term for 'a man, a fellow': cf. *Jack* and *Tom, Dick and Harry*, the commonness of the name giving rise to a generic sense. This may possibly be also the origin of *bob*, a shilling (from ca. 1800) and of the Winchester *bob*, a large white beer-jug; almost probably of *bob*, C18 slang for 'gin', and of the cant *bob*, a shoplifter's assistant, where, however, the idea may be that of *bobbing* in, out, or up; and probably of the *bob* in *wet bob* and *dry bob*. (See my *Dictionary of Slang and Unconventional English*, 1937, and *A Dictionary of the Underworld*, 1950.) Like the other endearments – except *Robin* – of *Robert* and like the original itself, it does not appear in proverbial English (Apperson).

BOBBIE, BOBBY. An endearment immediately of *Bob*, ultimately of *Robert*. In slang, it means a policeman, as do the slang derivatives *Robert* and *peeler*: from Sir *Robert Peel*, the institutor of the modern police force.

BOGUE. A very English form (now somewhat rare) of *Bevis*, q.v.

BONIFACE. Now seldom used, but in C17–early 19, popular as a font-name. From the L. for 'a well-doer': with amusing humour, it has, since Farquhar's *Beaux' Stratagem*, 1707, been applied generically to innkeepers. 'Cf. *abigail*. Much earlier is *Bonifazio* in a similar rôle in Ariosto's *La Scolastica*' (Weekley). 'Bonifacius . . . was the name of a martyr; then of a pope; and next was assumed by our Saxon Wilfred, when in the sixth century he set out to convert his continental brethren' (Yonge).

BORIS. Either from the Hungarian for 'a stranger' or, more probably, from the Russian for 'a fight', it is by Englishmen generally associated with Russia. Russian names – cf. *Alma* and *Ivan* – were, ca. 1917–40, under a cloud; and again since 1947.

BOTOLF. A contraction of *Bodvulf* or *Bodvuolf*, therefore a variant of *Biddulph*, q.v. The occasional spelling *Botolph* appears to be an attempt to make the best of two worlds.

BOYD. In Celtic, 'yellow'. Probably at first a nickname, it is more frequently heard as a surname than as a 'Christian'.

BRAM. A Dutch and, hence, American contraction of *Abraham*, q.v., but generally used in ignorance of its origin.

The only eminent *Bram* to which my memory turns is Bram Stoker, author of the ghoulish *Dracula.*

BRAN. From the Celtic for 'a raven', this *m.* name is rare outside of Wales and the Scottish Highlands. 'In Celtic mythology he was a god of the underworld, who later assumed the character of a hero, and finally was made the father of Caractacus, a convert to Christianity, and an introducer of that religion to Britain' (Harvey). Cf. at *Brian.*

BRAND. A mainly and originally Scandinavian name (lit., 'a flame; hence, a sword-blade'), which is the *m.* of the next. Its English use – now mostly as a surname – may in part result from a misconceived origin in (St) *Brandan* or *Brendan* (484–577) of Clonfert, Ireland. See also:

BRENDA. Probably the *f.* of *Brand.* 'The sword figures in northern and German nomenclature as Brand; . . . not from the verb *to burn* [cf., however, Weekley], but from *brandr*, an elastic [?pliable] staff, transferred to the blade of a sword. It would also mean the staff of a bow,' Yonge. Scott chose *Brenda*, originally of Zetland, to designate one of Magnus Troil's daughters in *The Pirate*, as Helena Swan reminds me.

BRIAN, BRYAN. Lit., 'strong' or, perhaps rather, 'strength' (Breton but cognate with Old Norse *Brján*; the L. form being *Brennus*). 'Brian has from very old times been a favourite . . . in both Brittany' – as *Brien* – 'and Ireland, the first no doubt from the Christian honours of [Bran the Blessed], the second from the source whence he was named. The great glory of Brian in Ireland was in the renowed Brian Boromhe' or Boru (926–1014), who fought twenty-five battles against the Danes, became chief king in Ireland in 1002, and was slain in his tent after his great victory at Clontarf on Good Friday. (Yonge; Harvey.)

BRIDE. A contraction of *Bridget* and the usual form of that name to be used in Scotland; seldom heard in Wales and not very common in Ireland, where the original is felt to be more dignified, partly because of its saintly associations. See:

BRIDGET; occasionally BRIDGIT, BRIGID or BRIGIT. (Originally and properly *Brighid.*) Perhaps 'strong girl', from Celtic *brigh*, 'strength'. It is, of all 'Christians', the most frequently given in Ireland: this popularity results directly from the fame of the late C5-early 6 virgin saint, who, the 'Mary of Ireland', was born of Christian parents at Fouchard in Louth. 'From her infancy Bride gave signs of the sanctity to which God's grace was leading her. . . . She founded the monastery of Kildare, the first Religious House of women in Ireland. Wonderful were the miracles she wrought, and equally marvellous her influence for good over the nascent Church of her country. . . . Her remains were enshrined with those of St Patrick, as . . . of the Second Patron Saint o' Ireland. . . . The Protectress of those engaged in dairy work (Benedictines). *Brigit* was originally a Celtic goddess. The clan of the Brigitantes was called after her. (See *The Golden Bough.*) See also *Biddy.*

BRIEN. Strictly, this is the Breton spelling of *Brian.*

BRIGID, BRIGIT. See *Bridget.*

BRONWEN, *f.* In Celtic, 'white-breasted': 'tis a Welsh name, now much less general than of old. Cf. Tennyson's 'lovely-breasted Ida'.

BRUCE, *m.*, is noted by neither Yonge nor Swan. It was originally, as it still is, a Scottish surname drawn from *Brieux* in France: cf. *Beaton* and *Cumming.* (Weekley, *Romance of Names.*)

BRUNHILD, BRUNEHILDA, BRUNHILDA. In Ger. – and it is a mainly Teutonic, especially Norse, name – the word is usually spelt *Brynhild(a)*; it must signify 'the breast-plate maid of battle'; literally 'breast battle', which doesn't make sense. As Charlotte Yonge so aptly says, 'A thorough Valkyr was Brynhilda, the maiden whom Odin had touched with his sleep-thorn . . . Sigurd aroused her, and won her for his own. . . . This is the . . . origin of our fairy tale of the *Sleeping Beauty*.' In the more Germanic version, she, 'like the Greek Atalanta, was only to be won by a champion who could excel her in games of strength, and her conquered suitors were all put to death'. She figures prominently in *The Book of Heroes* and in the *Nibelungenlied.*

BRUNO. Mostly, as at first, a Ger. name, it is occasionally – cf. the similar *Carlo* – bestowed in England and, more frequently, in the U.S.A. 'Brown' in Teutonic, it was, originally, a nickname: *Brúnn* is a frequent Norse nickname, as E. H. Lind's magistral *Norsk-Isländska Personbinamn*, 1920–21, makes abundantly clear. (Cf. the remarks at *Blanche.*) Its fame arose from that of that monk of Cologne who, in C11, founded the Carthusian order.

BRUSH. A very English contraction and transformation of *Ambrose*, q.v., it is one of those excellent names which are, heaven knows why, falling into desuetude.

BRYAN. A variant of *Brian.*

BUNTY. 'When we get to Bunty, Tottie and Wendy, it is time to stop theorizing' (*Jack and Jill*). Well, hardly! *Wendy* (q.v.) presents no insuperable difficulties; *Tottie*, euphemizing *Dotty* (q.v.), is a diminutive of *Dorothy*; and *Bunty* is an affectionate, sportive personification, either of the dialectal and colloquial *bunty*, (of a person) 'dumpy – i.e., short and stout', or of *Bunty*, a pet-name for a lamb.

C

CADELL. A Welsh *m.* 'Christian'. In Celtic, it means 'strength in war'. Now somewhat rare as a font-name, it flourishes as a Scottish surname. Cf.:

CADOGAN. Welsh *m.* Here the first element is the Celtic *cath* or *cad*, war, a battle or a defence; the etymology of the second element is obscure. Like *Cadell*, it has become a surname. Cf.:

CADWALLADER. Welsh *m.*: cf. the preceding pair of names and *Cadwallon.* In Celtic (*Cadwaladyr*), it signifies 'battle-arranger', one who, like the obsolete Welsh *Cathal*, was an admirable exponent of military tactics. (Yonge.)

CADWALLON. Welsh *m.* For the *Cad-*, see preceding trio of names; the *-wallon* may stand for 'lord' and is presumably from Celtic. In legend (?history), Cadwallon was the brother of the titular hero of Southey's fine poem, Madoc.

CAESAR. The name appeared first in the Julian *gens*, nearly 200 years before Julius Caesar. Perhaps from L. *caedere*, to cut; perhaps from *caesius*, blue-eyed (cf. *Eric Bright-eyes*); perhaps even from a Moorish word for 'elephant' – a member of the *gens* had slain one in Africa; but probably from the fact that the first Caesar had an abundance of hair (L. *caesaries*); Julius Caesar, oddly enough, was known as the bald-headed adulterer (see Oman's fascinating *Seven Roman Statesmen*). *Caesar* became a title and is the original of *Kaiser* and *Czar*. Not, in C20, much used in the British Empire as a baptismal name, it continues to be so used in America. (*Julius Caesar* is an extant traditional name; I first met with it, I remember, in the person of one of the worthy citizens of Gisborne, New Zealand.)

CAINTIGERN, *f.* An Irish name: in Erse, 'fair lady'. Cf. the Welsh St *Kentigern.*

CAL. The diminutive, seldom heard in Britain, of *Calliope, Calypso, Calvin,* and:

CALEB. In Heb., either 'a dog' or, more probably, 'bold, staunch'. In Judges, Caleb was the staunch and faithful spy, who, of the 600,000 persons that had come out of Egypt, alone went with Joshua into the Promised Land. In C16–17 England, current only among Puritans, it became, in C18, a fairly general 'Christian', free of cynical association and almost free of Puritan memories.

CALLIOPE. In Gr., '(she of the) beautiful voice'. In Gr. mythology, Calliope or Calliopea was 'the Muse of epic poetry, represented in works of art with a tablet and stylus, and sometimes with a roll of paper or a book' (E. H. Blakeney). Becoming rare.

CALVIN. Mostly American, it commemorates the great Protestant reformer (1509–64). Etymologically, it is a diminutive of L. *calvus,* 'bald'.

CALYPSO. Like *Calliope,* growing rare and derived from Gr. (*Καλυψώ,* from *καλύπτω,* I conceal): the nymph Calypso concealed Ulysses when he was shipwrecked on the island of Ogygia, whence, held by this love-sick daughter of Oceanus, he was, after seven years, released imperiously by the gods. (See Homer's *Odyssey.*)

CAMILLA. From Etruscan via L. and meaning 'attendant at a sacrifice' (Yonge) or 'freeborn servant of the temple' (Swan): she was dedicated to the service of Diana; as 'a warlike Volscian nymph', she was celebrated in the Aeneid. *Camilla* was adopted in that rage for classical names which characterized the English after the Reformation.

CAMILLE. An originally and mainly Fr. variant of the preceding.

CANDIDA. A L. name, meaning 'white': cf., therefore, *Blanche*. Its modern use dates from G. B. Shaw's delightful comedy, *Candida*, 1898. (Withycombe.)

CANUTE. Soon, apparently, to be obsolete. Originally Danish, where, as *Cnut*, *Knud*, or *Knut*, a hill or a barrow or even a protuberance; it is, therefore, cognate with our *knot*. The form *Canute* is caused by his L. name, *Canutus*, probably given as equivalent to 'white-haired'. Its use as an English font-name is probably, in large part, owing to the story of Canute and the disobedient waves – a story at least as famous as that of Alfred and the inconsiderate cakes.

CAR. See *Carmichael*.

CARA, *f.* Mostly an Irish name, it comes from the Celtic for 'friend'. In C20 non-Irish use, there is often an allusion to It. *cara* (dear girl): moreover, any woman so named invites the superlative, *carissima*. Cf.:

CARADOC, *m.* 'Beloved' (Celtic): cf. Gr. *χάρις* (grace) and L. *carus* (dear), and *Caradoc*'s Breton equivalent *Keridak*. Mostly Welsh, it occurs also in Scotland and is well known to the English reading-public through the satirical stories by Caradoc Evans (1883–1945).

CAREY or CARY. See Note at end of Introduction.

CARL. The anglicized spelling of the originally Ger. *Karl*, which is the general Teutonic 'shape' of *Charles*. Cf. *Carlo*, q.v.

CARLILE. Properly a surname (also in forms *Carlyle* and *Carlisle*), it is occasionally used as a 'Christian'. Probably from the ancient town in Cumberland: 'man of Carlisle'.

CARLO. The Italian form (cf. Sp. *Carlos*) of *Charles*, this name is, though not among manual workers, gaining ground in England and the U.S.A. Cf. *Carl*.

CARMEL, CARMELA, *f.* In Heb., 'vineyard' or 'fruitful field', the name is more frequent in Italy than in England; in the latter, indeed, it is now rather rare.

CARMICHAEL. In Celtic, 'friend of Michael', with especial reference to the Archangel St Michael: with the *Car*, cf. *Cara* and *Caradoc*. Mainly Scottish, it has become also a surname. Diminutive: *Car*.

CAROL, *m.* Either an Anglicization of Polish and Slovakian *Karol* (cf. Bohemian and Esthonian *Karel*) or a shortening of (Dutch and) L. *Carolus*; for etymology, see the English equivalent: *Charles*. (Yonge.) Cf. *Carolina*. It is also the pet-form of *Carolina* or *Caroline*.

CAROLA. The direct *f.* of L. *Carolus* (see *Carol*). Somewhat rare, it is advantaged by the growing fame of Carola Oman, biographer, historian, and historical-novelist.

CAROLINA, CAROLINE. Originally Continental forms – the former, predominantly Italian – corresponding to the Fr. and English *Charlotte* (q.v.), itself the *f.* counterpart to *Charles*. *Caroline* is deemed the more aristocratic (Royalty's influence, this), but both are, in C20, becoming slightly less fashionable. See also:

CARRIE; occasionally CARRY. The usual diminutive of *Carola*, *Carolina* or *Caroline*, as *Chatty* and *Lottie* are of *Charlotte*.

CASIMIR. Originally Polish ('show forth peace'), it had, in C19, considerable popularity in France and, perhaps thence, some little popularity in England, in which latter country it is rare in C20.

CASPAR; usually *Casper*. This *m.* name derives from the Persian for 'horseman'. Sometimes explained as a variant of *Jasper*.

CASSANDRA. In Gr., 'helper of men': cf. *Alexander*. Now rare, it appeared in England in the middle of C16; Jane Austen's sister bore it (Yonge). From that figure in Classical mythology of whom Sir Paul Harvey treats thus: – 'Cassandra, daughter of Priam, King of Troy, received the gift of prophecy from Apollo, who was enamoured of her. But as she slighted him, the god contrived that no trust should be placed in her predictions. After the fall of Troy she fell to the lot of Agamemnon, who took her back to Greece and to whom she foretold the calamities that awaited him. She was murdered by Clytemnestra.' Fig., *Cassandra* is used in much the same pejorative manner as *Jeremiah*. Diminutive: *Cassie*.

CATH, CATHIE. Diminutives of the next two names. Cf. *Kath*, *Kathie*.

CATHARINA, CATHERINE. English forms of *Katherine*, q.v.

CATHWG, *f.* A very Cymric form of *Katharine*.

CATO, *m.* Now rare; never general. From the fame of Cato the Censor (234–149 B.C.) and, especially, of Cato Uticensis the noble suicide, dramatized by Addison in the formerly celebrated tragedy, *Cato*. From L. *catus*, sagacious, probably reduced from *cautus*, wary, cautious.

CEC. (Pronounced *Sess.*) The diminutive, non-aristocratic, of *Cecilia* (etc.) and:

CECIL. Ultimately from L. *caecus*, blind, it derives from the Caecilian 'gens'; and, in actual practice, it may be described as the *m.* of *Cecilia*. In England, *Cecil* was originally a very aristocratic surname (cf. *Howard* and *Percy*), a fact that soon led to its adoption as a baptismal name. But note that the Burghley Cecils got their name from the family of *Sytsylt*, of Allt yr Ynys in Monmouthshire.

CECILIA. (For etymology, see *Cecil*.) The name owed its popularity much less to its notable connexions with Roman history than to the fame of the virgin martyr, St Caecilia (died ca. 176). A patrician, she converted to Christianity her betrothed husband and his brother; they too gave their lives that Christ might live in men's hearts. As a Christian, she was suffocated with the steam of a bath in her own house. (Benedictines.) – Also, she is noted as the patron saint of music: a choice determined by the fact that, in her martyrdom, she sang till she expired. An organ became her distinguishing mark, and thus she was credited with its invention. To her patronage of music (see especially Dryden's magnificent ode) was added that of poetry; she is therefore to be compared with Barbara, patron saint of art and architecture, and with Katharine, of literature and eloquence. (Yonge.) Whence:

CECILIE. An Englishing of the preceding. Probably:

CECILY represents a further step in adaptation. See also *Cicely*.

CEDRIC. In Celtic, 'war-chief,' it is thus one of many long-established *m.*, and a few *f.*, names in which war plays a part. That, at least, was Charlotte Yonge's opinion. Weekley, however, in *Jack and Jill* points out that it arose from Scott's mistake for *Cerdic*, the name of the first king of Wessex (d. 534). Gradually falling into disuse.

CEIRIDWEN, KERRIDWEN, *f.* A Welsh name – from that of a Celtic goddess. (Withycombe.)

CELIA. In C17, often *Coelia*, which points to a possible origin in L. *coela*, the heavens. In C17-mid 18 and in C20, often aristocratic; in C19, mainly proletarian and *petit bourgeois*, this latter prevalence being in part the result of association with Irish *Sheelah* (*Sheila*), in part the result of confusion with *Cecilia* (Yonge). This name was a favourite with C17 poets, both lyric and pastoral. One of the best of Sir Charles Sedley's 'songs' begins thus:

Not, Celia, that I juster am,
Or better than the rest,
For I would change each hour like them,
Were not my heart at rest.

CELINE. An originally and mainly Fr. form (*Céline*) of *Celia* via Fr. *Célie*.

CHARIS, *f.* (The *ch* is hard, i.e. as *kh.*) The C19–20 form of:

CHARISSA. From the Gr. for 'love', it came to mean 'charity' (Faith, Hope, and Charity). Introduced by Spenser in *The Faery Queen*. Cf.:

CHARITY. (For etymology, see *Charissa.*) Charlotte Yonge is not to be denied: 'A few ancient Greeks had names compounded of Charis . . .; but it was reserved for Christianity to give the word its higher sense. Charis, through the Latin caritas, grew to be the Christian's Charity. . . . And it was thus that, after the Reformation, Charity, [often] contracted into Cherry, became an English Christian name.' Helena Swan adds: 'It was very common in England in [C17], amongst the Puritans, and John Bunyan, in his *Pilgrim's Progress*, places Charity in the "Palace Beautiful".' Like *Faith* and *Hope*, it is still a frequent *f.* name.

CHARLES. Earliest as *Karl*, which in Teutonic languages means 'a man': cf. the A.-S. *ceorl*, whence *churl*. The form *Charles* seems to have been Fr. – from a blending of *Karl* (become *Carl*) and its L. 'shape', *Carolus* – long before it was adopted in England. As Charlotte Yonge says, our James I, thinking it a lucky – nay, a fortunate – name, and hoping to avert 'the unhappy doom that had pursued five James Stuarts in succession, . . . called his sons Henry and Charles'. The fate of 'the royal martyr' rendered Charles the most popular of all 'Christians' among the loyalists, and later among the Jacobites, both English and Scottish, so that, in late C17–20, *Charles* is, with *John*, *George*, *James* and *William*, the commonest of English font-names. (For derivative senses, see my *A Dictionary of Slang and Unconventional English*, especially under:)

CHARLEY, CHARLIE. Diminutive of *Charles*.

CHARLOTTE. Probably from Fr. *Charlot*, the pet-name for *Charles*. Carlota, or Charlotte, of Savoy, by marrying Louis XI, introduced *Charlotte* to the Fr. royal house. Its popularity in England arrived with George the Third's exemplary queen; a popularity probably increased by the sentimental aura attaching to the heroine in Goethe's *Werther*. (Yonge; Dr William Rose's introduction to his translation of *Werther*, 1929.)

CHARMIAN. Though from Gr. χάρμα (charma), a (source of) joy; delight, the *ch* is usually pronounced soft. In England, it appears hardly before C17: cf., in Shakespeare's *Antony and Cleopatra*, that Charmian who was the more attractive of the queen's two attendants ('Good sir, give me good fortune'). Etymologically, it may be compared with *Charis*. More correctly spelt *Charmion*.

CHATTY. A very English transformation (at first, only an endearment) of *Charlotte*: cf., therefore, *Lottie* (*-y*) and contrast *Carrie*(*-y*).

CHAUNCEY or CHAUNCY. Originally and still a surname, of French origin and probably from a place, it is rare in the British Empire but often enough used in the U.S.A. (Withycombe.)

CHERRY. See *Charity*. In C19–20, it is often used with an underlying reference to the bloom and colour of the fruit.

CHLOE. (Pronounced *cló-ee.*) In Gr., 'blooming' or 'verdant' (literally, 'a green and tender shoot'), *Chloe* was 'the summer epithet' of Demeter as 'the protectress of green fields' (Yonge). It owes its popularity partly to *Daphnis and Chloe*, but mostly to Horace's *Odes*. In late C16–17, the name figured largely in English pastoral, hence in lyric poetry: e.g. Dryden, in *A Rondelay*, writes thus,

> Chloe found Amyntas lying
> All in tears upon the plain;
> Sighing to himself, and crying,
> Wretched I, to love in vain!
> Kiss me, dear, before my dying;
> Kiss me once, and ease my pain.

(John & Constance Masefield, *Lyrists of the Restoration*, 1908.)

But by ca. 1850, it was almost confined to negresses in America and, by 1880, to spaniels in England (Yonge).

CHRIS. The usual diminutive of *Christopher* and *Christina* (or *-e*); an unusual one of *Christabel*. Cf.:

CHRISSIE, which is the familiar form of *Christina* (and *-e*) and

CHRISTABEL; occasionally CHRISTABELLE. From χριστός (L. *Christus*, the Anointed One) and L. *bellus*, *f. bella*, handsome. *Christabel* dates from ca. 1540 in Yorkshire, but it is now less general than *Christina* or *Christine*. To poetry-lovers the name has been endeared by Coleridge's unfinished poem (1816) thus entitled; it ranks with *Kubla Khan* and *The Ancient Mariner* as his greatest work; moreover, its metre was new.

CHRISTIAN. (Now rarely, though originally, *f.*) Direct

from L. *Christianus*, a follower of Christ, but certainly suggested, as a font-name, by *Christian* in its *f.* use: what with both *Christian* and *Christina*, the women were having it too much their own way! As *m.*, it was rendered much more popular by being used for the hero of Bunyan's great allegory.

CHRISTIANA. The *f.* of *Christian* (see Bunyan's *Pilgrim's Progress*); probably suggested by *Christina.*

CHRISTIE, CHRISTY. A diminutive of *Christopher*; now also a surname. Cf. *Chris*, *Kester*, *Kit*.

CHRISTINA. An alternative for, and the original of, *Christine*. It is the *f.* diminutive of *Christus* (see *Christabel*). Apparently the first person baptized thus, was St Christina, a Roman virgin of patrician birth, who was martyred in 295, (Yonge).

CHRISTINE. At first, it was rather Scottish (probably from France and Germany) than English, this mere variation of *Christina.*

CHRISTOPHER. In Gr., lit. 'Christ-bearing'. The St Christopher of legend, and the actual martyr to a less degree, popularized the name.

CHRISTY. See *Christie.*

CHRYSOSTOM. From Joannes *Chrysostomos*, John 'of the Golden Mouth', the eloquent C4 bishop, afterwards canonized. Now rare. (From the Gr.)

CHRYSTAL or CRYSTAL, *f.*, may be included among the jewel-names; but it is much less often bestowed than *Beryl* or *Ruby*.

CICERO. Seldom used in England; rather more often in U.S.A. After the great Roman orator, whose private letters are among the most interesting in any language. In L., lit. 'vetch': the first Cicero may have enjoyed local fame as a cultivator of vetches.

Cicely; Cicily. The latter probably deviates from the former, which in turn deviates from *Cecily*, q.v.

Ciprian, Cyprian, *m.* In L., 'inhabitant of Cyprus'. Rather uncommon in C19–20, when 'a Cyprian' suggests *meretrix Cypriana*; moreover, 'the Cyprian' is Venus regarded specifically as the goddess of lust.

Cis; Cissie. The latter is a further familiarization of the former, which represents a pet-name for *Cecily* and *Cicely*. Also *Sis*, *Sissie*.

Clair, Clare, *m.* The latter is the more English (via Norman) form, the former by now the no less English (though directly from Fr.) offset to the *f.*:

Clara, which is more often bestowed than its *m.* companions in the baptismal game. It is the *f.* of L. *clarus*, 'clear', hence 'renowned': cf. the etymology of *Clarence*. The earliest recorded *Chiara* (the It. form of the name) was that devoted follower of St Francis who, under his guidance, founded a religious order: the Sisters of St Clara, or 'poor Clares', from whom rapidly spread this name of *Clara* in various shapes and to all European countries.

Clare. See *Clair*. (Both these forms are occasionally – and, at first, incorrectly – apprehended as *f.*)

Clarence. From *clarens*, the present participle of *clarēre*, 'to be renowned,' in pre-classical L.; operative too, it would seem, were classical L. *clarus*, 'famous' – County *Clare* (admittedly after 'Red De Clare', stout Glos'ter's earl, the foe of Henry III) amplified as a dukedom into *Clarence* – and the Suffolk village of *Clare*. As a *m.* 'Christian', *Clarence* arose in late C16; it was popularized; William IV was Duke of Clarence (Yonge). Like *Algernon*, *Cecil*, *Cuthbert*, *Harold*, *Horace*, and *Percy*, the name has, among the more godless proletarians, become derisive: witness, e.g., Weekley, *W. & N.*, pp. 91–92.

CLARIBEL. An English *f.* derivative of *Clara*, and probably on the model of *Christabel*, since *Claribel* means 'clearly (i.e., brightly) fair'.

CLARICE. Lit., 'making famous,' from L. *clarus*, 'renowned' and *-ix*, the *f.* agent. At first It., the name travelled to France and then to England. Whence *Clarissa*.

CLARIMOND, *f.* An elaborately artificial name recorded at least as early as 1613; it is *Esclairmonde* (of Fr. medieval romance) in the later form, *Clairmond*. The *Clair-* is that of *Clarence*, *Claribel*, *Clarice*, and *Clarinda*, but the *-mond* is Old Ger. *munt*, yielding O.E. *mund*, 'protection,' as in *Rosamund*, q.v. (Yonge; Swan.)

CLARINDA. A fanciful *f.* name, from *Clara* on *Florinda* (?), coined about the same time as

CLARISSA. Richardson the novelist's adaptation of *Clarice*, q.v., in 1747–48.

CLARRIE. The diminutive of *Clarence*; also, occasionally, of *Clara* and its derivatives.

CLAUD, CLAUDE. The English form of *Claudius* (see *Claudia*). In C20, the irreverent are apt to poke fun at *Claud*: cf. the remarks at the end of *Clarence* and *Cuthbert*.

CLAUDIA, *f.* CLAUDIUS, *m.* Either from the old L. verb *clueo* (the Gr. *kleo*), 'I am famous,' hence meaning 'famous'; or, much more probably, from L. *claudus*, 'lame,' via the *Claudian* 'gens'. It is true that 'the Claudii were a family of evil fame, with all the darker characteristics of the Roman, and they figure in most of the tragedies of [imperial Rome]. . . . But the reign of the Emperor Claudius' – so ably and sympathetically drawn by Robert Graves in his two historical novels, *I Claudius* and *Claudius the God* – 'and the number of his freedmen, and new citizens, gave his gentile name an extensive vogue, and from his conquests in Britain was there much adopted,' Yonge. Moreover, in the first and second centuries of the Christian era, there were several remarkable British women bearing this name in the wake of several remarkable, though hardly so blameless, Roman women.

CLAUDIAN. A rather rare name; from *Claudianus*, a derivative of *Claudius*. The last of the L. classical poets – he died ca. 408 – bore this name.

CLAUDIE. A non-aristocratic 'endearment' of *Claud*, *Claudia*, *Claudian*, *Claudine*, and *Claudius*.

CLAUDINE. A Swiss and Fr. form of *Claudia* adopted in England. Probably via *Claudian*.

CLAUDIUS. See *Claudia*.

CLEM; CLEMMIE. Diminutives of:

CLEMENCE, *f.* rare and mostly French, the usual English *f.* being *Clemency*; CLEMENT, *m.* From L. *Clemens*, 'the merciful', *Clement* is a favourite with the Popes of Rome, of whom the first reigned ca. 91–100. Cf. *Clementine*.

CLEMENTIA. Originally and mainly Gr.; probably the immediate origin of:

CLEMENTINA. From the next as a specifically English variation thereof.

CLEMENTINE. Originally Ger. (*Klementine*: cf. Fr. *Clémen-*

tine), but popularized in England and U.S.A. in C19, especially in the song, 'My Darling Clementine'. A feminine diminutive from L. *clemens*.

CLEO. The diminutive of:

CLEOPATRA. In Gr., it means 'glory, fame, of [one's] father'. Cleopatra, who died in B.C. 30 at the age of 39, was the last of the Ptolemies in Egypt, which, on her death, became a Roman province. Beautiful, charming, and wise ('serpent of old Nile'), she figures in English literature less because of her early love-affair with Caesar (merely glanced at by G. B. Shaw, *Caesar and Cleopatra*) than because of her mature one with Antony – commemorated by Shakespeare, by Dryden (*All for Love* – the finest Restoration tragedy), and by Daniel (in a tragedy, 1594, in the Senecan manner); see also Rider Haggard's *Cleopatra*, 1889, as well as Jack Lindsay's historical novel, *Last Days with Cleopatra*, 1935. The name is now seldom bestowed among English-speaking people, though it is fairly common in Russia – or used to be. (Yonge; Harvey.)

CLIFFORD. As a place-name, *Clifford* signifies 'ford at or by a cliff or slope'; hence, as a personal name it signifies 'dweller by a cliff' or 'dweller on a slope'. Teutonic in origin, the two elements occur frequently in Old English; and as a surname, *Clifford* soon acquired a distinctive and distinguished connexion; it is the family name of the Cliffords of Chudleigh. Since the 18th Century it has often been bestowed as a front or given name. Diminutive *Clif* or *Cliff*; cf.:

CLIFTON. See Note at end of Introduction. Diminutive: *Clif*.

CLIVE became a 'Christian' in honour of 'Clive of India' or, as he is sometimes called, 'Clive of Plassey' (1725–74). He won notable victories at Arcot and Plass(e)y, 1751 and

1757. *Clive* is from *cliff*: cf. *Sutcliffe*, 'south cliff' (Weekley, *Romance of Names*).

CLO. The diminutive of *Chloe* and of the next three names.

CLODAGH is an Irish *f.* from a river name. (Withycombe.)

CLOTILDA; CLOTILDE. The former a mainly L., the latter a mainly Fr. name, they were fairly common in England in C19; but rather uncommon in C20. Perhaps 'famous battlemaid' (Teutonic); literally 'loud, i.e. famous, war'.

COELIA. An obsolete spelling of *Celia*.

COL. The pet-name 'shape' of *Colin*; occasionally of *Colbert*, *Colborn*, *Colman*, and *Columbine*.

COLAN, *m.* This is a Cornish name; meaning 'a dove', it derives from L. *columba*. The name sprang not only from the fame surrounding Columba or Columbus, the great C6 founder of a hundred monasteries, but also, in reinforcing part, from the sanctity investing Columba, a Christian virgin put to death by a heathen Cornish king, later canonized, and now the patron saint of two parishes in Cornwall. (Benedictines.)

COLBERT, *m.* In the Teutonic, 'cool brightness,' this is a French as well as an English name, the latter now somewhat rare. Cf.:

COLBORN, *m.* In Teutonic, 'a black bear'. It is akin to the preceding, for if in the former *col* is *kol*, 'cool,' and in the latter *kol* is 'black', that is because metal, once it has cooled, turns black.

COLETTE. This *f.* is properly Fr., but it is gaining ground in post-War England. It corresponds to *Nicholas* (p. 214), for it merely shortens the French *Nicolette* (as in the famous, and charming, medieval romance, *Aucassin et Nicolette*).

COLIN. (Cf. *Colan*, q.v.) Lit., 'a dove'. It derives from St *Columba* or *Columbus*, many of whose disciples were named *Gillecolum(b)* or *Mael(Maol)colum*, i.e. 'male servant of [St] Columba(-us)'; the reduction of *Columba(-us)* to *colum(b)* is typical in A.-S. and Celtic derivations from, or adaptations of, L. (or Gr.) names. The originally and, still, mainly Scottish *Colin* is sometimes confused with Fr. *Colin*, which is indubitably a diminutive of Fr. *Nicolas*. (Yonge.) Cf.:

COLMAN. Likewise from L. *columba*, 'a dove,' but not from the great St Columba(-us); the Church's intervention, here, is that of *Columbanus*, the Irish missionary who, finding the colleens much too alluring for his peace of mind, worked and suffered on the Continent, an influence strengthened and – in this matter of Christian names – given operative point by those five Celtic and English C7 saints who, by metathesis of *Columbanus*, bore the name of *Colman*. (See also *Colan* and *Colin*.)

COLUMBINE, *f.* From the It. *Colombina*, itself from the *f.* of *columbinus*, 'dove-like': 'an excellent thing in woman'.

CON. An occasional diminutive of *Constance* and *Conrad*. Cf. *Connie*.

CONAL. See *Connal*.

CONAN, *m.* In Celtic, either 'wisdom' or perhaps 'the high one' (cf. L. *Celsus*), this is a Breton as well as an Irish and Welsh name. 'Ossian' Macpherson calls a legendary man so named, 'Conan of small renown': contrast *Connal* and *Cormac*, both mighty figures in 'Ossian', that inflated prose epic which nevertheless has passages of haunting beauty. Also the name of a Celtic saint.

CONNAIRE. The Gaelic form of Irish *Connor*, it means in Celtic, either 'hound of slaughter' or 'great strength'.

CONNAL, CONNEL; CONAL. This Irish *m.* 'Christian' signifies, in Celtic, 'chief's, or high, courage'. (See also at *Conan.*) *Conal* has been endeared to the cultured English for its connexion with that remarkable Irish novelist and dramatist (like G. B. Shaw, long domiciled in England) who died in 1948 and whose lack of fame is the most flagrant example of neglect this century has the shame to offer, for even John Brophy's commendable efforts have failed to ensure him his due.

CONNIE. The most general diminutive of *Constance* and its cognates, as of its and their derivatives.

CONNOR. See *Connaire.*

CONRAD. In Teutonic, originally *Chuonrath* (cf. the old Mercian king, *Cenred*), 'able (or possibly "bold") speech'. A name famous in medieval European history, it bloomed brightest after – and mostly because of – the death of Conradin, 'the little Conrad,' who (1252–68) was King of Jerusalem and Sicily, only to be defeated in battle by Charles of Anjou and summarily executed; he was the third and last of the Hohenstaufen dynasty.

CONSTANCE. Less probably from L. *constans* (see at *Constantine*) than from *constantia* (see at *Constantia*), though admittedly *constantia* is, in L., a derivative of *constans*. It seems to have come to England from France, where it was for centuries a noble, a royal name; its general Fr. use arose in Provence, which took it from the other Romance countries, especially Italy. It fell away in post-Reformation England, but renewed its popularity in C17, mainly, it would seem, because of its prevalence among royalty and aristocrats. As *Custance*, now rather uncommon, it took a typically English shape as early as Chaucer.

CONSTANCIA. A variant (showing Portuguese influence) of *Constantia.*

CONSTANT, *m.* An English and Irish shortening of *Constantine*, in common with which it is, in C20, becoming rare.

CONSTANTIA; occasionally CONSTANCIA (q.v.). Direct from L., where, lit., it means 'constancy' or 'perseverance'.

CONSTANTINE, *m.* From L. *Constantinus*, originally a diminutive of *Constantius*, itself from *constans*, 'standing together,' hence 'constant, firm'. Its use in England is probably the direct result of the fame of Constantine the Great, who, in 313, gave Christians full citizenship in the Roman empire. Cf. the preceding quartet of names.

CORA. This Irish and American name comes from the Gr. (*κόρη*) for 'a maiden'; its popularity in the U.S.A. may owe much to Byron's poem (Yonge). Cf. *Corinna.*

CORAL, *f.* From the prettiness of coral; cf. *Pearl* and:

CORALIE. A French derivative from the preceding; not from the Fr. word for 'coral', for that happens to be *corail.*

CORDELIA. In Celtic, 'token of the flowing tide' or 'daughter of the sea': *Creiryddlydd*, Shakespeare's *Cordelia*, is the daughter of *Llyr* (Lear), 'the sea'; the modern form may be due to Ger. influence, for in the Ger. it is *Kordula.* 'Cordelia is hereditary in some Irish families; but it is chiefly used for love of Shakespeare's heroine of filial love' (Yonge): cf. *Imogen.*

CORDELLA. An English variant (cf. Ger. *Cordula*) of the preceding. Becoming rare.

CORINNA. From the Gr., hence the L., *f.* Christian name, presumably a diminutive of *koré* (see at *Cora*). The French form of the name is *Corinne*, now somewhat rare. English use – now verging on disuse – was very general in C17, especially among the lyric and pastoral poets, thanks to the influence of Ovid's Corinna. Sir George Etherege (in Southerne's *The Disappointment*) sings thus:

> See how fair Corinna lies,
> Kindly calling with her eyes;
> In the tender minute prove her;
> Shepherd! why so dull a lover?
> Prithee, why so dull a lover?

CORMAC. This Irish *m.* name means, lit., 'son of a chariot,' i.e. a charioteer. *Cormac* is a name prominent in Irish legend, in 'Ossian', in early Irish history, in the Irish Church, and, since C7, as a 'Christian' throughout Ireland.

CORMICK. A variant – more properly, a corruption – of the preceding.

CORNELIA, *f.*; CORNELIUS, *m.* The *Corn-* may be L. *cornu*, a horn, and therefore indicative of kingliness, a horn being the symbol of kingship; the *-elia*, *-elius* element is adjectival. In England, both these names verge on obsolescence; in the U.S.A., merely on comparative and perhaps increasing rarity: but their history is important. The Cornelian 'gens' (or clan) of Rome numbered many famous men and hardly less famous women, for Cornelia the mother of those two Republican trouble-makers the Gracchi had a firmer character than either of the two rather rash young men; of this 'gens' were the notable families of Sylla and Scipio; in addition to a rather obscure St Cornelia, there were at least three SS Cornelius, one of whom was a Pope of C3.

CORNEY. An Irish pet-form, hence an independent variant, of the preceding.

CORNIE, CORNY. 'Endearments' of *Cornelia*, *Cornelius*.

CORRIE. An occasional diminutive of *Cornelia(-ius)*, *Cora*, *Cordelia*, and *Cormick*.

COS. The diminutive – rarely heard – of:

COSMO. An Italian, thence English, contraction of It. *Cosimo*, at one time a very aristocratic name, meaning 'order': Gr. *κόσμος* (kosmos), whence, by philosophical evolution, our *cosmos*, the universe; indeed, we can now speak of 'cosmic order' and 'cosmic plan'.

COURTENAY. See Note at end of Introduction.

CRADOCK. An English contraction of *Caradoc*; now somewhat rare.

CRISPIAN; CRISPIN. The former represents L. *Crispianus*, the latter *Crispinus*: 'two brothers who accompanied St Quentin when he preached the Gospel in France. They settled at Soissons, and there, while pursuing their mission, supported themselves by making shoes until their martyrdom, A.D. 287. Shoemakers . . . adopted them as their patrons, and theirs was a universal holiday [October 25th]', Yonge. From L. *crispus*, 'curled,' hence 'curly'.

CRYSTAL. See *Chrystal*.

CURT. The diminutive of:

CURTIS, *m.* An American 'Christian' from the surname, itself from Middle English *Curthose*, 'short hose,' or from Old Fr. (*le*) *curteis*, '(the) courteous (man)'. Weekley, *Surnames*.

CUTHBERT. A.-S. *Cūthbeorht*, lit. 'famous-bright', hence probably 'famous splendour.' It was St Cuthbert (d. 687) who, from a shepherd lad becoming a saintly bishop, invested the name with reverential glamour. Despite its essential Anglo-Saxonism, it is now, among the lower orders (and others), a name of derisive connotation (in which respect cf. *Algernon*, *Clarence*, *Harold*, *Percy*); 'the comic sense of this name apparently dates from a pre-War music-hall song describing the adventures of three gilded youths, "Cuthbert, Clarence and Claude" ' (Weekley, *W. & N.*).

CUSTANCE. See towards the end of the entry at *Constance*.

CY. A diminutive of *Cyrus*.

CYMBELINE, *m.* Rare outside Cornwall and now, even there, seldom heard. From the Celtic ('lord of the sun'), it is, by most of us, remembered as the title of a play in which Shakespeare freely mingled Holinshed with Boccaccio.

CYNTH; CYNTHIE. Diminutives of:

CYNTHIA. The goddess Artemis (Diana) was so called because she was born at Mt Cynthus in Delos, the smallest of the Cyclades in the Aegean Sea. The name is, or was, a favourite with the lyric and pastoral poets of Europe.

CYNTHIE. See *Cynth*.

CYPRIAN. See *Ciprian*, of which it is the original and more correct form.

CYRIL. Gr. *Κύριλλος* (Kyrillos), lit. 'lordly' (Gr. *κύριος*, 'a lord or master'), this name 'fell to the lot of two great doctors of the Church – patriarchs, the one of Alexandria, the other of Jerusalem; also to two martyrs . . ., and thus it became widely known. The Welsh had it as Girioel, which . . . is nearer the pronunciation than our own . . . soft C.' (Yonge.)

CYRUS. In C19–20, much more common in America than in the British Empire, *Cyrus*, from the Gr. *Kŭros*, transliterating a word from Persian ('the sun' – cf. *le Roi Soleil* and

Pharaoh; or, say others, 'a throne'), owes its popularity to the founder of the Persian empire. Cyrus, a mighty conqueror whose fame attracted French writers, died in 529 B.C. History has not yet finished disentangling the ravelled skein of legend, fable and romance occasioned by his many and spectacular activities.

D

DAFFY. A diminutive of *Daphne.* So is *Daff.*

DAFOD. A Welsh form of *David.* Cf. *Dawfydd.*

DAGMAR. Originally and mainly Danish, it represents 'Dane's joy' and is the name of 'the favourite queen of the Danes, whose only fault was lacing her sleeves on a Sunday', as Charlotte Yonge of the quiet humour and cultured wit observes.

DAI. A Welsh *m.* 'Christian', possibly – like Fr. *Dé* – from a Celtic word meaning 'fire'. (Celtic *dei*, to shine.)

DAISY. Said by Helena Swan to be 'an English pet-name for Margaret ("pearl")', it is, in sober fact, the flower, which is A.-S. '*daeges eage*, day's eye, from its opening in the morning and also from its appearance' (Weekley).

DALY. See *Elaine.*

DAMIAN. Gr. *Damianos*, it signifies 'taming', 'one who tames,' from δαμάω (damaö). There are four Saints Damian, including the famous mid C7–early 8 Bishop of Pavia 'distinguished for learning and piety' (Benedictines). With the variant *Damien,* this name is now bestowed rarely except among Catholics.

DAN. Both a diminutive of *Daniel* and a *m.* 'Christian' in its own right. In Heb., *Daniel* means 'God is my judge'. It has no connexion with that odd phrase, apparently first used derivatively by Sterne (who took it from 2 *Samuel*, xvii, 11) in his novel, *Tha Sentimental Journey*, 1768: *from Dan to Beersheba,* from one end of the land to the other; these two cities being at the extreme north and the extreme south of Canaan. (Harvey.) Nor is it to be confused with the *dan* of *Dan*

Chaucer, this *dan* equalling the Sp. *dom*, from L. *dominus*, a master. – See also *Daniel*.

DANDIE. A Scottish *m.*, it is a corruption of *Andrew*. In Scott's *Guy Mannering*, Dandie Dinmont was 'a sturdy hospitable Liddlesdale farmer, and the owner of a special breed of terriers' (Harvey).

DANIEL. In Heb., 'the judging God – God is my judge – the Lord is judge'. Daniel of the Lion's Den – cf. the Misit Mark of the Daniel Press at Oxford (*misit angelum suum*, 'He sent His angel') – may be said to have implanted the name in popular imagination; it has flourished in both the East and the West, and 'in Ireland it was adopted as the equivalent to Domnall, Donacha, and other names from Don (or brown-haired), thus causing Dan to be one of the most frequent of Irish contractions', Yonge.

DANNIE. A diminutive of the preceding. Cf. *Dan*.

DAPH. A diminutive of the next; cf. *Daffy*.

DAPHNE. In C19 rather fashionable, in C20 tending to go below-stairs, this *f.* name, deriving from the Gr., means a bay-tree: which etymology reminds the romantic that mythological Daphne, pursued by amorous Apollo, was by the gods, on her supplication, transformed into this tree, henceforth Apollo's favourite; not that Apollo, any more than the other gods, came to believe in sublimation!

DARBY, like *Dermot*, is the commonly employed English variant of the Irish *Diarmid* or *Diarmaid*, a freeman. As to 'Darby and Joan', it was 'first used of attached old couple in song in *The Gentleman's Magazine* (1735), perhaps characters from real life' (Weekley).

DARCY, D'ARCY. This is the English form of the Irish *Dorchaidha*, or patronymic *O'Dorchaidhe*, which has also been corrupted to *D'Orsay* and even *Darkey*, which translates it. (Yonge.) Often, however, it comes from the French surname *D'Arcy*, 'he of Arcy'.

DARIUS. In Persian 'wealthy', this name is now comparatively rare even in the U.S.A. There were three Persian kings named Darius; of these, much the greatest was the first (521–485 B.C.). Cf. *Caesar*.

DARKEY. See *Darcy*.

DARREL(L); DARYL. This attractive *m.* name means 'darling' and derives from an A.-S. word.

DAVE. A diminutive of *David*.

DAVID. ' "The man after God's own heart" was well named from the [Heb.] verb to love, David, still called Daood in the East. It was *Δαυίδ* in the Septuagint; *Δαβίδ* and *Δαυείδ* in the New Testament; and the Vulgate ['s *Davidus*] made it the name well known to us. . . . The Eastern Church . . . seems to have adopted David . . . long before it was revived among the Jews'; like *John*, it strikes very few people as being Hebraic. Early in C6, a princely Welshman, Dawfydd (i.e. David), lived so holy a life that his bishopric became known as St David's, 'the principal Welsh see having been there transplanted in his time': it was he who came to be 'the Patron Saint of Wales and perhaps the most illustrious of the ancient British Bishops', and his day is March the 1st. (Whence *Taffy* and *Tafline*.) The name spread to Scotland, to Ireland, where it was often treated as though it were synonymous for *Dathi* and *Diarmaid*, and to England. (Yonge; Benedictines.)

DAVIE, DAVY. Diminutive of the preceding. Cf. *Dave*.

DAWFYDD. The usual Welsh form of *David*. Cf. *Dafod*.

DAWN, *f.*, is the English answer to *Aurora* (p. 47).

DAY. An Anglicization of *Dai*: except as a Cornish *m.* name, when it may represent (St) *Deicolus*, 'God-server'.

DEB, DEBBY. The usual diminutives of *Deborah*.

DEBERAH. An English variant of *Deborah*.
DEBIR. " " contraction of *Deborah*.

DEBORAH. In Heb., 'a bee' and, rather later, 'eloquent' (from the bee's humming, it would seem). It became popular among the Puritans as the name of 'Rebecca's devoted nurse' and that of 'the wife of Leppidoth – she who was "a Prophetess and Judge" in Israel' and who, with Barak, freed Israel from the oppression of the Canaanites. (Swan.) Confined, virtually, to Jews and to mindful descendants of Puritans.

DECIMA, *f.* See:

DECIMUS; DECIUS. The latter is a contraction of L. *decimus*, 'the tenth,' probably applied originally to a tenth son, and applied to a notable Roman clan (the *gens Decia*). 'Decimus and Decima are now and then to be found among us in unusually large families,' Yonge.

DEINIOL. The Welsh 'shape' of *Daniel*. There is a St Deiniol.

DEIRDRE (less often, *Derdre*) has, in C20, become fashionable among actresses, authoresses, and women artists. From Old Celtic *Derdriu*, 'The Raging One': ? she who causes fear in the manly breast. (Webster.)

DELIA. A 'surname' of Artemis, as *Delius* is of Apollo; from the Gr. island of Delos. *Delia* has been popular with English lyric and pastoral poets: cf. *Celia*.

DELICIA. The English form of It. *Delizia*, 'delight(ful)'. Becoming rare.

DELLA 'seems to be purely fanciful' (*Jack and Jill*): perhaps a blend of *Delia*+*Bella*.

DEMETRIUS, *m.* Gr., 'of Demeter,' originally 'vowed to, working for Demeter', the goddess protecting all the (vegetable) fruits of the earth. 'One of the most popular names in all the Eastern Church' (Yonge), but increasingly less used in Britain, where it has never been common.

DEN. A very colloquial abridgement of:

DENIS, DENNIS. Ultimately from *Dionysos*, the Gr. god of wine and revelry, by way of the adjective, *Dionysios*, L. *Dionysius*. 'Denis is a very frequent Irish name, as a substitute for Donogh; and, to judge by the number of the surnames, Dennis, Dennison, and Tennyson or Tenison, it would seem to have been more common in England than at present,' Yonge. Rarely: *Denys*.

DENISE, properly a Fr. name, is the *f.* companion to *Denis*.

DENZIL or, less correctly, *Densil*, is a mainly Cornish *m.* name, perhaps cognate with *Denis*.

DEODATUS. 'God-given,' i.e. by God. Now rare. Cf. *Dorothy*.

DEREK. The most general C20 form of *Derrick*, q.v. Something of a favourite with actors (for themselves) and with authors (for their other selves).

DERMOT. See *Diarmaid*.

DERRICK; DEREK (q.v.). From the Teutonic (cf. Ger. *Dietrich*, 'the people's wealth'), this is a Dutch pet-form of the name corresponding to *Theodoric.* As *Derrick,* it is also a surname.

DESMOND is an Irish clan-name become a surname, become a given name; literally 'South Munster'.

DETTA. An English contraction of *Henrietta* (cf. *Harriet*), says Swan. But it may in some instances be a shortening of It. *Benedetta* (cf. *Benedict*).

DHUGAL, *m.* (Cf. *Fingal,* q.v.). In Celtic – it is a solely Celtic name – it means 'black, i.e. swarthy, stranger'. Also *Dougal.*

DI. The diminutive of both *Dinah* and *Diana.*

DIAMOND, *f.* A 'jewel-name': cf. *Beryl, Emerald, Pearl, Ruby.*

DIANA. 'An ancient Italian divinity, whom the Romans identified with the Greek Artemis. . . . At Rome Diana was the goddess of light, and her name contains the same root as . . . *dies* [day] . . . Diana . . . represented the moon' (Blakeney). 'The name slept as a mere pagan device till the' C16, when it became fashionable with Sp., then Fr., and then, especially during the Restoration period, English poets. 'In the lower classes, Diana seems to be at times confused with the Scriptural Dinah,' Yonge, 1884; in C20, the confusion has ascended to those who should know better.

DIARMAID. A Celtic name, meaning 'a freeman', frequently heard in both Ireland and Scotland. (See also the next.) It figures prominently in legend – though not in Macpherson's *Ossian* – and in history. Diarmaid, King of Leinster, 'acted the part of Paris, and ruined his country by the abduction of Devorgil of Meath' (Yonge). Anglicized as *Dermot.*

DIARMID. A variant of the preceding and, in C19–20, the more usual spelling. The Old Celtic form was *Diarmait.*

DICK. A shortening of obsolete *Diccon*, an English transformation of *Richard.* For the numerous slang and colloquial senses of, and phrases built on, *Dick* and *Richard*, recourse should be had to a dictionary of slang.

DICKIE, DICKY. A more familiar form of *Dick.*

DIGBY. See Note at end of Introduction.

DIGGORY, says Charlotte Yonge, 'is a highly romantic name, derived from an old [Fr.] metrical tale of a knight, properly called D'Egaré, the wanderer, or the almost lost, one of the many versions of the story of the father and unknown son'. But 'the apostrophe is a misprint . . . Possibly the name was *Desgaré*, an Anglo-French substitute for O.F. *esgaré* (*égaré*), lost' (*Jack and Jill*).

DINAH. Heb. 'judged'. The Biblical Dinah was the daughter of Jacob and Leah. A non-aristocratic name: see also at *Diana.*

DIONYSIUS. Gr., 'of Dionysus,' i.e. of Bacchus. A rather rare English name, it owes its use to the fame of six notable characters in history: two tyrants of Syracuse (405–343 B.C.); the great Gr. rhetorician of Halicarnassus (C1 B.C.); Dionysius the Areopagite, concerning whose period there is some doubt; Dionysius of Alexandria (C3 A.D.), and Pope Dionysius, d. 269. (Harvey; Benedictines.) Compare *Denis.*

DODO. An English contraction and transformation of *Dorothea*: cf. *Doll.* The novel with which, at the age of 26, E. F. Benson made his name, in the early 'nineties, was entitled *Dodo.*

DOLL, DOLLY. An English telescoping of *Dorothea.* In C16–18, it was considered rather vulgar, as Shakespeare's harlot *Doll Tearsheet* and Jonson's low criminal *Dol(l)*

Common testify. Cf. the preceding, which has always been respectable.

DOLLY. See *Doll*. – Also a diminutive of *Adolphus*.

DOLORES. Originally and mainly Sp. ('sorrows': cf. Our Lady of Sorrows: *Maria de Dolores*), from L. *dolor*, 'grief', 'pain,' and 'often given to children born in time of sorrow' (Swan). In late C19–early 20 there flourished an opera singer thus pseudonym'd; without the glow of Patti, or the tonal vigour of Melba, she yet had more charm than either; she was just a little inferior to both as a singer.

DOMINIC. By way of Fr. *Dominique* from L. *dominicus*, as in *dies dominica*, 'the Lord's day,' it means 'child born on Sunday'. Popularized by the renown of the Sp. St Dominic, founder of the Dominicans or Black Friars. There is an occasional *f.*: *Dominica*.

DOMNECH. An Irish form of the preceding.

DON. A contraction and pet-form, as is *Donnie*, of:

DONALD. An Anglicization of Gaelic *Domhnall*, 'world-ruler,' though glossed by many pre-1890 Irish scholars as 'proved chieftain'. A Donald was the earliest Christian king of Scotland. (Yonge.)

DONOGHUE. From the Celtic and usually explained as 'brown chieftain'.

DORA. Adapted from Ger. *Dore*, a contraction of *Dorothea*. In English use, it is occasionally a shortening of *Dorothea*; but usually it is independent and not, as so often explained, 'a gift of God' (that is *Dorothea*), but Gr. δῶρα θεῶν: *dōra theōn*, gifts of the Olympian gods. The most famous Dora in fiction is David Copperfield's wife. Many puns have been made on 'Dora', an anagram for the Defence of the Realms

Act, 1914: of which some inept clauses are allowed by a too patient people to remain.

DORCAS. Gr., 'gazelle'. 'One of the names of the widow whom Peter raised from the dead. Her deeds of charity have, in England, caused her name to become a synonym for charitable working-societies' (Swan) and thus less popular as a 'Christian'.

DOREEN. Originally Irish (*Doireann*), it is from the Celtic for 'sullen' or 'moody'. So Yonge and Withycombe; 'but possibly a mere diminutive of Dora' (*Jack and Jill*).

DORI. A mostly American pet-form of the next, it is occasionally bestowed independently; occasionally, too, it represents *Dorothea* or *Dorothy*.

DORINDA. 'A fashionable English fancy embellishment' rather of *Dora* than of *Dorothea* or *Dorothy*: cf. *Florinda* for *Flora*. (Yonge.)

DORIS appears in neither 'Yonge' nor 'Swan', yet it is a frequent *f.* name, rather avoided by the aristocracy. It is direct from the L. *f.* name of the wife of Nereus and of the wife of Dionysius I, Tyrant of Syracuse, also the name of a Gr. girl in Juvenal and Propertius. Lit., 'a Doric girl'.

DOROTHEA. Lit., in Gr., 'a gift (*dōron*) of God (*Theos*)': cf., therefore, *Dora* and *Tudor*, qq.v. Of this widespread European name, the Ger. and Portuguese form is the same as the English (though the more English 'shape' is *Dorothy*), the Fr. *Dorothée*, the It. and Sp. *Dorotea*, the Polish *Dorota*. Under Hanoverian rule, *Dorothea* and *Dorothy* fell into disfavour, but by 1880 it was, as it still is, fashionable with all classes. (Yonge.)

DOROTHY. The specifically English form of *Dorothea*, perhaps influenced by Fr. *Dorothée*.

D'ORSAY. See *Darcy*.

DOT. A diminutive of *Dorothea* and *Dorothy*.

DOTTY. A diminutive of the same: it is to be avoided because of its slang connexion.

DOUCE, *f*. An English contraction of *Dulcibella*; sometimes direct from the Fr.

DOUG. The diminutive of *Douglas*.

DOUGAL. See *Dhugal*.

DOUGIE; incorrectly DUGGIE. Like *Doug*, a diminutive of:

DOUGLAS. Originally and mainly a Scottish name, from a Celtic word meaning 'dark stream'; from a clan-name, it became a surname, then a given name. It is prominent in Scottish history and legend, especially in the two men named *the Black Douglas* and *Douglas 'Bell-the-Cat'* (the 5th Earl of Angus).

DOWAL. An Irish form of the Scottish *Dougal* and *Dugald*. For etymology, see the latter.

DREDA, *f*. A Cornish, or mainly Cornish name. Possibly connected with Middle English *dreden*, whence our *dread*; but more probably represents a shortening of *Etheldreda* (p. 110).

DREW, *m*. Brought to England by a follower of William the Conqueror, this name (*Dru*) seems to have been derived from a Teutonic word meaning 'carrier'.

DRUSILLA. A *f*. diminutive of the L. *Drusus*, '(a) strong (man)', a well-known Roman surname of the Livian family; less probably the name comes from the Gr. and signifies 'dew-watered'. Now rare. English pet-form: *Drucie*.

DUCIA. See *Dulcibella.*

DUDLEY. See Note at end of Introduction.

DUFF, *m.* This Scottish font-name represents a modern form of Celtic *Dhu,* lit. 'the black man', i.e. 'he of the swarthy countenance'.

DUG. A diminutive of:

DUGALD. In Celtic, lit. 'dark stranger': cf. the etymology of *Duff.* 'Dougall and Dugald have been from time immemorial Highland names, and, together with Donald, serve as the national nickname of the Gael among the Lowlanders' (Yonge). Complementary to *Fingal,* q.v.

DUKE. See Note at end of Introduction; cf. *Earl.* Both *Duke* and *Earl,* as given names, are rare in the British Empire and common in the United States. More ambitious than envious. – Also see *Marmaduke.*

DULCE, DULCIE; DULCIA. *Dulce* and *Dulcia* are interchangeables; *Dulcie* a diminutive of the other two. For etymology, see:

DULCIBELLA. L. *dulcis,* 'sweet' or 'mild' (cf. *la douce France*), 'is explained by Spanish authors to have been the origin of their names of Dulcia, Aldonça, Adoncia . . ., so that it was most correct of [Cervantes] to translate . . . Aldonça . . . into . . . Dulcinea . . . Dulcia lingered in the south of France, became Douce, and came to England as Ducia in the time of the Conqueror, then turned into Dulce, and by-and-by embellished into Dulcibella, and then by Henry VII's time fell into Dowsabel' (Yonge). *Dowsabel* has long been dead; *Dulcibella* is moribund.

DULCINA. A variant of:

DULCINEA. A diminutive of *Dulcia*: cf. Dulcinea del Toboso in *Don Quijote*.

DUGGIE. See *Dougie*. – Also, it is the correct diminutive of *Dugald*.

DUNCAN. Of Celtic origin, this Scottish 'Christian' represents either *Donnachu*, 'brown warrior,' or, less probably, *Donncean*, 'brown head'. Like *Donald*, *Duncan* occurs in the medieval Icelandic saga of Burnt Njal; the gentle, saintly king of Scotland in Shakespeare's *Macbeth* is the C11 Duncan I of Scotland. (Yonge.)

DUNK. (More properly *Dunc.*) The diminutive of *Duncan.*

DUNSTAN. An A.-S. name equivalent to 'hill-stone', presumably in reference to physical strength or moral firmness: cf. *Peter*. The name, now rather uncommon, was popularized by the fame of that Dunstan who, after a turbulent love-affair, became a monk at Glastonbury and soon its abbot, and in 960 (aged 35), prime minister and Archbishop of Canterbury until his death (988) after a wise ministry and vigorous reform. (Dawson.)

DURAND. Adopted from the Fr. but now rare. Like the It. *Durante*, it means 'enduring' and derives from L. *durare*, to last. Cf. the famous sword *Durindana* or *Durandal*, which, after being Hector of Troy's, became Roland's.

DYLAN is a Welsh *m.* name, 'very common and attractive', as the *Morning Post* reviewer of the first edition of this book remarked; it graces a notable poet. In Cymric, *dylan* is the sea, the ocean.

E

EACHAID; EACHAN. These Gaelic *m.* 'Christians' are from Celtic for 'a horseman' (literally 'a horse').

EADITHA. An English variant of *Edith*; now seldom used.

EAMON. The Irish for *Edmund*.

EARL or EARLE. See Note at end of Introduction.

EASTER, *f.* Lit. (in Teutonic) 'a child born at Eastertide'. It is becoming rare.

EB; EBBIE. Diminutives of:

EBENEZER, *m.* In the old Testament, Ebenezer is a stone that, erected by Samuel, commemorates the defeat of the Philistines. It is a Heb. word meaning 'stone of help', i.e. 'God is our help': cf. George Baker's arresting novel, *Ebenezer Walks with God*, 1931.

ED. A very familiar pet-name for *Edgar*, *Edmund*, *Edward*, *Edwin*.

EDA. Originally a diminutive – perhaps, rather, a shortening – of *Edith*.

EDDIE. A diminutive, rarely of *Edward*, mostly of *Edwin* and *Edmund*.

EDGAR. In A.-S., *Eadgar*, from a Teutonic word meaning 'felicitous spear'. In C20, it shows signs of disuse, despite notable associations with literature and with Edgar King of all England in 959–975, – who, despite being 'a loose liver', is now venerated as a saint (Dawson).

EDIE. The usual 'endearment' of:

EDITH. In A.-S., *Eadgyth*, 'prosperous war'. As used by the Normans in England, it lumps together the A.-S. names *Eadgyth*, *Eadgifu* ('rich gift'), *Eadgifa* ('giver of bliss'), and even *Adelgifu* ('noble gift') and *Aelgifu* ('elf-gift'). There are two English saints of this name: 1, Edith of Polesworth (C10) – divided by martyrologists into three, and, even so, confused with 2, Edith of Wilton, also of C10. (Yonge; Dawson.)

EDITHA. A mere spelling variant of *Eaditha*.

EDMOND, EDMUND. In A.-S., *Eadmund* ('happy protection'); the *-ond* form is Gallic. 'One of our most English names, belonging to the king of East Anglia [ca. 840–70], who, as the first victim of the Danes, became the patron saint of Bury St Edmund's, and the subject of various legends,' Yonge. Like *Edgar* and *Edwin*, it is much less used in C20 than in C19.

EDNA. A contraction of the long-obsolete *Edana*, it means either 'rich gift' or 'perfect happiness'; if the former, cf. *Edna* with *Edith*. It is not, however, certain that it was not formed as the *f.* of Scottish *Edan*, which in the Celtic means 'fire' and which has a Latinized shape, *Edanus*. In *Jack and Jill*, Ernest Weekley makes a strong case for an origin in obsolete *Edina*, itself probably the *f.* of *Edwin*; Heb., 'rejuvenation' (Webster).

EDWARD. In A.-S., *Eadvard* or *Eadward* ('rich ward' or 'guard' or 'guardian'). Charlotte Yonge hymns it as 'the most really noted of all our own genuine appellations. . . . It comes to light in our royal line with the son of Alfred, and won the popular love for the sake of the young king whom St Dunstan and the English called the martyr.' Edward the Confessor, feeble as a ruler, became a patron saint of England; 'in the ardour of embellishing his foundation of Westminster Abbey, it was natural to give his name to the heir of the crown, afterwards "the greatest of the Plantagenets".

The deaths of his three children bearing Norman or Spanish names confirmed this as the royal name, and the third king so called spread it far and wide.' But rarely has it been more effectively borne than by Edward VII.

EDWIN. In A.-S., *Eadwine*, lit. 'rich friend' or 'happy friend'. This was the name of 'the first Christian king of Northumbria, whose conversion [forms] the most striking portion of Bede's history' (Yonge). After his marriage with St Ethelburga, we learn, he 'zealously promoted the conversion of his subjects. He fell at Hatfield Chase, A.D. 633, fighting against Cadwallon of Wales and the Pagan tyrant of Mercia' (Benedictines).

EFFIE. A contraction and diminutive of *Euphemia*, but in C20 often bestowed independently. Cf. *Phemie*.

EGBERT. In A.-S., *Ecgbeorht*, literally 'edge-bright', hence 'formidably bright'. There is a noted St Egbert, an Englishman, who went, in late C7, to Ireland 'to frequent its renowned schools of piety and learning'; his influence there was tremendous. (Benedictines.)

EGMOND, EGMONT. The former is, properly, Ger.; the latter, English: but in neither form has it been a very common English name. In the Teutonic, it means 'sword protection', hence 'terrible protection', i.e. a protector dreaded by the protégé's enemies.

EILEEN is often said to be an Irish form of *Helen*, q.v. Miss Withycombe, however, has pointed out that it is a genuinely Celtic name: *Eibhilin* or *Eibhlin*.

EILUNED is a Welsh *f.* name that is, in C20, becoming more general, – which is a good thing, for Welsh *f.* names are, most of them, very attractive.

ELAIN (rare), ELAINE. A variant of *Ellen* and *Eileen*, i.e. of

Helen, of which *Elaine* (probably influenced by Fr. *Hélène*) is the most mellifluous variation. Now adjudged, rather gratuitously, as 'pretty but Victorian', it has gained a wistful charm from Tennyson's idyll, *Lancelot and Elaine* (1859), discreet, somewhat namby-pamby, yet of a touching beauty. Diminutive, *Daly*. Cf.:

ELEANOR, ELEANORA, ELEANORE. English variants, perhaps shaped in part by the Ger. *Eleonore* and the It. *Eleonora*, of *Helen*; directly, however, *Eleanor* and *Eleanore* derive from the Provençal *Aliénor*. *Eleanor* was, in England, a royal name throughout the latter half of the Plantagenet period. (Yonge.)

ELEAZAR, *m*. In Heb., 'God has helped' – loosely 'the Lord's help', – it is now somewhat rare.

ELI has two independent existences. A diminutive of the next three names, especially of *Elias*, it is also a Biblical name in its own right (see 1 *Samuel*, i, 9), with the literal meaning, in Hebrew: 'height': ? 'the exalted'.

ELIAS. Heb. 'God the Lord', through the Gr. (cf. Elias in the New Testament). Its use in England, where it now occurs but rarely, may have been, in part, occasioned by its employment in Holland. It is therefore cognate with the next two names; indeed, it is best treated as a form of:

ELIJAH. 'The noblest prophet of the kingdom of Israel was called by two Hebrew words, meaning God the Lord, a sound most like . . . Eliyahu, the same in effect as that of the young man who reproved Job and his friends, though, in his case, the Hebrew points have led to his being called in our Bible Elihu, while we know the prophet as Elijah, the translators probably intending us to pronounce the *j* like an *i*,' Yonge. The lit. sense is 'Jehovah is God'.

ELIHU. A Hebrew name, meaning either 'God is Jehovah'

(cf. *Elijah*) or perhaps 'God – or, the Lord – himself'. Both *Elijah* and *Elihu* are rare in England, not quite so rare in the U.S.A.

ELINOR. A mere variant of *Eleanor*.

ELIOT. See *Elliot*.

ELISABETH. See *Elizabeth*.

ELISE. Properly and mostly Fr., this is a variant of *Eliza*, which is, in sense, the same as *Elizabeth*. *Elise*, pronounced Fr. fashion, is much prettier than *Eliza*.

ELISHA. In C19–20, chiefly in the U.S.A., where most of the 'prophets' reside. In Heb., 'God is [my] salvation' but, lit., 'to whom God is saviour', it becomes *Eliseus* in the New Testament. Next to Elijah, Elisha was perhaps the greatest of the Old Testament prophets. 'It is possible that the frequent Ellis of the middle ages may spring from it,' Yonge.

ELIZA. A 'contraction, introduced by the Elizabethan poets, of Elizabeth' (Swan); often so dissociated from its original that it is apprehended as an independent name: 'Eliza and Elizabeth are sometimes to be found in the same family' (Yonge). Cf. *Liz*, *Liza*.

ELIZABETH, ELISABETH. Heb., 'God hath sworn' or 'God is an oath' or 'oath of God': 'in memory of the covenant made with Abraham' (Swan). It is known in many forms: see *Eliza*, *Bessy*, *Betsy*, *Betty*, *Liz*, *Lizzie*, *Liza*, *Lisa*, *Libby*. Moreover, *Isabella*, *Isabel*, and their derivatives represent a Romance variation of the Biblical form. The original name was *Elisheba*, and this has developed through the Greek *Elisabet* (cf. the It. *Elisabetta*) and the Latin into *Elisabeth*: whence *Elizabeth*, a form not improved by those poets who turned Queen Elizabeth into Eliza. *Elizabeth* has been famous in history both politically and ecclesiastically; spelt with an *s*, it is borne by four saints, the earliest being the mother of St John the Baptist, the latest that daughter of Peter II of Aragon who, married to Dionysius, King of Portugal, became 'for the King and Court a striking pattern of every virtue' and who, on his death, 'took the habit of the Third Order of St Francis, and devoted herself to good works' until her death in 1336 (Benedictines).

ELLA. As *m.*, it is long obsolete and perhaps A.-S. *Aella*, 'elf-friend'; but in C19–20, it is only *f.* and a quite independent word – in short, either a variant of *Ellen* or from Old Ger. *Alia*, 'all' (Withycombe).

ELLEN. A Scottish (hence English) pronunciation of *Helen*: the change is not for the better.

ELLIE. A diminutive of *Eleanor* and *Helena*.

ELLIOT, ELLIOTT; ELIOT. A very English derivative of *Ellis* and therefore ultimately from *Elisha*.

ELLIS. (For etymology, see *Elias*.) In C18–20, it is mostly a surname, but, as a 'Christian', it is still a name of considerable merit.

ELLO. Lit., in Heb., 'God's oath' (cf. the first element in *Elijah*, *Elihu*, and *Elisha*), it is now used only as a reduction of *Elliot*.

ELMA, *f.* As a Gr. derivation, it signifies 'love'; as an A.-S., 'like an elm' (Loughead).

ELMER is merely an American metamorphosis of *Aylmer*: witness Elmer Rice, the quietly dynamic writer, and those two well-known characters of fiction, Sinclair Lewis's Elmer Gantry and Talbot Mundy's Elmer Rait.

ELOISA, ELOISE. These may be *f.* forms and derivatives of

Lewis (*Louis*), which in the Teutonic means 'famous war'; but Fr. influence it is which, by virtue of *Héloïse*, has been mainly instrumental in popularizing the name in England. Thus the old explanation. Miss Withycombe, however, shows that the name more probably Gallicizes the Old German *Helewidis*, a rather odd compound of *haila*, 'healthy, hale', and *vid*, 'wide'.

ELSA, ELSE. Originally Ger., as *Else* has mostly remained when it is not used as an endearment for *Elsie*. In Teutonic it means 'noble maiden': and therefore it has no justifiable connexion with *Elizabeth*.

ELSHENDER. A Scottish contraction of *Alexander*.

ELSIE. An English and Scottish contraction of *Elizabeth*.

ELSPAH. A Scottish contraction of *Elizabeth*; cf. *Elsie* and:

ELSPETH, ELSPIE. Scottish derivatives from *Elizabeth*.

ELUNED. A variant of *Eiluned*.

ELVINA, like *Malvina* (p. 190), is a Celtic *f.* name of romantic associations and decreasing viability; 'friendly' or 'wise friend' (Loughead).

ELVIRA. A Sp. name, perhaps from Old German *Alverat*, 'Elf-Counsel'. (Withycombe.)

ELZA. A rather affected spelling (and pronunciation) of *Elsa*.

EM. Now the diminutive, but originally the etymon, of *Emma*.

EMANUEL; EMMANUEL. (In Italy, frequently preceded by *Victor*.) Originally *Immanuel*, it derives from Heb., where it means, lit., *immanu*, 'with us': probably 'God with us'. First used, as a Christian name, by the Greeks; then by the Italians, from whom it spread rapidly. It rarely occurs nowadays: people feel that it is a little too God-like for common clay.

EMELINE. See *Emmelina*.

EMERALD. A girl's name from the precious stone: cf. *Ruby* and see *Esmeralda*.

EMERY. A variant of *Emmery*.

EMILE. Originally and mainly French, it was introduced into England by the Huguenots, I fancy; corresponding probably to the Fr. *Emilie* (our *Emily*), it derives from L. *Aemilius*, the name of a Roman clan (*gens*) that furnished Rome, all Italy, with some remarkable men and distinguished women; there was, too, a Veronese poet, Aemilius Macer, who, a friend of Ovid and Virgil, wrote on birds, reptiles, and plants. *Aemilius* is a variant of L. *aemulus* (our *emulous*), itself the origin of *aemulari*, to strive emulously with, to excel. Little used in England since C18.

EMILIA, *f.* Connected, I believe, with *Emile*, q.v., rather than with Teutonic *amal*, 'work'.

EMILIE, EMILY. Better *Emily*, for the former baldly repeats Fr. *Emilie*. For etymology and connexions, see *Emile*.

EMLYN. A Welsh *m.* name used as a variant of *Ermin*; an English *f.* name, which, in the Teutonic original, means 'work serpent', according to some; perhaps rather from L. *Aemilianus*.

EMMA. (Not to be confused with, nor treated as an etymological equivalent of, *Emilia* and *Emily*.) 'Emma comes, *via* Imma, from Irma, short for some such name as Ermintrude, in which the first element is the name of a Teutonic deity and the second as in Gertrude' (*Jack and Jill*). 'As a name it was at first exclusively Frank. . . . The first Emma mentioned was the daughter of Charlemagne'; at first it was 'considered so un-English' that it was 'translated into Aelgifu'; but soon there were Emmes, Ems, and Emms. By 1500, *Emma* was common enough in England, partly because clergymen used it as a translation both of *Amy* and of *Em.* (Yonge.)

EMMANUEL. See *Emanuel.*

EMMELINA, EMMELINE. Originally diminutives, now regarded as elaborations of *Emilia* and *Emily.*

EMMERY; EMERY. A pleasant Anglicization of *Almeric(k).*

EMMIE, EMMY. A diminutive of *Emma*, *Emilia*, *Emily*, *Emmelina*; cf. *Em.*

EMMOTT, *f.* and, derivatively, *m.* A mainly North of England name, probably extruded from *Em*, the original English form of *Emma.*

EMMY. See *Emmie.*

EMRYS, *m.* This Welsh name represents a thorough Cymrization of *Ambrose* or its L. predecessor *Ambrosius*, known to the Welsh through the zeal of missionaries.

ENA. Perhaps from Gr. αἴνη or αἶνος, 'praise,' and therefore constituting the *f.* of *Aeneas*; or else a contraction of *Edana* (for which, see *Edna*); or, more probably, simply the name-ending, *-ena*: cf. *Ina.*

ENID. This is one of those names which would entail on its owner a very grave responsibility, if in the Celtic it means 'spotless purity', as some have held. (According to Miss Withycombe the origin is obscure; she very tentatively associates the name with Welsh *enit*, 'a woodlark'. In Arthurian romance, Enid was the metaphorical torch-bearer of virtuous and noble womanhood. 'In the Middle Ages no higher praise could be bestowed on a woman than to be called "a second Enid",' Helena Swan: in the present century, any self-respecting woman would face-slap a husband that offered to treat her as Tennyson's Geraint did Enid in the Idyll bearing their names. (*Geraint* I had imagined to be long dead and buried: and yet you will see the name attached to a contributor to *Lovat Dickson's Magazine*, February, 1935. It commemorates a Cornish saint of that name.)

ENIE. The diminutive of *Ena* and:

ENOCH. In Heb., 'dedication', hence 'dedicated' (to God). In the Bible, Enoch, father of Methuselah, had himself attained the not inconsiderable age of 365 when a possible record was spoilt by his translation to heaven; he was the sixth in descent from Adam. Tennyson's *Enoch Arden*, published in 1864, tells a noble story of self-sacrifice, and may thus have done something to perpetuate the name, which is now rarely found outside of rural districts. The sub-title of H. A. Vachell's *Vicar's Walk* (1933) runs thus: 'A chronicle of certain adventures and misadventures, traffics and excursions, in the life of Enoch Saint, chorister, soldier, and dean's verger' (in the ancient town of Wells).

ENOS. Also from Hebrew, in which it signifies 'mortal man', and also becoming rare. Any boy so named risks being called Eno's.

EOGHAN. In Celtic, 'young warrior'. Originally an Irish name, it is in Scotland 'indiscriminately translated by Evan, Ewan, and Hugh' (Yonge). See also *Owen*.

EPHRAIM. Heb., 'two-fold increase' or 'doubly fruitful': a sense that may, in these birth-controlled times, increase the deceleration in its use. In the Old Testament, he was the second son of Joseph.

EPPIE, *f.* An English diminutive of *Euphemia.*

ERASMUS. From Gr. *erao* (ἐϱάω), 'I love': cf. the *Iras* mentioned under *Ira*; strictly, the Gr. word should be *erasmios.* The earliest historical Erasmus 'was tortured to death in Diocletian's persecution' in the early C4. The great Dutch scholar assumed it – incorrectly – as a translation of his name *Gerhard*; it was his visit to England which introduced it there, though it is now seldom bestowed among us.

ERIC. Literally it is perhaps 'ever king'. Its early – its Norwegian – form was *Eirik* (Old Norse *Eyrekr*), the *ei* being *aye* (as in *ever and aye*), although both Weekley and Withycombe say that this element is of doubtful meaning; *ric* is the *rich* of Old Ger., *ryce* of A.-S., and *rex* of L. 'Our adjective *rich* is its sordid offspring, and in France a wealthy peasant is *un richart*' (Yonge), though in C20 *un richard* is any rich vulgarian. The name was debased by Dean Farrar in *Eric, or Little by Little*, which the present writer, name-lured, read at the formidably mature age of seven; it was more nobly used by Sir Henry Rider Haggard in that stirring 'juvenile', *Eric Brighteyes.* By 'Johns' and 'Toms' and 'Dons', it is often, as I discovered at school, despised as pretty-pretty. Diminutived as *Ricky* or even *Rex.*

ERICA. The female form of the preceding.

ERMIN, *m.* If a Welsh name, it would mean 'lordly'; 'probably a legacy of the Roman Herminii' (Yonge). But modern research has shown that *Ermin*, the name of a Teutonic demigod, is Teutonic rather than Celtic.

ERMINIA. The *f.* of the preceding.

ERMINTRUDE. (In Ger., *Irmentrud* or *-de.*) See *Emma.*

ERN. A (by some, thought rather vulgar) diminutive of *Ernest*, *Ernie* being held preferable.

ERNEST. Originally Ger. (*Ernst*), it was, by 1860, 'working its way into England, though not yet with a naturalized sound'. Charlotte Yonge questions whether it may not derive, not from Ger. *Ernst*, 'earnestness', but from Scandinavian *aar*, Ger. *ar*, A.-S. *earn* (in Scottish, *erne*), 'an eagle,' especially as the older Ger. form was *Arnust* (with this etymology, cf. that of *Arnold*); unfortunately the predominant Old Ger. form was *Ernust*.

ERNESTINE. A melodious *f.* derivative from the preceding. Originally Ger., in which language, as in Fr. after it, *-ine* is a very common *f.* suffix, probably from L. *-ina*, the diminutive of *-a*.

ERNIE. A diminutive of *Ernest*.

ERROL, *m.* Ultimately from the L. and signifying 'wandering' or 'wanderer' (Loughead).

ESAIAS. The Gr., hence Ger. and English, form of *Isaiah*, 'salvation of the Lord'. In Gr., *-ias* is a frequent suffix in *m.* names and some few *f.* names.

ESAU. Heb. 'hairy'. Popularized in England by the Biblical story of Esau, that elder son of Isaac and Rebecca who sold his birthright to his brother Jacob for a mess of pottage. It is dying out.

ESMÉ, *m.* and *f.* Not, I believe, bestowed before mid C19 in England, but current in Scotland since mid C16. 'Apparently the past participle of O.Fr. *esmer*, to esteem' (Weekley); hence, like *Amabel*, from the L. *amare*, 'to love'.

ESMERALDA. Mostly a Sp. name, it is, lit., 'an emerald': cf. *Pearl*. It derives from the Gr. σμάραγδος (smaragdos), perhaps from μαρμαίρω, marmairo ('twinkle' or 'sparkle'). 'The rainbow of St John's vision was "in sight like unto an emerald". Thus Smaragdos was one of the early martyrs,' Yonge.

ESMOND. 'Desmond, Esmond and Redmond were taken to Ireland by the vikings' (*Jack and Jill*). Teutonic, *Esmond* perhaps means 'divine protection': *mund* certainly means 'protection', but the first element is in doubt.

ESSIE. A diminutive of *Esther*, but occasionally used as a self-contained name independent of any reference thereto. Cf.:

ESTELLE. A diminutive of *Esther* influenced by L. *stella* (a star): cf. *Estella*, in Dickens's *Great Expectations*.

ESTHER. From Persian *satarah* or Assyrian *sitarch* (perhaps, as Weekley suggests, from the Persian for 'the planet Venus'), through Gr. ἀστήρ (*astēr*), 'a star,' hence 'any luminous body, e.g. a meteor', which in the Septuagint becomes, as a name, 'Εσθήρ (*Hesthēr*) and among the Romans *Esthera* or *Hestera*; 'whence the . . . variations in English of Esther or Essie, and Hester or Hetty'. But 'not till the days of [Racine's sacred drama *Esther*, 1689, based on the life of the Jewish captive of King Ahasuerus] was Esther much in vogue'; the play, performed by the young ladies of St Cyr, popularized the name in France, where 'it vied with the cumbrous splendours taken from the Scudery cycle of romance'; Swift's two most famous women friends were named Esther, they were born about 1690, and he renamed them Stella and Vanessa. Cf. *Vashti*.

ETHEL. In A.-S., *Aethelu*, 'noble,' never stood alone as a *f.* name and only rarely (witness Searle) as a *m.*; usually it preceded a noun, the pair forming such names as *Ethelgiva*, 'noble gift'. In 'the Benedictines' there are no saints named *Ethel*, but nineteen whose names begin therewith. It is one of the most Anglo-Saxon of all our *f.* 'Christians'. Cf. the next six names.

ETHELBERT. 'Aethelbryht, or Noble Splendour, named our first Christian king of Kent, also a brother of King Alfred's, and a missionary of the royal blood of Northumbria, who preached in southern Germany, and died about the year 700, at Egmond, where, as St Adelbrecht, he became patron,' Yonge. Now rare.

ETHELBURGA. In Teutonic, 'noble fortress' – hence 'noble protectress', *Ethelburga* lingers on in the land, mainly because it is that of three C7 Saints, to two of whom numerous English church buildings – especially those at Lyminge and Barking – have been either dedicated or in some way indebted for part of their fame. (Benedictines.) Sometimes shortened to *Ethelburg*.

ETHELDRED (now rare), ETHELDREDA (not quite so rare). A.-S. Aethelthryth, 'noble might'. It is popularly connected with the Ger. *Ediltrud*, 'noble maiden,' for, as Charlotte Yonge points out, 'most likely names ending in *trut* had been brought to England, and as the Valkyr sense was forgotten, the native meaning of *threat* was attached to the word, and the spelling adapted to it.' See also at *Audrey*.

ETHELFLEDA. (The variant *Ethelfledh* has long been obsolete.) Literally 'Nobly beautiful', this is an A.-S. *f.* name of Teutonic origin. Now seldom bestowed.

ETHELIND, ETHELINDA. Either 'noble maiden' or 'noble snake', the latter connoting wisdom; it is, in either interpretation, of Teutonic origin. The name is becoming rare. Cf. also *Ethel*, q.v.

ETHELRED; ETHERED. 'Aethelred, Noble-speech or counsel, the brother of Alfred, was almost canonized by his subjects, and is sometimes called Ethered, whence the Scottish Ethert' (Yonge). Becoming rare.

ETHERT. See the preceding.

ETTA. An English shortening of *Henrietta*; also a diminutive of *Esther*.

ETTIE, ETTY. A diminutive of *Esther*: cf. *Etta*.

EUGENE, *m.* In Gr., 'well-born,' this is one of a group of names beginning with εὖ, 'well' or 'happily': cf. the next five 'Christians' and see *Evangeline*. The Gr. *Eugeneios* became the Latin *Eugenius*, the Fr. *Eugène* and the German *Eugen*. It was Prince Eugene of Austria whose fame as a general against the Turks and the French (for the French have ever been chivalrous foes) for a full score of years (1697–1717) popularized his name in both France and, through his association with Marlborough in 1704–09, England.

EUGENIA. This convenient *f.* of *Eugene* has not 'caught on' in England; in France, as *Eugénie*, it has been fashionable since Eugénie de Montijo married Napoleon III in 1853. Among the Irish, *Eugenia* often represents *Eughania*, an Erse *f.* of *Eoghan* (q.v.).

EUNICE. It derived from the Gr. εὖνις, 'a wife,' though probably with some influence from εὖ, 'will' + νίκη, 'a victory', i.e. happy or glorious or fortunate victory. *Eunice* was by the Jews given a slight moral twist to make it denote 'one who conquers by virtue'; we find it in the New Testament as the name of Timothy's mother. (Helena Swan.)

EUPHEMIA. (In Scotland, at first often and now occasionally *Euphame*.) In Gr., the word means 'fair speech' and 'abstinence from foul speech', the latter having a connotation of 'silence', hence of constancy, as in the legend of that virgin martyr (307 A.D.) of Bithynia who gave to the name its far-flung popularity. It is difficult to determine why *Euphame, Euphemia* should be so often used in Scotland, so rarely in England; perhaps it is 'only another attempt to translate the Keltic Aoiffe' (Yonge). The pet-form is *Effie.*

EUPHRASIA, *f.* Gr., 'good cheer'; hence, probably, 'cheerful'. It has appealed to the devout, for a worker of minor miracles so named died, after long years of strict religious observance, in the Thebaid early in C5.

EUSTACE, *m.* This Gr. name probably means 'rich in ears of corn', i.e. 'happy in harvest' (*Εὔσταχυς*, Eustakhus; L. *Eustachius*), hence 'fruitful' or 'blooming'. Owing to its saintly fame, *Eustace* existed in England before the Norman Conquest; it was popular in C12–16; now it is seldom bestowed. The *f.*, *Eustachia* or *Eustacia*, hardly impressed the English, among whom it has not been used since C17.

EVA, EVE. (For the etymology, see *Zoe.*) In Book IV of *Paradise Lost*, Milton stresses far too much his opinion that Eve ('For softness she and sweet attractive grace') was in subjection to Adam, but one can hardly quarrel with:

'So hand in hand they pass'd, the loveliest pair
That ever since in love's embraces met,
Adam the goodliest man of men since born
His sons, the fairest of her daughters Eve.'

EVADNE, *f.* In neither 'Yonge' nor 'Swan', this name, which is that of the most important woman in Beaumont and Fletcher's *The Maid's Tragedy*, 1619, recurs in *The Fortunes of Evadne*, a novel by Dorothea Conyers. Rather fanciful, it is also unusual – and, because of its trisyllabic pronunciation, avoided by the illiterate. 'Tis Evadne (*ē-vād-nē*), the wife of Capaneus, one of 'the seven against Thebes', as in the play by Aeschylus: she leapt into the flames that were consuming her husband's body, to be herself consumed. (Most of 'em remain widows for quite six months.) In Gr., her name was *Εὐάδνη*, *Euädnē*, ? 'the well-tamed'.

EVAN, like *Ewan*, is a correct Anglicization of Celtic *Eoghan*, which, when it went to Scotland, was translated as *Evan* and *Ewan*. (Yonge.) But it is also the Welsh form of *John*. *Evan*, a very agreeable 'Christian', has been perpetuated by Meredith in his novel *Evan Harrington*, 1861.

EVANGELINE. Lit., 'happy messenger' or 'bearer of good tidings'. The *eu* of the Greek was changed to *ev* early in the course of alphabetic evolution. Thus we have *Evangelist*, one of the four narrators of Christ's personal history, and *Evangeline*, which Longfellow apparently invented for the heroine of his poem (published in 1847): 'whence many of the name have sprung up in America' (Yonge).

EVE. See *Eva*.

EVELEEN. In Celtic, 'pleasant,' this is the original and in Ireland by far the commonest form of *Eveline* (and *f.* *Evelyn*); in Erse it is *Eibhlin*. Ultimately, the name may go back to the Heb. word for 'life': see at *Zoe*.

EVELINA. An ornamental variant (cf. Fanny Burney's novel, *Evelina*, 1778) of:

EVELINE. (For etymology, see *Eveleen*.) This, not *Evelyn*, is 'the true English feminine form', as Helena Swan declares.

EVELYN. Originally *m.* and perhaps from the Celtic for 'pleasant', it has, in C19–20, been used for both sexes; for the *f.*, both *Eveleen* and *Eveline* (qq.v.) are undeniably preferable, except when *Evelyn* is meant to represent the surname *Evelyn* ('the old French form of the Latin *avellana*, a hazel', Yonge; Old German *Avelina*, says Withycombe).

EVERARD. 'Strong or courageous as a wild boar' in Teutonic, it was once a frequent *m.* in both France and England; in the latter, it is, except among the cultured, seldom bestowed in C20. The old pronunciation, *Everett*, sometimes occurs as a modern variant.

Evie, Evy. A diminutive of *Eva, Eve.*

Evircoma. A Celtic *f.*, meaning, lit., 'pleasantly amiable'.

Evy. See *Evie.*

Ewan. See *Evan.* Sometimes spelt *Euan* or *Ewen.* It may be apprehended as a variant of *Owen.*

Ewart. An English contraction of *Everard.* In this form and in its derivative variant *Ewert*, it is also used as a surname.

Ewen. See *Ewan.*

Ezekiel. Since, in Heb., it signifies 'God will strengthen', it should be compared with *Hezekiah*, 'strength of the Lord'; but, like it, it is now seldom bestowed. Ezekiel was a prophet at the time of the Jewish exile in Babylon (C6 B.C.).

Ezra. 'Ezra's name is thought to be the same as that of Zerah, son of Judah, the rising of light, from whom likewise Heman, the writer of the 88th Psalm, is termed the Ezrahite' (Yonge); more probably, however, *Ezra* derives from the Heb. for 'help'. It was Ezra who, ca. 536 B.C., led the Jews back from the Babylonian captivity: see the Book of Ezra. The name is becoming rare except among Americans: cf. the 'prophetical' Ezra Pound, notable American expatriate writer.

F

FABIAN, *m.* L., 'bean-grower,' from *faba*, a bean; whence our *Fabian*, via the *gens Fabia* (the Fabian clan), especially Fabius Cunctator (the delayer): cf. *Fabian tactics*.

FAITH. (See also *Charity* and *Hope.*) This Scriptural-virtue *f.* name appealed to the Puritans, survives in rural districts, and is still fairly common among Nonconformists. 'One of St Sophia's daughters was thus called, and, like her sisters Hope and Charity, she laid down her life for her faith' (Swan) at the age of nine; and in 303, Faith, a French virgin, who was burned to death, set, in her martyrdom, so brave an example that a number of bystanders declared themselves Christians and were forthwith beheaded (Benedictines).

FAN. A diminutive of *Frances* or, simply, of:

FANNY, which was originally, and often still is, used as a pet-form of *Frances*, but which has also, in late C17–20, been treated as wholly independent: though etymologically it is manifestly the same, for it means 'free', 'frank': see *Frances*. 'By an odd caprice, it has lately been adopted in both France and Germany instead of their national contractions [*Fanchon, Fanchette; Franze*]', says Charlotte Yonge in 1884; in 1905, Helena Swan remarks that 'it is now falling out of favour in England' – but the process seems to be somewhat slow. (See also at *Myfanwy.*)

FARQUHAR. In Celtic it is reassuringly 'manly', it derives from Fearchur, a Scottish king, and it is everywhere becoming rather uncommon as a given name.

FAY, *f.* A variant of *Faith* (q.v.) and therefore a revival of archaic *fay*, as in *by my fay*. It is borne by a charming and very well-known English actress.

FEE. A diminutive of *Felicity* and:

FELICIA. A variant, as in Felicia Hemans the once famous poetess, of:

FELICITY. A natural English adaptation of Fr. *Félicité*, *Felicity* comes from L. *felicitas*, 'happiness,' itself from *felix* (see the next). The font-name arises either from the fact that Felicitas was the Roman goddess of happiness, 'in the form of a matron, with the staff of Mercury [the *caduceus* of Hermes] and a cornucopia,' which latter attribute – Blakeney does not suggest this – might seem to suggest that the Romans had some equivalent to 'May all your troubles be little ones!'; or, more probably, from the famous saint.

FELIX. Direct from L. *felix*, 'happy' or 'fortunate'. Common to Britain, France, Spain and Russia, it is a name particularly significant in the annals of the Church, especially the Catholic Church: Felix was that Roman governor of Judea before whom St Paul was arraigned; four Popes and one anti-Pope were thus named; and there are some sixty-five other saints bearing this name (Benedictines). Two Phelim O'Neills, who changed *Phelim* (q.v.) to *Felix*, have been styled *infelix Felix*, 'unhappy' or 'unlucky Felix' (Yonge).

FENELLA. See *Finella*.

FERDIE. A diminutive of:

FERDINAND. From a Teutonic compound signifying 'venturous journey' or 'adventuring life', perhaps equivalent to 'one who leads an adventurous life', a knight errant. It is an English, Fr. and Ger. name, popularized by that saintly king of the first half of C13: Ferdinand III, King of Castile and Leon. 'A brave soldier, he won back from the Moors . . . Seville and Cordova, and gave its deathblow to their rule in Spain.' 'The idol of his people,' he was 'heedful to do no wrong to the least of his subjects' (Benedictines). It has, ever since early C 11, been a kingly, princely, and aristocratic name.

FERGIE. (The *g* is hard.) A diminutive of:

FERGUS. A Celtic – mainly Irish and Scottish – *m.* 'Christian', it derives from a Celtic word meaning 'man's strength', hence 'manly strength'. Those of Caesar's foes whom he names *Vir-* had a name in *bri*, a Celtic root signifying 'force': cf. the Sanscrit *virja* and L. *virtus*, 'valour,' and *vir*, 'a man'. This is the Gaelic *fear* – *Feargus* or *Fearghus* is an old spelling of our name – and the Cymric *gwr.* Thus Yonge; both Weekley and Withycombe, however, state that the Celtic *Fearghus* means 'super-choice', i.e., 'excellent choice'.

FINELLA, FENELLA. In Celtic, 'she of the white shoulders', and thus connected with Finn or Fionn, 'the grand centre of ancient Gaelic giant lore'. The ancient *Fionn-ghuala* ('white shoulder') naturally became *Finnuala*, for that is how the 'tough-looking name' is pronounced; whence *Fenella* or *Finella.* 'In the clouds at the opening of Scottish history, we find Fynbella, or Finella, recorded as the cruel Lady of Fettercairn, who, in 994, killed King Kenneth III' (Yonge).

FINGAL. In Celtic, it is 'fair stranger'; contrast Dugald, 'dark stranger': both were originally epithets of racial designation, *Fingal* for a Norseman, *Dugald* for a Dane. Among the compounds of *Finn* – cf. *Finella* – is the Swedes' *Finngaard*, 'which their pronunciation contrives to make sound like Fingal, with what is called the "thick *l*"; and in modern times it is so spelt in allusion to Macpherson's hero' (Yonge). The legendary Scots-Irish bard for whom Macpherson acted in 1765 as 'mouthpiece' is reputed to have flourished ca. 300 A.D.; whence Fingal's Cave.

FINNUALA. See *Finella.* Now rare.

FIONA. Lit., 'white (girl)': from Gaelic *fionn.*

FLAVIA. L. *flavus* and *fulvus* both mean 'yellow', the former being the lighter, *fulvus* denoting a tawny hue. Adjective is also *flavius*: and, oddly enough, the Romans had both a Flavian and a Fulvian *gens* or clan. The former *gens* rose, in C1 A.D., to the throne with Vespasian, Titus, and Domitian. Like *Flavian, Flavia* is now but rarely heard as an English, or American, font-name.

FLAVIAN. L. *Flavianus*: for etymology see *Flavia.* There are six saints so named.

FLEUR is the Fr., *Flower* the English form of the flower-name *par excellence.* One of John Galsworthy's Forsytes is *Fleur*, the more fashionable shape.

FLO. A diminutive of *Flora* and *Florence,* as are *Florrie* and *Flossie.*

FLORA. This *f.* name owes its popularity to *Flora* (L. *flos*, 'a flower'), 'the Roman goddess of flowers and spring, whose annual festival (*Floralia*) was celebrated from the 28th of April till the 3rd of May, with extravagant merriment and lasciviousness' (Blakeney). Cf.:

FLORENCE, *m.* This Irish name, 'so common among the peasantry' – though often as *Flory*, 'is intended for Finghin, or Fineen (fair offspring); also for Flann, Fithil, and Flaithri', Yonge. As equivalent to L. *Florentius* (from *florens*, 'blooming'), it has been obsolete for centuries. Cf.:

FLORENCE, *f.* L. *Florentia,* from *florens*, 'flourishing,' is the name of a late C6–early 7 virgin saint more generally known – in contradistinction, doubtless, to the fifteen male saints Florence or Florentius – as Florentina, 'the scion of an illustrious . . . family, and the only sister of . . . Bishops Leander, Fulgentius, and Isidore of Seville,' who became an abbess

(Benedictines). 'The recent revival is chiefly owing to the name having been given to English girls born at the Italian city so called' and, during and after the Crimean War, to the fame of Florence Nightingale (Yonge).

FLORRIE. A diminutive of *Flora* and *Florence*. Cf. *Flossie*.

FLORY. See *Florence, m.*

FLOSS. A shortening of:

FLOSSIE. A diminutive – by many deemed vulgar – of *Flora* and *Florence*.

FLOWER. See *Fleur*.

FRAN. A frequent diminutive of *Frances* and a comparatively rare one of *Francis*.

FRANCE. A pet-name for either *Francis* or *Frances*.

FRANCELIA. An affected, but in C20 rarely used, variant of:

FRANCES, *f.*; FRANCIS, *m.* 'Mary Tudor, . . . in memory of her brief queenship of France,' or as a compliment to King Francis of France, 'christened her first child Frances – that Lady Frances Brendon . . . who had numerous namesakes among the maidens of the Tudor court'; these girls mostly spelt it *Francis*. 'The masculine came in at the same time, and burst into eminence in the Elizabethan cluster of worthies – Drake, Walsingham, Bacon; but it did not take a thorough hold of the nation, and was much left to the Roman Catholics. It was not till Frank had been restricted to men that it took hold of the popular mind, so as to become prevalent,' Yonge. *Francis* derives from Old Ger. *Frang*, *Franco*, 'a free lord'; and the *Franci*, 'the free men', were 'a confederacy of German tribes', who, 'after carrying on frequent wars with the Romans, . . . at length settled permanently in Gaul, of which they became the rulers under their king Clovis, A.D. 496' (Blakeney). There have been many very illustrious men called *Franciscus*, *Francisco*, *Franz*, *François*, and *Frank*, and not a few such women called *Francisca* or *Francesca*, *Frances* or *Françoise*; and *Français*, 'a Frenchman,' is obviously the same word.

FRANCESCA. This, the Italian, form of *Frances* has been adopted, in strict moderation, in Britain in C19–20, partly because of the moving story of Paolo and Francesca, which, in addition to being brilliantly translated by Byron from Dante, forms the subject of Leigh Hunt's narrative poem, *Story of Rimini*, 1816, and of a temporarily fashionable play by Stephen Phillips, 1899.

FRANCIE. A diminutive of *Frances*. Cf. *Fran* and *France*.

FRANCIS. See *Frances*.

FRANK. The more Teutonic form of *Francis*. Perhaps influenced by Fr. *franc*. See also at *Frances*.

FRANKIE. A pet-name for either *Frances* or *Francis*, or simply for *Frank*.

FRANKLIN, properly a surname (lit., 'freeholder'), has, in the U.S.A., been often bestowed as a 'Christian', since ca. 1785, in honour of Benjamin Franklin (1706–90), statesman, scientist, writer; a popularity increased by the fame of that even greater man, Franklin Delano Roosevelt (1882–1945), President from 1933 until his death.

FRED; FREDDIE or FREDDY. Pet-names for a person bearing any of the next five. *Fred*, however, is rarely applied to a Frederica.

FREDA. A pet-form of *Winifred* rather than an Anglicized variant of *Frida.*

FREDERIC. A variant of *Frederick.*

FREDERICA. A Portuguese and English *f.* – cf. It. *Federica* – of *Frederic(k)*, it was rare before the C19; and increasingly less general after it.

FREDERIC or FREDERICK. In Fr., *Frédéric*; in Ger., *Friedrich* (whence *Fritz*); in Old Ger., *Frithuric* (cf. A.-S. *Freodhoric*): lit., 'peace-rule', hence 'peaceful ruler', which seems unsuitable for Frederick Barbarossa and Frederick the Great. (Withycombe.)

FREDRIC. A variant of the preceding, or, more precisely, of *Frederic.*

FREE. See:

FRIDA; more generally FRIEDA. A Ger. *f.* name (lit., 'peace': cf. A.-S. *frith*) that has, in C19–20, gained some hold in England. Diminutive: *Free.*

FRITZ. Occasionally heard in England as a diminutive of *Frederic(k)*, it is properly the pet-form of the Ger. equivalent *Fri(e)drich.* During the war of 1914–18, it was the Tommies' generic name for a Ger. soldier, though *Jerry* was rather more frequent during the last two years: see S. and S. In that of 1939–45, *Fritz* was little used.

FULBERT. A long-established, but decaying English *m.* 'Christian', it derives from Teutonic, where it means 'exceeding bright'. It is therefore a variant of the Fr. *m. Philibert* or *Filibert.* Héloïse (Abélard's Héloïse) was the niece of an old Fr. canon named Fulbert.

FULK or FULKE is a fine old *m.* name, but it is more properly to be regarded as a surname. From Old Ger. *Fulco*, 'one of the *folc* or people'. One of its noblest owners was Fulke Greville, friend of Sir Philip Sidney and himself a notable poet.

G

GABE. An English diminutive of:

GABRIEL. In Heb., it means either 'man, or hero, of God' or 'God is my strength' (? 'source of merit'), and it is 'common to England, France, Germany, and Spain' (Swan). Gabriel was that archangel who 'strengthened Daniel, and who brought the promise to Zacharias and to the Blessed Virgin. His name is chiefly used by the Slavonians' (Yonge), and is becoming rare in the British Empire.

GABRIELA. See:

GABRIELLA, GABRIELLE, *f.* Etymology as for *Gabriel*, except that 'hero' necessarily becomes 'heroine' and 'man' – 'woman' or 'girl'. *Gabriella* is primarily It. and Sp., as *Gabrielle* is primarily Fr.: English hospitality has done the rest.

GAIL. This diminutive of *Abigail* is sometimes – and increasingly, especially in U.S.A. – bestowed as an independent *f.*

GARETH. See *Garth.*

GARNET. As *m.*, probably 'little Warren': Anglo-Norman *Guarin* + the diminutive suffix *-et.* As a *f.*, it is apparently of entirely independent origin – straight from the Common Noun *garnet*; cf. *Amber*, *Pearl*, *Ruby*. (Withycombe.)

GARRET or GARRETT. A variant of obsolete *Garrath*: see *Garth.*

GARRIE, GARRY. The diminutive of *Garret* and *Garth.*

GARTH, *m.* This is a modern form of *Gareth*, knightly as in

Tennyson's Idyll, *Gareth and Lynette*, 1872, and current as a Welsh name (witness the brilliant Gareth Jones bandit-killed in China in August 1935). The A.-S. is *Garrath*, 'firm spear'. (See also at end of *Gerald*.)

GASTON, *m.* Properly and mostly Fr., it may derive from Sp. or, more precisely, Basque, in which not so ancient language it is thought to mean 'beautiful town'. Others think that it may be a variant of *Gascon* and therefore designate racial origin.

GATTY, *f.* A contraction, typically English in its thoroughness, of *Gertrude*.

GAVIN. A mainly Scottish name (*m.*), *Gavin* in its Celtic original perhaps means 'hawk (*gwalch*) of the month of May'; Ernest Weekley, however, thinks with Camden that it is a made-up name. It is better known in the form:

GAWAIN, GAWAINE; now usually GAWEN. This is the English equivalent of the Scottish *Gavin*, q.v., and was popular in the Middle Ages. A Sir Gawain appears thrice in notable English literature: in the medieval verse-romance, *Sir Gawain and the Green Knight*, in *The Mabinogion*, and in Tennyson's *Idylls of the King*. As a Knight of King Arthur's Round Table he is, by many, considered inferior only to the King himself and to Sir Lancelot. Than the former he had more character, knightlier virtue than the latter. Ultimately, it would seem, Gawain is Gwalchmai, who, in Welsh pedigrees, is King Arthur's nephew: golden-tongued, learned, courteous, as indeed was that young man of letters (literary London did not know his worth) whom, as *Gawen*, it adorned: who it adorned: Gawen Brownrigg (†1938).

GAWEN. See the preceding.

GAY. A woman's name, direct from the adjective.

GEMMA. Another female name, direct from It. *Gemma*, 'a precious stone'. (Withycombe.)

GENE. The usual diminutive of *Eugene*, *Eugenia.*

GENEVIEVE. Perhaps 'fair girl', it comes through French, from late L. *Genevefa*, from Celtic.

GENEVRA. An English contraction of *Guinevere*; for etymology, see *Gwendolen.* The contracting may have been influenced by Fr. *Geneviève* of independent origin.

GEOFF. The usual diminutive of :

GEOFFREY; occasionally GEOFFROY. The former seems the more English, the latter a Gallicized form (Fr. *Geoffroi*): actually *Geoffrey* (*-froy*) is the Gallicized form of *Godfrey* or rather of its Teutonic original (*Gottfrid*, *Gottfried*), meaning 'God's peace'. One naturally looks to see whether so utterly fortunate a name – implying no fatalistic quietism but a suffusion by the inner light – has any notable religious associations: there are two canonized abbots and a saintly and most kindly bishop more usually remembered as St Godfrey. (Benedictines.)

GEORDIE. A Scottish and North Country variant rather than diminutive of:

GEORGE. The Gr. *γῆ* (*gē*), 'earth' and *ἔϱγω* (*ergō*), 'I work,' formed *γεωϱγός* (*geōrgos*), 'an earth-worker', i.e. 'a husbandman'. The usual early 'Christian' was *Georgios* or *-ius* and it became general through the fame of St George, who in C4 gained a signal victory over the devil (picturesquely bodied forth in a dragon) – a fable as baseless in animal-fact as is the denial of his existence. It was this St George who was mightily hailed by the Crusaders and who, from C13, 'came to be regarded as Patron of England, partially displacing St Edward the Confessor' (Benedictines). Yet 'scarcely a single George appears in our registers before 1700, although afterwards it multiplied to such an extent as to make it doubtful whether George, John, or Charles [or Thomas] be the most common designation of Englishmen' (Yonge). *George*, moreover, has for half a century been a common (non-aristocratic, however, and non-cultured) form of address to a man whose name is unknown; *Jack* is employed in the same way, and *Tommy* is the usual address by those speaking to a boy unknown. *George* is also the generic husband.

GEORGIANA; GEORGINA. These *f.* derivatives of *George* were unbestowed in England before C18 and were rare before ca. 1750; they are slowly losing their popularity, which has never been comparable with that of *Ann* or *Elizabeth*, *Margaret* or *Mary* and at least another twenty *f.* names.

GEORGIE, GEORGY. A diminutive of *George*, *Georgiana*, *Georgina*. Also it is the *f.* form of *George*.

GEORGINA. See *Georgiana*.

GEORGY. See *Georgie*.

GER; GERRIE or GERRY. Pet-names to *Gerald*.

GERAINT. This Welsh *m.* has become very rare; see at end of the *Enid* entry. From the name of one of Arthur's knights.

GERALD seems to arise from a confusion of the Teutonic *Gerwald*, 'spear-wielder' and the mainly Ger. *Gerhard*, 'spear [that is] hard,' i.e. 'firm spear'. The original form was *Gerhold*, and, as Helena Swan says, 'A good many Gerholds came to England with William the Conqueror, and from England the name was carried to Ireland, and there became naturalized'; note, however, that the Gerhold who founded the monastery of Tempul Gerald (etymologically, a most fascinating name), died in 732, and became a saint famed in Irish legend, was an Anglo-Saxon migrant (Yonge). But some of the Irish and Welsh Geralds have had parents confusing Gerhold with Celtic Gareth.

GERALDINE. The English *f.* of *Gerald* looks as if it were prompted by both It. *Giralda* and Ger. *Gerhardine*, which are *f.* For 'suggestibility', cf.:

GERARD. An English variant of *Gerald*; probably influenced by Ger. *Gerhard.*

GERLINDA. An English variation on *Geraldine*, perhaps by way of an unrecorded *Geralinda* influenced by the various *-linda*'s.

GERRY. See *Ger* and contrast *Jerry.*

GERT; GERTIE or GERTY. Diminutives of the next; *Gert* is thought rather vulgar.

GERTRUDE. The first element is that in *Gerald*: the Teutonic *ger* or *gar*, 'a spear'; the second, a Teutonic word for 'might, strength'. The first *Gertrude* appears to have been a Valkyr named *Geirthrud* or *Gerdrud*; 'for, alas! the pretty interpretation that has caused so many damsels of late to bear it, as meaning *all truth*' – wrongly based on modern Ger. *gar*, 'quite,' and a complete ignorance of the etymology of *truth* – 'is utterly untenable, unless they will regard themselves as allegorically constant battle-maids, armed with the spear of Ithuriel,' as Charlotte Yonge, amicably disdainful of such folk-etymology as rides rough-shod over well-proved origins; she, however, had believed the second element to signify 'maiden'. And such prettiness is unnecessary if one remembers that there are three Saints Gertrude; two in C7 and one in late C13–early 14. The very English transformation, *Gatty*, is unfortunately disappearing.

GERTY, GERTIE. See *Gert.*

GERVAS (rare), GERVASE or GERVAISE. The third form is a fusion of the second and Fr. *Gervais*; the origin is either Classical and obscure, or Teutonic and signifying 'spear-eagerness' (cf. *Gerald*) or, in another interpretation, 'spear-servant'. There is one St Gervase, who, a C1 martyr, was a son of that other much-esteemed martyr, St Vitalis, and a brother of yet another, St Protase (Benedictines). Hence the English shapes, *Jarvis* or *Jervis*.

GIBBIE. A Scottish contraction of *Gabriel*. Cf. *Gabe*.

GIBBON is an English transformation of *Gilbert*. Perhaps influenced by:

GIDEON. 'A destroyer', 'a feller' (of men) – in other words, a great soldier – in Hebrew. The Biblical Gideon, whose martial exploits seem to have impressed both the Huguenots of the civil wars in France and the Puritans of the Civil War in England, was that Old Testament judge of Israel who freed his people from the yoke of the Midianites. (Yonge.) Now rather rare.

GIL. A diminutive of:

GILBERT. In Old Ger., *Gisilbert*, *Giselbert*, *Gislebert*, 'bright pledge'; whence, by contraction, *Gilbert*. (Not, as sometimes explained, *gelb-bert*, 'yellow bright'.) 'There were four saints so called, namely, an abbot of Fontenelle, a great friend of William the Conqueror, an Auvergnat knight in the second Crusade, the English founder [C12] of the order of Gilbertine monks, and a bishop of Caithness, and it has been a prevalent name in England, Scotland, and the Low Countries,' Yonge. The first element, *gisl*, *gisel*, *gisil*, reappears in *Gisela*, a *f.*

GILCHRIST. In Celtic, 'a servant of Christ,' this is a Scottish *m.* 'Christian' which has become also a surname. Cf.:

GILDAS. 'Servant of God' in Celtic (cf. *Gilchrist*), this is the

Latinization of Gaelic *gilla*, 'a servant,' the *das* being L. *deus*. It is Gildas who, a Welsh historian, 'rates all the contemporary princes so soundly' (Yonge). Now rare.

GILES. This English and Scottish name, popular enough at one time to have become a surname and, in C20 as a 'Christian', finding aristocratic favour in England, is of doubtful origin. Probably it is referable to *aegis* – the aegis or aigis of Pallas Athene, whose shield was originally the skin of an *αἴξ* (aix) or goat – and, if so, must mean 'with the aegis' and therefore, via Fr. *Gilles*, 'stock name for a stage simpleton' (Weekley, *W. & N.*), a contraction of *Aegidius*, the name, as it happens, of a mid C7–early 8 saint who, born a Greek, 'passed his life as a hermit in the South of France' and who is known as St Giles.

GILL. A contraction, or rather, a shortening of *Gillian*. Occasionally it is equivalent to the *Jill* of 'Every Jack has his Jill'.

GILLESPIE, *m.* and *f.* Properly a Scottish name, derived from the Celtic for 'the servant of a bishop' (cf. *Gilchrist*), the *espie* being an early (Irish or) Scottish attempt at L. *episcopus*.

GILLIAN, *f.* An English variation of *Julia* on the analogy of the *m. Julian*, or, perhaps, rather a reduction and transformation of *Juliana*: Professor Weekley upholds the latter view; '*Gillian* is the popular form of *Juliana*, which, for some unknown reason, was a favourite medieval font-name'.

GILLIE. A diminutive of *Gilbert*.

GILLIES, *m.* In Celtic – it is a Scottish name – it represents 'servant of Jesus': cf., and see, *Gillespie*. The *-ies* represents *Iesus* (pronounced *yésus*). It has become also a surname. Cf. also *Gilmour*.

GILMOIR. A Gaelic 'shape' of:

GILMOUR, *m.* This Scottish 'Christian' and, derivatively, surname is lit., in Celtic, 'servant of Mary'. For others of the religious 'servant' group, see *Gilchrist*, *Gildas*, *Giles* (perhaps), *Gillespie*, and *Gillies*.

GIP; often GYP or GIPP. An Anglicized shortening of *Gilbert*.

GIRZIE. A Scottish diminutive of *Griseldis*, *Grizel*.

GISELA. See *Gilbert*, at end.

GITHA, GYTHA. Perhaps it is a contraction of A.-S. *Eadgifa* (see *Edith*), but more probably it represents simply the second element ('gift') of that word; it may, however, be a Norwegian name, from *guthr*, 'war' (Withycombe).

GLAD. A familiar and almost vulgar shortening of *Gladys*.

GLADUSE. The Cornish form of *Claudia*. Cf.:

GLADYS. The Welsh form of *Claudia*. Sometimes spelt *Gwladys*, which seems to be a pseudo-erudite affectation.

GLAUD. The Scottish form of *Claud*.

GLORIA; pet-form, *Glory*. A *f.* name common in C19, less bestowed in C20. From L. *gloria*, fame. Cf. *Gloriana*, 'one of the names under which Queen Elizabeth is indicated in Spenser's *Faerie Queene*' (Harvey).

GLORY. See the preceding.

GODDARD. In Ger., *Gotthard*, from Old Ger. *Godehard*, this English *m.* font-name (now unusual) and surname means 'God-strong; hence, pious; virtuous' (Webster).

GODFREY. From Teutonic, it denotes 'God's peace'; the

Dutch is *Godfried*, the Ger. *Gottfried* (earlier *Gottfrid*: Old Ger. *Godafrid*). Godfrey, abbot of St Quentin in the early C11, 'named two godsons, the canonized bishop of Amiens [1066–1115], and the far more famous Gottfried of Lorraine, who might well, as leader of the crusading camp, bequeath his name to all the nations whose representatives fought under him, and thus we find it everywhere. . . . We received one Godfrey from the conqueror of Jerusalem' – Gottfried of Lorraine, i.e. Godfrey of Bouillon (1060–1100) – 'but previously the Gottfried had been taken up by the French, and was much used by the Angevin counts in the Gallicized form of Geoffroi', Yonge. (See also *Geoffrey*.)

GODWIN. Teutonic for 'God-friend', i.e. excellent friend. Now also a surname.

GORDON, *m.* From the Scottish surname, it owes some of its late C19–early 20 use to the fame of General Gordon († 1885).

GORONWY. A Welsh *m.*, of obscure origin. Perhaps cf. *Gawain*.

GRACE. Cf. those other theological abstractions: *Faith*, *Hope*, *Charity*, *Mercy*, and *Prudence*, qq.v., and yet others – mostly obsolete. Like them it became popular so soon as parents perceived that the Reformation was firmly established. Its survival is in part the result of that very amiable mistake made by the Irish in which they equated it to their *Grainé* (q.v.) and so whole-heartedly adopted it that *Grace* (or *Gracie*) may usually be found wherever there are Irish associations and connexions. Not 'graceful' or 'slight of stature' (L. *gracilis*), as some have supposed, but 'thanks' or 'gratitude', 'favour' or 'bounty'; more relevantly, it served to translate the Gr. χάρις – see both *Charis* and *Charity*. (Yonge.)

GRACIE is a diminutive of the preceding, but sometimes it is bestowed as an independent font-name.

GRAHAM. See Note at end of Introduction.

GRAINÉ, GRAINNE, GRAINA. *f.* An Irish 'Christian' now often supplanted by *Grace* (q.v.), it represents, in Celtic, 'love,' and, in the Celtic cycle of romance, Grainne was daughter of Cormac MacArt, one of the five Kings of Ulster, a lady of great wit, the belovèd of the mighty Fionn and the lover of Fionn's nephew Diarmaid.

GRANT. See Note at end of Introduction. Mostly American.

GRANUAILE. This Irish *f.* is an elaboration of *Grainé*.

GREG (Northern) and GRIG (Southern). These are the sole diminutives (so far as I know) of *Gregory*; but it is also an independent Scottish *m.* name, in Celtic meaning 'fierce', with phonetic variant *Greig* (also a surname).

GREGORY. This *m.* 'Christian' is, on two counts, as delightful as it is dignified: it is, in itself, euphonious without being luxurious, clangorous without harshness; and it has a brilliant ecclesiastical representation. As Charlotte Yonge – a lady whom it were as uncouth as it is difficult to withstand – has very aptly said, '*Γϱηγόϱιος* [Grēgorios] came from *γϱηγοϱέω* [grēgoreō], a late and corrupt form of the verb *ἐγείϱω* [egeirō] (to wake or watch). A watchman was a highly appropriate term for a shepherd of the Church, and accordingly Gregorios was frequent among early bishops.' The shortened *Gregor* is mainly Scottish.

GRETA. Either an Anglicization of *Grete*, a Ger. contraction of *Margaret*, or, more probably, an adoption of the Swedish *Greta*, likewise a contraction: cf. the Old Norse *Gretta*. The fame of Greta Garbo, the magnificent Swedish film-actress, has rendered the name almost as popular in England as in America.

GRIFFIN. See:

GRIFFITH. An English and Welsh *m.* name, the Welsh original being *Gruffydd*, wherein the *u* approximates to short *i* and *dd* is pronounced *th*. The Welsh merely adapted *Rufus*, 'red (-haired)' or 'ruddy (-cheeked)', and in the same way turned the derivative *Rufinus* into *Gruffyn*, i.e. *Griffin*. *Griffith* was borne by numerous Welsh princes, many of whom invested it with an aura of honour and even with a halo of romance; its popularity had the inevitable result – it became a common surname.

GRISELDA. The English form of the mainly Scottish:

GRISELDIS. In Teutonic, 'grey battle-maid' (lit., 'grey battle'). In C13, the English lady, Graesia de Bruere [Fr. *bruyère*] doubtless drew her name from the Old Ger. *grisja*, 'grey'. 'Griselda was the perfectly patient wife' – nowadays she would be condemned as 'soft' – 'whose tale was told by Boccaccio, and narrated by Petrarch to Chaucer, who told it in his own way'; the lady was also commemorated by Dekker, Chettle and Haughton in their comedy, *Patient Grissil*, 1603. 'The Scots seem to have been peculiarly delighted with the lady Griselidis – and Grizell or Grisell acquired fresh honour with Lady Grisell Baillie. Grizzie or Girzie are the contractions,' Yonge.

GRISELIDIS. A variant of the preceding.

GRISELL, GRISSEL, GRISSIL. Once common, now rare variants of *Grizel*.

GRITTY. A Scottish diminutive, and occasionally independent font-name, from *Griseldis*; an English one of *Margaret*.

GRIZEL, GRIZELL or GRIZZELL; GRIZZIE. A Scottish contraction of *Griseldis*. Cf. *Gritty*.

GRUFFYDD. The Welsh original – cf. *Dawfydd* for *David* – of *Griffith*.

GUENDOLEN, diminutive *Guen.* See *Gwendolen.*

GUENEVER, GUENEVERE. See *Guinevere.*

GUIDA. This *f.* of *Guy* comes from Italy, where it is the obvious *f.* of:

GUIDO. This Italian 'shape' of *Guy* has occasionally been used in England as a doublet of that name.

GUILLYM. This is a Welsh form of *William.*

GUINEVERE, GUENEVERE. Celtic, this name has a first element (*guen, gwen*) that means 'white' (cf. *Gwendolen*); and the entire name appears to mean either 'white wave' (cf. *Gwenhuyfar*, q.v.) or, less probably, 'white phantom' (? 'pure-spirited'). It is still bestowed occasionally, especially by the cultured in honour of the wife of King Arthur in the Arthurian romance-cycles: notably in the versions by Malory and Tennyson.

GUS. The usual diminutive of *Augustus.* Although now regarded as rather vulgar, it is nevertheless free of the absurd connotations of:

GUSSY, which is still more familiar and is, though decreasingly, applied to a rather effeminate man.

GUSTAVUS. This English name is dying out, despite its rich historical associations, whereas in France *Gustave* (cf. Ger. *Gustaf*) remains very popular. In Teutonic, it signifies either 'the divine staff' or 'the staff of the Goths' (cf. *pillar of the Church*).

GUY. Perhaps from Celtic ('sense'), more probably from Old Ger. *Wido* of obscure meaning (? 'leader'), it has been inextricably entangled with L. *Vitus*, perhaps because of the fame of the St Guy, more generally known as St Vitus (martyred ca. 302 A.D.). It came to us from France, has been the name of two famous medieval heroes celebrated in verse – Guy of Gisborne and Guy of Warwick, and, though temporarily eclipsed by the Gunpowder Plot and though a pejorative in slang, it is nevertheless popular in C18–20; moreover, it is perpetuated in two well-known novels, Scott's *Guy Mannering* (one of his best), 1815, and G. A. Lawrence's *Guy Livingstone*, 1857. (Yonge; Benedictines; Harvey.)

GWALCHMAI. A Welsh form of *Gavin*.

GWEN; GWENDA. Diminutives of *Gwendolen*. There are two Saints Gwen.

GWENDALINE; GWENDDOLEN. Variants of:

GWENDOLEN (or -IN), which is the modern form of a Celtic name doubleted with *Guinevere* (earlier *Gwenever*); often spelt *Guendolen*. The first element means 'white'; the second has occasioned dispute, for Charlotte Yonge defines the name as 'white-browed', whereas Helena Swan says that it represents 'white bow', symbolical for 'the new moon'. The latter lady is tersely adequate on the etymological implications of this mainly aristocratic *f.* 'Christian'. '*Gwen*, "white," is constantly found in Welsh names: in composition it becomes *wen*, and ramifications . . . are almost endless . . ., names seemingly widely divergent being ultimately reducible to this word. From Gwen, or Guen, . . . "white" come Gwendolen, Guinevere, Gwenhwyfar, Genevra, Jennifer, Gwynne, Winne, Wenefrid, Winefred, [Winefrid], Genevieve, Vanora, and many others,' qq.v.

GWENDOLINE is a variant of the preceding; it seems to be the form preferred by the Catholic Church, which has canonized two Gwendolines, a Welsh virgin of C6 and an C8 abbess of Alsace. (Benedictines.)

GWENFREWI. A Welsh form of *Winifred*. (Cf. *Gwalchmai* for *Gavin*.)

GWENHWYFAR. A Welsh variation of *Guinevere*, though, lit., it means 'swelling white wave'.

GWENNIE, GWENNY. A diminutive of *Gwendolen*.

GWENWYNWYN, *m.* From the Celtic and perhaps meaning 'thrice-white' or ? 'thrice-fair': *gwen* and *wine* (*wene*) are mere variants of the Celtic for 'white'. But 'thrice-blessèd' (cf. *Gwyneth*) is more likely.

GWILYM is the Welsh form of *William*; but as *William* and Ger. *Wilhelm* are racial cognates, so possibly are *Gwillym* and Fr. *Guillaume*.

GWLADYS. A Welsh form of *Claudia*: cf. *Gladys*.

GWYDYR, *m.* A Welsh 'Christian' meaning 'wrathful'. Not a particularly happy name, one would have thought.

GWYNETH. A mainly Welsh *f.*, meaning 'blessed': cf. *Beatrice*.

GWYNNE, *f.* In Celtic, 'white'. Cf. the first element of *Gwendolen*.

GYP. See *Gip*.

GYTHA. See *Githa*.

H

HACO, HACON. Both are from a Scandinavian etymon, connoting 'useful'; the former is a Latinized derivative of the latter. With *Hacon*, compare the Norwegian *Haakon.* Now rather rare in English.

HAGAR, *f.* This now somewhat obsolescent name owes its English use to Hagar, the concubine of Abraham and the mother of Ishmael (Genesis, xvi). The Heb. form is *Haghar*, akin to the Arabic *hajara*, 'to forsake'.

HAGGAI, *m.* Heb., 'festival of the Lord'. Rare except among Jews and Russians, it was originally borne by that minor prophet who, flourishing ca. 520 B.C., addressed hortatory encouragement to the Israelites.

HAGGY. A variant of *Aggie* and now rare. It is 'the maidservant's name in Southey's *Doctor*' (Yonge).

HAÏDÉE. A Fr. *f.* that has, since ca. 1930, become fairly general on the stage; often Anglicized as *Haidee* and pronounced *Háydee.* From the Gr., it should mean 'modest'.

HAL; rarely HALL. A diminutive, much less common than it used to be in C15–16, of *Henry* or, rather, of *Harry*, q.v.

HALBERT. This, a Scottish *m.*, represents, in Teutonic, 'bright stone' or perhaps 'stone-bright' and, derivatively, 'stone-hard'.

HALDANE, *m.* Lit., 'half-Dane,' it derives from Teutonic. It has become more frequent as a sur- than as a font-name.

HALLAM. This surname – the same word as '*Hallam*shire' – has been used as a baptismal only since 1833, the year which witnessed the death of historian Hallam's extremely gifted son, aged only 22: the Arthur Henry Hallam immortalized by his Cambridge friend, Alfred Tennyson, in *In Memoriam*, 1850 – one of the three greatest elegies in the language.

HAMILTON. See Note at end of Introduction.

HAMISH. This is the Gaelic form of *James*.

HAMLYN. A diminutive of:

HAMO. This English and Norwegian *m*. 'Christian', deriving from Teutonic, means 'home'; it is dying out in Britain. Occasionally, *Haymo*.

HANK. An American diminutive of *Henry*. Probably influenced by Ger. *Hanke* (for *Heinrich*).

HANNAH. Once both English and Scottish, this doublet of *Anne* is now mainly English. For etymology, see *Anne*: *Anne* probably varies *Anna*, which is unaspirated Greek for the Heb. *Chaanah*, 'grace'.

HANNIBAL. Phoenician, 'grace of Baal'. 'The far-famed Hannibal himself'—the Carthaginian general (246–182 B.C.) who defeated the Romans at Cannae only to be himself defeated by Scipio, fourteen years later (202) – 'answered exactly to the Hananiah or Johanan of the Holy Land, saying that it was the grace of Baal that unhappily he besought by his very appellation,' Yonge. The prevalence of *Hannibal* among the Cornish peasantry perhaps indicates Phoenician influence in that county. But *Hannibal* and *Hanno* were once fairly common in the Midlands.

HANNO. This mainly Cornish *m*. name is from the word that forms the first element of *Hannibal*. 'Hanno, so often occurring in the Punic wars, was another version of the Hebrew Hanan' (Yonge).

HANNYBALL. An occasional Cornish spelling of *Hannibal.*

HARDING. An English *m.* 'Christian' from Teutonic *Hardwin,* it means, lit., 'firm friend'. Now much more general as a surname than as a font-name.

HAROLD. In Danish and Norwegian *Harald,* and *Harivald* in Old Norse (it is essentially, predominantly, a Norse name), it is a compound denoting 'army-wielder', hence perhaps 'powerful general'. It owes its English prevalence to *Harold, the Last of the Saxon Kings* – the title of Bulwer Lytton's historical novel published in 1848. This king was Harold II and he has been even more finely celebrated in Tennyson's strangely neglected drama, *Harold,* 1876; but then Tennyson's three historical dramas, nervous and arresting, are too little read in C20. There was also 'a Christian child' – now St Harold – 'put to death by Jews infuriated against Christianity, at Gloucester (1168). This strange outbreak . . . is also held responsible for the martyrdoms of St William of Norwich and St Robert of Bury' (Benedictines).

HARRIET. In Teutonic, 'home-rule' – which seems to be an ominous name with which to embark upon married life – *Harriet* is the *f.* of *Harry* (see therefore *Harry*), but it was probably influenced by Fr. *Henriette,* for *Henrietta* is the *f.* of *Henry.* (Is there a lost *Harrietta*?) Since ca. 1870, *Harriet,* generally as *'Arriet,* has been generic for a coster-girl: she and 'Arry are often depicted and described as a coster couple. Their coat of arms, I suggest, should figure a lusty male and female form rampant on 'Ampstead 'Eath.

HARRIOT. A variant of the preceding. *Hawyot* was once the usual pronunciation of *Harriet*; therefore *Harriot* may be a blend.

HARRY, sometimes in C19–20 bestowed, like *Jack,* as an independent font-name, is a very old pet-name for *Henry*; its great popularity dates from the exploits of Henry V

(1387–1422). *Old Harry* is the devil; Congreve employs the politer *by the Lord Harry*, a strange apotheosis of the traditional enemy of God. But *Tom, Dick and Harry*, for the populace, hardly antedates 1800; Minsheu, in 1617, speaks of '*Jac* and *Tom, Dic, Hob* and *Will*' (Weekley, *W. & N.*).

HARTLEY is apparently in neither Yonge nor Swan: it would therefore seem to have derived from the surname ('hard lea', perhaps 'stony meadow'). Its two most famous 'exponents' are Hartley Coleridge, the luckless poet (1796–1849), and Hartley Withers, sane and brilliant writer on economics. But a boy so named in this irreverent century runs the risk of being nicknamed 'Jam' or 'Jams'.

HARTY. An English variation of *Hester*; also a transformation of *Harriet*.

HARVEY. Either Celtic, 'bitter,' the original *Houerf* becoming *Houerv*, which in turn became *Hervé* – the name came to England with the numerous adventurers out of Brittany – as Charlotte Yonge, who relates a beautiful legend of the first Harvey, upholds; or, preferably, Fr. *Hervé*, from the heroic Ger. *Herewig*, 'warrior-war,' i.e. '(land-) war warrior', as Weekley holds (*Romance of Names*).

HATTY. An English transformation of *Harriet*; sometimes bestowed independently.

HAWKIN, HAWKINS, now almost wholly a surname. A derivative of obsolete *Halkin*, itself a diminutive of *Hal* from *Harry* from *Henry*; *-kin* is the diminutive suffix, as in *lambkin.*

HAYMO. A variant of *Hamo.*

HAZEL, *f.* From the tree and nut so named; from a common Teutonic radical. Cf. *Ivy*.

HAZZY, *m.* The diminutive of *Ahasuerus,* occasionally used in the U.S.A. Nowadays – when bestowed at all – *Hazzy* frequently bears no reference to its original; it is 'just a name'.

HEATHER, *f.* From the shrub. Perhaps influenced by its flower, the *heather-bell*. Not before C19. Cf. *Hazel*.

HEBE, *f.* To be avoided, for it has become generic for a barmaid. Hebë, from Gr. *ἡβάω* (hēbaö), 'be in the flower of youth,' is the goddess of youth – the Romans, in fact, called her Juventas – and a daughter of Zeus and Hera. 'She waited upon the gods, and filled their cups with nectar, before Ganymedes obtained this office' (Blakeney).

HEC. A diminutive, generally considered rather vulgar, of:

HECTOR. Gr., 'defender'; Gaelic, 'horseman'; Norwegian, 'hawk of Thor'. Although it is true that the Gr. 'name comes from the Trojan hero, the Scottish from the Gaelic *eachan* [a horseman], and the Norwegian from Hagtar' (Swan), it is fairly certain that the Scottish and Norwegian etymologies have been superimposed, by nationalistic philologists, upon that Hector who was 'the chief hero of the Trojans in their war with the Greeks. . . . He fought with the bravest of the Greeks,' only to be slain by Achilles. Besides being a great warrior, he is distinguished by the virtues of a man: 'his heart is open to the gentle feelings of a son, a husband, and a father' (Blakeney). For his character, see esp. Taylor, *Ancient Ideals*, I, ch. vii; for a sidelight on his fame, note that, 'in medieval romance he is the great hero of the Trojan War' (Harvey). But his name does not form the origin of the quaint American asseveration, *by heck*! : that is merely a euphemism for *by hell*!

HEDLEY. See Note at end of Introduction.

HELEN; HELENA. The former is an English and Scottish shortening of the latter, which is very rare in Scotland.

Helena, found also in Sp. and Portuguese, Ger. and Dutch, represents the Gr. *Helenë* ('Ἑλένη), the *f.* of *Helenos*, lit. 'the bright' or 'the light' from a radical (*ele*) signifying heat or light: cf. *Hēlios*, the sun-god, and *Selēnē*, the moon-goddess. The Gr. is the most noted of all Gr. *f.* names, since it is that of the 'fatal beauty' who, after an adventure in her youth (and before – she was one of Zeus's many children), was married to the noble Menelaus, only to be seduced by handsome Paris and carried off to Troy: whence the Trojan War, towards the end of which, on the death of Paris, she married his brother, Deiphobus, and betrayed him to the Greeks. She became reconciled with Menelaus and, according to the most persistent legend, lived happily with him till her or his death; one legend, however, makes her, Menelaus dead, marry Achilles and bear him a son. (Blakeney.) With Aeschylus's pun on her name (ἑλένας, 'ship-destroying') and his 'Wherefore else this fatal name, That Helen and destruction are the same', relate Marlowe's variation on the '*femme fatale*' and 'ship' themes: 'Is this the face that launched a thousand ships,' etc.; a description known to many who, of poetry, know but this.

HELOISA, *f.* Perhaps a blend of Fr. *Héloïse* and It. *Eloïsa*, it connotes, in Teutonic, 'famous holiness'.

HENNIKER. A derivative, now rare, of *Henry*, perhaps influenced by Sp. and Portuguese *Enrique* and Dutch and Danish *Hendrik*.

HENRIETTA. The *f.* of *Henry*; cf. *Harriet*. Probably Fr. *Henriette* with a L. ending.

HENRY. 'Where Heimrich' – Old Ger. *Heimirich*, modern *Heinrich*, and lit. 'home-rule' (Teutonic) – 'first began does not appear' although the name is blood-brother to *Heimdall*, 'the third sword-god of the old Teutonic mythology [and] the mysterious watchman whose duty it was to protect Asgard, the heaven of the early Scandinavians' (Swan); 'it sprung into fame with the Saxon emperor called the Fowler, and his descendant [972–1024] won the honours of a saint, whence this became a special favourite in Germany. . . . From the Kaisers, the third Capetian King of France was christened Henri, a form always frequent there. . . . It must have been from the reigning French monarch that William the Conqueror took Henry for his youngest son, from whom the first Plantagenet king received . . . it' in 1068 and made it an English kingly name in 1100 (Yonge).

HEPSY. The diminutive of:

HEPZIBAH. Heb., 'My delight is in her', it is a Biblical name (2 *Kings*, xxi, 1). In 1905, Helena Swan observed that 'though now rarely met with in the British Isles this name is still common in America'. Is New England to be regarded as its spiritual home?

HERB. A pet-name, not wholly free from vulgarity, for:

HERBERT. In Teutonic, it means 'bright army', hence perhaps 'glorious warrior'. A Norman brought it to England ca. 1070, and 'one of the many Herberts founded a family in Wales, which, in the time of Henry V [1413–22], was one of the first to follow the advice to use one patronymic instead of the whole pedigree of names. It is probably owing to the honours in [politics, war, poetry, and philosophy] of the branches of this family that Herbert has . . . become an exceedingly prevalent Christian name in England' (Yonge).

HERBIE; HERBY (rare). An affectionate diminutive of *Herbert*; cf. *Herb*.

HERCULES, *m.* Now rare, it is in honour of the Classical equivalent of Samson. The Gr. Ἡρακλῆς (Hērаklēs: 'lordly fame') became in Etruscan *Hercle*, whence L. *Hercules*. Cf. *Achilles*, q.v.

HERMAN. A Ger. (Teutonic 'army man'), hence an English name rarely bestowed since the war of 1914–18 and still more rarely since Hermann Goering rendered it odious in 1939–45.

HERMIA. Either the *f.* of the Gr. *Hermēs* or a variant, by abridgement, of:

HERMIONE. Gr., 'daughter of Hermes'. Hermione, lovely daughter of Menelaus and Helen, after having been forced by her father to marry Neoptolemus, was able, the latter murdered, to marry Orestes, to whom she had, years before, been promised. In Shakespeare's *A Winter's Tale*, she is the loved and much-wronged wife of Leontes.

HERO. In Gr., 'a lady' or 'mistress of the house', *Hero* is therefore cognate with *Hera*, the white-armed queen of Olympus. It is a name of some note, for 'it belonged first to one of the Danaïdes, then to a daughter of Priam, then to the maiden whose light led Leander to his perilous breasting of the Hellespont [see also *Leander*], and from whom Shakespeare probably took it for the lady apparently "done to death by slanderous tongues"' (Yonge). Now rare.

HESKETH: See Note at end of Introduction.

HESTER. A variant of *Esther*.

HETTY. A diminutive of both *Esther* (and *Hester*) and *Henrietta*. Cf. *Etty*.

HEW; HU. An English and, more particularly, Welsh *m.* 'Christian' from a Celtic word signifying 'mind': ? therefore 'brainy'.

HEZEKIAH. See at *Ezekiel* for the origin. This is the name of that King of Judah, C8–7 B.C., who abolished idolatry – or thought that he did. It has, except in America, become exceeding rare.

HI. Short for *Hiram.*

HILARIA, *f.* A derivative of:

HILARY, *m.* and occasionally – and derivatively – *f.* By way of *Hilarius* from L. *hilaris,* 'cheerful'. The name recommended itself to the early Christians: there are three Saints Hilaria, two Saints Hilarinus, two Hilarions, as well as eight Saints Hilary, of whom the most important is that C4 Bishop and Doctor of the Church who, known in his own day as Hilarius, so ably defended the central faith against the Arian heresy. (Benedictines.)

HILDA. Chief among the Valkyries was Hild, Hildr, Hildur, or Hiltia. In Teutonic the word means 'battle' and has thus passed to the principal battle-maid; from her it has descended to any maiden. In Germany, it was originally used only in combination (cf. the *Ethel* of those far days), as in *Hildiridur,* 'battle-hastener,' and *Hildegunda,* 'battle-maid of war'. It appeared, by itself, only in Scandinavia and in England; the princess Hildur became the abbess Hilda of Whitby, who, succeeding St Begga, died in 680: her vision is still to be seen 'hovering in the sunny air' by those who have a sufficiency of faith; and her name is still a favourite about Whitby. (Yonge; Swan.)

HILDEBRAND, *m.* From Old German for 'battle sword'.

HILDEGARD or -GARDE, *f.* Another name from Old Ger.: lit., 'battle-wand', hence 'battle maiden'.

HILDEMAR. 'The glory of Hilda' in Teutonic, this *f.* is somewhat rare. See also *Hilda.*

HIPPOLYTUS. Gr., 'he who sets horses free': cf., therefore, *Philip.* In mythology, he was a son of Theseus (who seems to have been rather a libertine) by Hippolytë, queen of the Amazons; in martyrology, the most important Hippolytus is the C3 St Hippolytus of Porto, concerning whom 'the modern speculations . . . literally fill volumes' (Benedictines). The *f.*, *Hippolyta*, is not unknown.

HIRAM, *m.*, is rare in England. It is related to the old-fashioned *Hierom*, which led to *Jerome* (p. 159); in Heb., it means 'most noble'.

HOBART. English variant of *Hubert.*

HOEL or HOWELL. This Welsh *m.* 'anglicizes' Welsh *hywel*, 'lordly'. (Withycombe.)

HOMER. Much less frequent in England than in America, it obviously implies a compliment to one of the world's three – or is it four? – greatest poets. The Gr. name *Homēros* appears to be related to a Gr. word meaning 'a security' or 'pledge'.

HONOR, *f.* Direct from the L. for 'honour': cf. *Grace.* At Rome two temples were built in honour of *Honor* (or *Honos*), the personification of that virtue. (See also at *Vera.*)

HONORA, HONORIA. (From the preceding.) The former probably derives from the latter, for in the late Roman empire there was one Justa Grata Honoria – who, in point of fact, dishonoured her three honourable names. (Yonge.)

HOPE, *f.* Originally Puritan, it has no longer any marked puritanical connotation. It is of the same class as *Honor*, *Faith*, and *Charity* (or *Mercy*): qq.v.

HORACE. 'The Horatian gens was a very old and noble one, memorable for the battle of the Horatii, in the mythic times of early Rome'. If derived from L. *hora*, 'an hour,' it means 'the punctual (man)', but this is probably an instance of folk-etymology; 'the family themselves derived it from the hero ancestor, Horatus, to whom an oakwood was dedicated.'

Its traditional use in the Walpole family – where it alternates with *Robert* (after the C18 statesman) – arises probably from admiration for the great lyric and satiric Roman poet. The name now causes amusement – as do *Algernon, Cuthbert* and *Clarence* – among derisive half-wits.

HORATIA. The *f.* of:

HORATIO. A variant of *Horace* probably suggested by It. *Orazio*. Its C19–20 use, sadly diminished, is mainly prompted by hero-worship for Horatio Nelson.

HORRIE; generally HORRY. The diminutive of the names in *Hora-*.

HORTENSIA. The *f.* of the obsolete *Hortensius*, 'a gardener,' it is now verging on the obsolescent. The L. originals were members of the ancient and honourable *gens* (clan) *Hortensia*.

HOSEA; properly HOSHEA. Rare in C19–20 except among the Jews, it represents, in Heb., 'salvation': and should therefore be compared with *Joshua*.

HOWARD. From the surname, which, like *Percy* and *Stanley*, is very aristocratic in its connexions. '*Howard*, which is phonetically Old Fr. *Huard* ["an osprey"], is sometimes also for *Harward* or *Haward* (Hereward)', lit. 'the sword-guardian', or 'for *Hayward*', Weekley, *Romance of Names*. Sometimes also for Old Ger. *Hugihard*, 'mind-strong, firm-minded' (*Jack and Jill*).

HOWELL. See *Hoel*.

HU. A variant of *Hew*.

HUBBARD. An English variation of *Hubert*. Now mostly a surname.

HUBERT, *m.* At one time wrongly explained as 'bright of hue', *Hubert* is, in Teutonic, 'mind-bright' or '(of) bright mind'. Hubert of Tongres was converted while out hunting, a sport to which he was much addicted: he has thus become the patron saint of hunters. Becoming a bishop, 'he translated St Lambert's relics and See to Liége' in 727, and died in that same year. (Benedictines.) Cf.:

HUGH. From a Teutonic, especially a Scandinavian word meaning 'mind, thought' (which is still *hu* in Scandinavia; cf. Dutch *heuge*); it derives from an old verb for 'to think' (in A.-S. it is *gehygan*). Weekley, in *Jack and Jill*, says that *Hugh* is short for *Hubert*; cf., therefore, *Howard* in the interpretation 'mind-strong'. It was long spelt without a *g* in France, and its popularity in Britain results in part from its adoption in Cymric countries as resembling the famed Hu Gadarn, from whom probably sprang Hugh of Wales, a national figure. It has been a famous name in both Church and State.

HUGHIE. The pet-name for all such Hughs as deserve it – or don't.

HUGO. Originally the L., then, much later, the Ger. form – cf. It. *Ugo* – of *Hugh*; hence an English one. Much less common now than in the Middle Ages.

HULDA, *f.* Mostly in U.S.A.; from Norwegian *Huldr*, lit. 'muffled'. But *Huldah* is Heb.: 'a weasel'.

HUMBERT, *m.* A Teutonic name signifying 'bright (*bert*, A.-S. *beorht*) giant' (*hum*, as in *Humfrey*).

HUMFREY or *Humfry*; usually and barbarously, HUMPHREY. Teutonic, 'giant peace': for the first element, cf. *Humbert*, for the second cf. *Frieda.* At first an aristocratic name – *dine with Duke Humphrey*, by the way, indicates 'going without a meal' – it was in C18 mainly a peasant's; it is now middle-class.

HUMPS, like *Numps*, is a diminutive of the preceding.

HYACINTH. An Irish *m.* name from the *Hyacinthus* (lit., 'purple') of Gr. mythology, it is extremely rare outside Ireland, where its prevalence (esp. as *Sinty*) has been caused by the eight Saints Hyacinth and the famed St Hyacintha of Mariscotti.

HYLDA is a rather affected shape for *Hilda*.

I

Ian; Iain. This Scottish *m.* is a variant of *John*, and *Iain* – affected by C20 novelists – is the more Gaelic form (cf. Erse *Eoin*).

Ianthe, *f.* Gr., perhaps 'violet flower'. Popularized by W. S. Landor. (Withycombe.)

Ida. Not from the Mount Ida in Phrygia, nor that in Crete; nor, except perhaps in parts of Ireland and Scotland, from the ancient *Ita*, 'thirsty' in Celtic; but short 'for Idonia, once a common name' (*Jack and Jill*). The name seems to be falling, ever so slightly, from grace.

Idris is a Welsh *m.*, frequently bestowed.

Ifor. The Welsh form of *Ivor.*

Ignatius. The origin is rather obscure, but it may reside in L. *ignis*, 'a fire,' and the name therefore mean 'fiery'; others hold that it simply derives from the Gr. *Ignatios*, of unknown etymology. It has never, in the British Empire, been in any way frequent except among Catholics, for whom it is rightly an imposing, and an endearing, name: Ignatius, Bishop of Antioch for some forty years, was thrown to the Amphitheatral beasts of Rome ca. 114; Bishop Ignatius of Constantinople, a C9 denouncer of Byzantine vice; and Ignatius of Loyola (d. 1556), who, after being a soldier, 'turned . . . to the more arduous service of the Militant Church' (Benedictines). Diminutive: *Iggie.*

Ikey. An English transformation and diminutive of *Isaac.* Also generic for a Jew.

Imagina. A variant, originally and mainly Ger., of *Imogen.*

IMMANUEL. For this now rare form, see *Em(m)anuel.*

IMOGEN; IMOGINE. An old English *f.* name of doubtful etymology: H. A. Long supposes it to mean 'last-born'; Charlotte Yonge thinks that it may be 'a Shakespearean version of Ygnoge, daughter of Pandrasus, emperor of Greece, and wife of Brutus'; Professor Weekley indicates that *Imogen* is a First Folio misprint for Holinshed's *Innagon* or *Innogen.* Its modern use – e.g. in A. E. W. Mason's novel, *Sapphire* – owes much to the charm of Shakespeare's Imogen in *Cymbeline.*

-INA. See at *Ernestine.* – Hence *Ina,* a *f.* in its own right: cf. *Ena.*

INES, INEZ. Occasionally used in England, these forms are an approximation to Sp. *Iñez,* which corresponds to our English *Agnes,* itself probably an approximation to Fr. *Agnès,* which represents L. *agnus.* The early C14 Castilian and Portuguese Iñez de Castro, of the tragic death, has been celebrated by Camoens and Landor.

INGRAM, *m.* (Now mostly a surname.) In Teutonic, 'Ing's raven'. Ing was the son of Tuisco ('the divine word . . . the original stock of Teutonism') and perhaps the name-father of the Angles, the Anglo-Saxons, the English. *Ingram* is not to be derived from *engelram,* 'angel-purity'. (Yonge; Swan.)

INGRID. This pleasant *f.* name, unheard in England before C20, is Norwegian: 'Ingir's ride'. Ingir was a national hero. (Withycombe.)

INIGO. This contraction or metathesis of *Ignatius* was originally Sp. and has never been common in England.

INNOCENT. From the genitive, *innocentis,* of L. *innocens,* 'harmless,' later 'innocent'. Since it has provided the name of thirteen popes and one anti-pope, it is a mainly Catholic name.

IOLANTHE; (obsolescent) YOLANDE, *f.* Probably from Old Fr. *Violante*, which is only very doubtfully connected with *Viola*. W. S. Gilbert's opera *Iolanthe*, 1882, has done much to preserve this form of the name.

IOLO is the Welsh form of *Julius* (q.v.) perhaps influenced by It. *Giulio* and Sp. *Julio*. It is borne by a noted, and notable, anthologist and bibliographer.

IRA, *m.* Wholly American, is the Heb. for 'watchful' or 'a watcher'. Rare in Britain but common in the U.S.A.

IRENE is from *Eirēnē*, the Gr. goddess of peace, the name denoting 'messenger of peace' and the L. form being *Irene*; the name is, properly, trisyllabic, with the stress on the second syllable. At Rome, however, the goddess was known as *Pax*. 'She was worshipped at Athens and Rome; and in the latter city a magnificent temple was built to her by the emperor Vespasian . . . Pax is represented on coins as a youthful female, holding in her left arm a cornucopia, and in her right hand an olive branch or the staff of Mercury' (Blakeney). There are four Saints Irene, all martyrs (Benedictines).

IRIS, *f.* A transliteration of Gr. ἶρις, 'a rainbow'. In Gr. mythology, Iris is the personification of the rainbow, 'the swift messenger of the gods': in the *Iliad*, Iris is an unpersonified messenger of the gods.

IRMA, *f.* See *Emma*.

IRVING. See Note at end of Introduction.

ISA. An occasional American *f.* name. Is it the Ger. *f.*

'Christian', *Isa*, 'iron'? Or Gr. for 'equal'? In England it is a pet-form of *Isabel.*

Isaac, in Heb., signifies 'laughter'. It is little used except among the Jews, who often bestow it in honour of that patriarch Isaac, who, son of Abraham and Sarah, figured in a dramatic episode, which he survived to marry Rebecca and of her beget Jacob and Esau. Variant *Izaak*, as in Izaak Walton (1593–1683), author of *The Compleat Angler*, 1653, the most famous of fishing books.

Isabel, Isobel. Originally *Elisabeth*: see *Elizabeth.* 'Scotland and France are the countries of Isabel; England and Germany of Elizabeth': in C20, however, *Isabel* or *Isobel* is very common in England too. 'Elisabeth of Hainault, on her marriage with Philippe Auguste [King of France, 1180–1223], seems to have been the first to suffer the transformation into Isabelle, the French being the nation of all others who delighted to bring everything into conformity with their own pronunciation. The royal name thus introduced became popular among the crown vassals.' (Yonge.) But it has also an independent origin as a Biblical name (1 *Kings*, xvi, 31).

Isabella, Isobella. An elaboration of the preceding.

Isadora, *f.* Originally and mainly Sp., it would seem to constitute the *f.* of *Isidor(e)*, q.v. It has been adorned by the famous American interpretative dancer, Isadora Duncan (1878–1927).

Isbel. A Scottish form of *Isabel.*

Iseult. The same as *Ysolt* (q.v.), but more directly from Fr.

Ishbel. The original, the 'Celtic' form of *Isbel.*

Ishmael, *m.* Heb., 'God hearkens'. Now rare, largely because it has become generic for 'an outcast'.

Isidor, Isidore, *m. Isidor* is mostly the Teutonic, *Isidore* the Fr. *m.* form of a name that Ernest Weekley brilliantly conjectures to signify 'gift of Isis'. Mostly a Jewish name. There are nine Saints Isidore.

Isobel (affectedly, *Ysobel*); **Isobella**. See *Isabel* and *Isabella.*

Isold, Isolda, Isolde. A Romance form of *Iseult.* See *Ysolt.*

Israel. Heb., 'contending with the Lord'. Rare except among Jews.

Ita. A Celtic form of *Ida*, q.v.

Ivan. The Russian form of *John, Ivan* was fairly common in C19–early 20, but it has, in the British Empire, been seldom bestowed since the Russian Revolution of 1917. Cf. *Boris.*

Ivo. In origin, this *m.* is a Breton name: *Yves,* which is 'the Old French nominative of *Yvain,* identical with Evan and John . . . From it are derived the female names Yvette and Yvonne' (*Jack and Jill*).

Ivor. An Irish, Scottish, and (as *Ifor*) Welsh form of the Viking name, *Ingwar,* ? 'protector of Ing'.

Ivy, *f.* In Teutonic, 'clinging,' it is obviously from the plant. Cf. *Hazel.*

Izaak, Izack. 'Saxon' forms of *Isaac*; both are now rare.

Izod. See *Ysolt.*

Izzy. The diminutive of *Isidor* and, occasionally and loosely, of *Ishmael.* Also of *Isaac* and *Israel.*

J

Jabez, *m.* Heb., 'he will cause pain' or 'causing pain or sorrow'. Cf. *Ita* and Celtic *Una*, qq.v.

Jacintha, *f.* Gr. 'purple'. It is from the same word as *Hyacinth*, q.v., and is probably an importation from the Romance languages. Now rare.

Jack. The usual diminutive or, rather, pet-form of *John*, it is sometimes bestowed independently. It is frequently used in names personifying human types and non-human aspects: the Australian *jackaroo*, modelled on *kangaroo*; *Jack Frost; Jack Adams; Jack Robinson; Jack Sprat; Jack a' Lent*, the Shakespearean equivalent of *Aunt Sally*. 'To enumerate all the transferred and colloquial senses of *Jack*,' continues Professor Weekley (in *W. & N.*), 'would require a fair-sized book. As applied to people it is usually contemptuous or hostile. . . . Even *Jack Tar*, now admirative, was . . . originally used by those who thought, with Dr. Johnson, that no man ever went to sea who had wit enough to get himself inside a gaol.' (See also my *Dictionary of Slang and Unconventional English.*) In America, the derivative *Jackson* (Jack's son) is not only a surname but, thanks to the fame of General Andrew Jackson (1767–1845), the seventh President (1829–37) of the U.S.A., and of General Thomas Jackson (1824–63), better known as 'Stonewall' Jackson, a not infrequent given-name.

Jackie, Jacky. A diminutive rather of *Jack* than of *John*. (Cf. *Johnnie*.) See also *Jacqueline*.

Jacob. Heb., 'a supplanter'. Jacob, the patriarch, is noted for his dream and for his twelve sons, who founded the twelve tribes of Israel. See also *James*. Diminutive: *Jake*.

JACOBINA, *f.* A fairly common Scottish name coined as a counterpart to *Jacob*.

JACQUELINE, a Fr. *f.* derivative of *Jacques*, is being adopted in post-1918 England. Diminutive: *Jackie* (or -*y*).

JAGO, rare outside of Cornwall, is an adoption of the Sp. form of *Jacob*.

JAKE. The diminutive of *Jacob*. Both forms are employed far more in America than in England.

JAMES. The Gr. *Iάκοσος* (which may be transliterated further as *Jacobos*) derives from the Biblical *Ja'akob*, from Heb. *akeb*, 'the heel,' because, as the Prophet said, 'he took his brother [Esau] by the heel in the womb' and duly supplanted him in his birthright. *Jacobos* became L. *Jacobus* (originally pronounced *yakobus*); whence French *Jacques*, whence 'in a way puzzling to phoneticians' Sp. *Jayme*, later *Jaime* (pronounced *Hah-ee-may*), whence, with the L. and Fr. ending in -*s*, our *James*. 'In Gaelic, James became Hamish, while Ireland spells it Seumas (Shamus)': Ernest Weekley in *Jack and Jill*. The popularity of the name has been caused by its prevalence among European royalty and by its eminence in the annals of the accredited saints. Pet-form: *Jamesie*; usually diminutive: *Jim*.

JAMESINA. The *f.* – mainly Scottish – of the preceding.

JAMIE. A Scottish variant rather of *Jimmy* than of *James*, it is, however, bestowed occasionally as a self-sufficing font-name.

JAN. A Welsh form of *John*, it is also a shortening of *Janet* and a variant of:

JANE. An English contraction and transformation of *Joanna*. Diminutive: *Jenny*. Cf.:

JANET; occasionally JANNET. A Scottish *Jane*, of which it was originally a diminutive.

JANETTA. An elaboration and diminutive, now rare, of the preceding.

JARETT. A variant of *Garret(t)*.

JARVIS. See *Gervas*.

JASMINE. Another flower-name for the use of girls. Variant: *Jessamine* (diminutive: *Jess*), rare in C20.

JASPER, *m.* In Persian, 'master of the treasure' – even if it be only of his own integrity. Most jewel-names are *f.*: e.g., *Beryl*, *Ruby*. The variant *Caspar* is rare.

JAVOTTE, *f.* Celtic, 'white stream'. Originally Fr., it is a diminutive of *Geneviève*: cf. the Fr. *Vevette* and the Ger. *Vevay*. An uncommon name.

JAY, originally a nickname (from the discordant bird) and then a surname, has in America become a Christian name; for instance, of the millionaire, Jay Gould.

JEAMES. 'The original spelling of the name James, which was thus pronounced, though now it is a nickname for flunkeys,' Swan.

JEAN, *f.* A Scottish variant of *Jane* and *Joan*: see *Johanna*, from which, in C19–20, it is frequently used quite independently. *Jean* (cf. Fr. *Jeanne*) has become much more popular than *Jo(h)anna*.

JEANIE. A diminutive of the preceding.

JEDEDIAH. Heb., 'God is my friend'; diminutive, *Jed*. Only in U.S.A. (Withycombe.)

JEFF. A diminutive not of *Geoffrey* but of *Jeffery* or *Jeffrey*.

JEFFERSON, strictly a surname, has, in C19–20 U.S.A., been frequently bestowed as a 'Christian', commemorative of Thomas Jefferson (1743–1826), third President (1801–09) of the U.S.A. and a great, practical-idealistic statesman. He has never had quite his due of praise.

JEFFERY, JEFFREY. An English variant of *Geoffrey*.

JEHU, *m.* Now rare, even among the Jews, it represents, in Heb., 'the Lord is he'. It has long been a colloquialism for a coachman, because Jehu, King of Israel, drove 'furiously'.

JEM; JEMMIE, JEMMY. Diminutives of *James*; cf. *Jim*, *Jimmy*.

JEMIMA, JEMIMAH. In Arabic, 'a dove'; in Heb., 'handsome as the day', this, the name of one of Job's daughters, is now rare except in the provinces: elsewhere, it is used derisively. Diminutive: *Mima*.

JEMMIE (or -Y). See *Jem*.

JEN. A very familiar diminutive of *Jennifer* and *Jenny*.

JENKIN. A Welsh and English diminutive of (*Jan* or) *John*.

JENNIFER. A delightful English adaptation of the Celtically derived *Winifred* or *Winifrid*, q.v. Unfortunately, it seems to show signs of decay – except in Cornwall. Since ca. 1930, however, it has regained some of the lost ground.

JENNY. An English contraction, both of *Johanna* and of *Jane*, but now generally bestowed without reference to its original.

JEREMIAH. 'As Judah sinned more and more, and her fate

drew on, Jeremiah stood forth as her leading prophet'; he flourished ca. 650 B.C. 'His name meant exalted of the Lord, and became Jeremias in the Greek, Jeremy in vernacular English,' Yonge: more precisely, the Heb. means 'Jehovah has appointed'.

JEREMIAS. A Fr. and English variant, now very unusual, of *Jeremiah*, q.v.

JEREMY. See *Jeremiah.* It is one of the best of our *m.* names.

JERMYN. This ancient English *m.* derives from Fr. *Germain*, L. *Germanus*, a German: compare those other two racial names, *Francis* and *Norman.* (*Jack and Jill.*)

JEROME. Gr., 'holy name'. *Hierōnumos* became, in L., *Hieronymus*, whence the It. *Hieronimo* and *Geronimo*, Ger. – harking back to L. – *Hieronimus*, Fr. *Hiéronôme*, later *Jérôme*, and M.E. *Hierom.* Much of the name's dignified popularity must be attributed to the renown attaching to St Jerome (ca. 331–419), who 'was a fierce controversialist, and wrote many letters and treatises against various heresies' (Dawson). Occasionally written *Jerram.*

JERRY. The diminutive of *Jeremiah* (or *-ias*) and, occasionally, of *Jeremy* and *Jerome* and, loosely, of *Gerald.* Among the Tommies, *Jerry* (properly *Gerry*) designated the German, esp. the German soldier; one often heard the phrase, *poor old Jerry*, both in 1914–18 and in 1939–45.

JERVIS. A modernization of *Gervas*, of which (q.v.) it is, in a sense, an Anglicization, for, after all, *Gervas* was, fundamentally, a Norman name. Cf.:

JERVOISE. A variant of the preceding. By Fr. influence: cf. *Gervaise* for *Gervas.*

JESS, *f.* The pet-form of *Jessamine*, *Jessica* and *Jessie.*

JESSAMINE. See *Jasmine.*

JESSE, *m.* Heb., 'the Lord is'. Perhaps the first Jesse was a staunch and impressive affirmer of the existence of 'the true God'. The position to-day is rather that he who asserts a theological God is rash, and that he who denies *a* God is a cretin.

JESSICA. This very attractive name was originally Jewish (Heb. for 'God is looking'): see *Genesis*, xi, 29.

JESSIE; occasionally JESSY. Properly, this is a pet-form either of *Jessica* or of *Janet,* but in the Dominions *Jessie* is often bestowed as a self-contained *f.* 'Christian' by parents that have never heard of *Jessica.*

JEVAN, JEVON. A Welsh variant of *Evan,* q.v. Cf. the Jevan Dovy of Welsh national songs. Sometimes anglicized to *Jevon.*

JILL. The more usual form of *Gill,* the shortening of *Gillian* (q.v.). 'Now a favourite name for sprightly heroines' (*Jack and Jill*).

JIM; JIMMIE, JIMMY. Diminutives of *James.* More accurately, *Jim* is a pet-name, *Jimmie* its diminutive.

JINNY. A diminutive of *Jane.* Cf. *Jenny.*

JO. The pet-form of *Josephine* and, loosely, a variant of *Joe.*

JOACHIM. An English – and Ger. and Russian – contraction of the Heb. *Jehoiachim* or *Jehoiakim,* '(the) appointed of the Lord' – lit., 'God has set up'. Jehoiachim was the luckless king who was carried into captivity in Babylon.

JOAN. A contraction of *Johanna,* this pretty name is now used without reference to its original.

JOANNA. See *Johanna.*

JOB. The Biblical Job, whose historicity requires a considerable amount of acute analysis, originally bore – according to the Alexandrian version – the name of *Jobab*, 'shouting'; the most general theory is that *Job* means 'persecuted'; but the most suitable (though not, therefore, the best) is that it denotes 'penitent', as Mohammed believed. (Yonge.) It is *'Ιώβ* in the Septuagint; in Heb., *Eyob* – two syllables.

JOCELIN, *m.* L. *jocus* (cf. our *jocose*), 'merry,' 'sportive'. In *Jack and Jill*, however, we read that 'Its origin is mysterious, but it seems to be a double diminutive, -el -in, of Josse or Joce, the name of a famous Breton saint, who is "latinized" as Jodocus'. This melodious name is unfortunately falling gradually into disuse. Earlier etymologists frequently made it the *m.* of:

JOCELINE, *f.* Perhaps a diminutive from L. *justus*, 'just'; nevertheless, it is probably the same word as *Jocelin.*

JOCELYN. A variant of both *Jocelin* and *Joceline.*

JOCK. As *Jack* is the English, so is *Jock* the Scottish pet-form of *John.* In late C19–20, *Jock* is generic for a Scot.

JODOCA, *f.* A Welsh variant of obsolete *Jocosa* (now *Joyce*).

JOE; JOEY. Of these diminutives of *Joseph,* the latter is usually bestowed on animals.

JOEL, *m.* Heb., 'Jehovah is God,' especially in the favourable sense.

JOEY. See *Joe.*

JOHANNA; JOANNA, the more usual, although a 'derivative' of the other. Once a fairly common name, and a dignified (cf. Joanna Baillie, the poetess), it is now rather uncommon and apt to provoke derision, the more so as, in rhyming slang, it represents *pianner*, which the educated spell – and pronounce – *piano*. 'This name' – in Heb., 'grace of the Lord' (lit., 'Jah is gracious') – 'comes from the same root as Hannah and Anne – i.e., . . . *chaanach*, "favour," . . . "grace," combined with *Iah*, . . . Jehovah, together giving Johanna, the feminine form of Johannes [L., from Heb. *Iohanan*] of which John is a contraction,' Swan.

JOHN. (See also *Jack* and, for the etymology, *Johanna.*) This name owes most of its universality to the Evangelist; its brevity and strength have contributed to make it, in the minds of the majority, the finest of all *m.* 'Christians'. As Professor Weekley (in *W. & N.*) remarks, 'Taking the European languages as a whole, the dominant name is *John*'. Of forms of the word, Charlotte Yonge lists four in English, three in Scotch, two in Welsh, two in Erse, one in Gaelic; three in Ger., five in Danish; three in Fr. and five in Belgian; eight in It., two in Sp.; six in Russian and six in Lithuanian; seven in Modern Gr.; and so on. 'On the whole,' continues Weekley, '*John* has, in English, preserved a little more dignity than *Jack. John Chinaman* is a shade more respectful than Defoe's *Jack Spaniard* . . . [In short,] *John* and *Jack* predominate among personifications': cf. *John Company* and *John Barleycorn.* (See also at close of the entry at *Joseph.*)

JOHNNIE, JOHNNY. A diminutive of *John.* In late C19–early 20, generic for a fashionable young man-about-town.

JOLYON, *m.*, as in *The Forsyte Saga*, may be *John* influenced by Continental forms; or else from Fr. *joli.*

JON. A rare variant of *John*, though in some instances it appears to be a contraction of *Jolyon.* The name of perhaps the most attractive character in the whole of Galsworthy's *The Forsyte Saga.*

JONAH, *m.* Heb., 'a dove'. Jonah, sent in C9 B.C. to prophesy against Nineveh, sailed instead for Tarshish. In a tempest, he was, by lot, cast into the sea; he was swallowed by 'a great fish' – *not* a whale, obviously – and, after some uncomfortable moments, ejected upon the land. The name is seldom bestowed, for it has come to be generic for a bearer of ill-luck.

JONAS. A Greco-Latin form of the preceding and now somewhat rare.

JONATHAN. Heb., 'the Lord's gift' (lit., 'Jehovah gave'): cf. *Deodatus* and *Dorothy*, qq.v. The friendship of Saul's son with David did much to promote the use of the name, which is, now, seldom bestowed except in the United States: and even there it is falling into some disfavour because *brother Jonathan* has, since ca. 1802, become synonymous with *uncle Sam.* (R. H. Thornton, *An American Glossary*, 1912.)

JORDAN. Heb., 'descender' (lit., 'going down'), the river Jordan being derived from *jared*, 'to descend,' for it flows with exceeding swiftness. 'It was probably this custom [of bathing purificatorily therein] that led to the adoption of Jordan as a baptismal name,' Yonge. It is now mostly a surname.

JOS is short for *Joseph*; cf. *Josh.*

JOSCELIN, JOSCELINE. A drastic English recasting of L. *Justus* or perhaps rather of *Justinus* (English *Justin*). Despite authoritative warning, I still think that *Joscelin* cannot be cut wholly off from *Jocelin*, q.v.

JOSEPH. Heb., 'he shall add', 'increaser', 'addition', 'increase'. Unless as a compliment to father's virility or mother's fertility, this, for intelligence, rivals any such imaginary name as *Extra* or the not wholly imaginary *Increase.* The name was for ever endeared to the Jews by Pharaoh's prime minister, who flourished ca. 1900 B.C.; and, as with all the other such Jewish names (notably *John*) as have achieved generality, Gentile parents seldom think of its Semitic connexions when they invest young hopeful therewith. It may be interesting to know that whereas there are some eighty-four Saints John, there are only fourteen canonized Josephs (Benedictines).

JOSEPHA. The *f.* properly of L. *Josephus*, hence of *Joseph.* Cf.:

JOSEPHINE. A *f.* diminutive of *Joseph*; falling into decay. Cf. *Josepha.*

JOSH. A diminutive – very familiar it is, too! – of the next. 'Josh was Mrs White's *nom de caresse* for Mr White, who had been baptised Joshua,' Horace Annesley Vachell in *The Disappearance of Martha Penny*, 1934.

JOSHUA. Originally *Jehoshea: Hoshea*, 'salvation' + *Je*, 'the Lord,' the whole (in Hebrew) therefore meaning 'the Lord (is my) salvation', a fitting name for him who led the Israelites to the Promised Land. *Joshua* is *Jesus. Jesus* is merely the Gr. form of *Joshua.* (Cf. *Jehovah* for *Yahweh.*)

JOSIAH. Heb., 'Jehovah supports'. Josiah, King of Judea, was a great religious reformer killed in battle in 609 B.C. The Gr. form is *Josias.*

JOSIE. A diminutive of *Josephine.*

JOSSELYN. An incipiently moribund English variant of *Joscelin.* Cf. *Joycelin.*

JOY, *f.* An 'abstract-virtue' name: cf. *Mercy*, *Hope*, *Honor*, etc.

JOYCE, *m.* and *f.* Formerly said to derive from L. *jocosus*, *jocosa*, 'merry'; now known to derive, partly via the Latinized *Joceus*, *Jocea*, 'from Old Ger. *Gozo*, from *Gauta*, the root of the folk-name *Goth*' (Withycombe).

JOYCELIN probably represents a contamination of *Joscelin* by *Joyce*.

JU. A diminutive of *Judith* and *Judy*.

JUDE, *m*. A contraction of the obsolete *Judah* and its variant *Judas*, it derives, as one would expect, from Heb. and signifies 'praised' or 'praise' or 'praise of the Lord', though, even of the earliest holder of this name, it would be more true to say that he got no further than being his father's, or more probably his mother's, joy. *Judah* was besmirched by *Judas*, the traitor; even the nobility of Judas Maccabaeus and the eloquent apostolate and gallant death of St Jude (brother of James the Less) have not freed the name of all stigma; nevertheless, *Jude* lingers in rural England and is green in literary memory because of the realistic power of Hardy's *Jude the Obscure*, reprinted in 1895 from Harper's Magazine.

JUDITH, *f*. originally *Jehudith*, is a racial name (cf. *Francis* and *Norman*) – 'a Jewess'; and it 'belonged primarily to the Hittite wife of Esau, . . . but its fame is owing to [that] heroine of Bethulia' who slew Holofernes, the general of Nebuchadnezzar (605–562 B.C.), King of Babylon, and 'whose name is, however, said rather to mean a Jewess than to be exactly the feminine of Judah. Indeed some commentators, bewildered by the difficulties of chronology, have supposed the history to be a mere allegory in which she represents the Jewish nation' (Yonge); the Book of Judith appears not to antedate C1 B.C.

JUDY. Usually a diminutive of *Judith*, but occasionally employed as an independent font-name.

JULE. A somewhat familiar diminutive of:

Julia. This, the natural *f.* of Julius, dates from early Roman times. It was at its English height ca. 1720–1890. See *Julius.*

Julian. L. *Julianus*, a derivative of *Julius* (q.v.). 'The unpopularity which might have clung to it as . . . the name of two apostates was counteracted by its being that of ten Saints': no, Helena Swan, for whereas there are about thirty saints, whose influence assuredly outweighs that of one-third that number, there was much in the character of Julian the Apostate *par excellence* (331–363) to excite the admiration of all but narrow Christians, and his dying *vicisti, Galilaee* (Christ, thou hast conquered) is merely the figment of a pious wish.

Juliana. The *f.* of the *preceding*, q.v.; its Latinity was effectively disguised in *Gillian*, q.v. The anchoret Juliana of Norwich (d., a centenarian, in 1443) influenced later medieval England by her XVI Revelations of Divine Love. (Harvey.) Cf. *Juliet.*

Julie. A softened form, influenced by Fr. *Julie*, and sometimes independent of: *Julia.*

Juliet, Juliette. From It. *Giulietta*, the diminutive of *Giulia*, L. *Julia.* Its use in England was inaugurated by Shakespeare and has been much reinforced by the charm exercised by the heroine of *Romeo and Juliet.*

Julius. (Cf. *Julian*, q.v.) Virgil sings that

> The boy Ascanius, now Iulus named—
> Ilus he was while Ilium's realm still stood,

thus relating him to the river Ilus (whence *Ilium*); commentators say that Ascanius was named Iulus from Gr. *ἴουλος* (ïoulos: 'first growth of the beard') because he was yet a beardless youth when he slew Mezentius. Virgil continues:

A Trojan, by high lineage shall arise—
Caesar . . . .
Called Julius, from Iulus, mighty name.

But *Iulus* may be a diminutive of L. *diuus*, 'divine'. The imperatorial name and fame have ensured that, even to this day in Caesar-defeated England, *Julius* remains fairly frequent and, like *Julian*, of a distinguished nature. (Yonge.) Diminutive: *Jule*.

JUNE, *f.* This attractive name – cf. *April*, more charming in its Fr. dress (*Avril*) – was unheard before C19 and extremely rare before C20.

JUSTIN. From L. *Justinus*, a *m.* diminutive of *justus*, 'the just,' from L. *jus*, 'right,' 'law'. The most noted Justinus is known to us as Justin the Martyr: one of the greatest early Church writers – in fact, he was the most instructive of the C2 writers – he was beheaded at Rome in 167.

JUSTINA. The *f.* of *Justin*, q.v. Its use has been largely determined by the fame of St Justina of Padua, a virgin martyr of C1; there are four other Saints Justina, but their history is obscure. The name is becoming rare.

K

KAREN. See *Kay* (as a girl's name).

KARL. The Teutonic spelling of *Carl*, Charles.

KATE. A diminutive, sometimes bestowed as an independent font-name, of the next three: –

KATHARINA. A variant of the next. Cf. the relation of *Anna* to *Ann(e)*.

KATHARINE. The name is a diminutive formed from χαθαρά (the *f.*), 'pure,' 'clean,' 'unsullied'; and *Katharina* (*Catharina*) may have been the earlier shape of the word. 'Three other attributes are supposed to attach to Katharine – beauty, grace, and intellectual devotion. Several' – in Benedictines, it is six – 'Saints of the Roman Catholic Church have given lustre to the name, and hence, no doubt, its popularity in the Middle Ages' (Swan); it still is popular – indeed, one of the four or five most frequently bestowed of *f.* Christian names.

KATHERINE. A variant of the preceding.

KATH; KATHIE. Diminutives of *Katharine* and *Kathleen.* Cf. *Kitty* and *Katie* and, despite pronunciation, the Ger. *Kathi* and *Kathei.*

KATHLEEN. The Irish form of *Katherine.* (The ending, *-leen,* is typically Irish.)

KATIE, KATY. A diminutive of *Katherine.*

KATRINE. An English shortening – and hardening – of *Katharine.* Perhaps influenced by It. *Caterina.*

KATTY. An Irish diminutive of *Kathleen*, q.v.

KAY, *m.* and *f.* As *m.*, it represents the L. *Caius* and is cognate or, rather, identical, with a Teutonic word signifying rejoicing. In the Arthurian legend, Sir Kay, a member of the Round Table, acted as seneschal to the King. As *f.*, it may have been suggested by *Katie* or simply by the *K.* prevalent among those who address their friends by the initial of their 'Christians'; more probably, however, it constitutes, originally, a diminutive of *Karen*, which, rare in English but frequent in Danish, signifies 'pure' and therefore ranks as a cognate to *Katherine*.

KEAN, *m.* From Celtic *cian*, 'vast', it is an Irish name; though it may derive from Celtic *cean*, 'head'; *Kean*, moreover, is sometimes said to be short for *Cornelius*: but the 'vast' etymology is that which most philologists accept. 'So common was it once that fifty Cians were killed in the battle of Magh Rath' (Yonge).

KEELDAR, *m.* A Scottish name, becoming unusual, it derives from a Teutonic word meaning 'battle-army'.

KEITH, *m.*, was originally the surname of a Scottish line of earls. In Gaelic, it means 'the wind': the original bearers of the name were wind-swift or perhaps wind-blusterous. (In part: Loughead.)

KEN. Usual diminutive of *Kenneth*.

KENELM, *m.* Of Anglo-Saxon origin, it signifies 'bold (*cēne*), helmet (*helm*)'. (Webster.)

KENNETH. (For an early reference, see at *Finella*.) Deriving from Celtic – it is Scottish – it means 'handsome'. There is a canonized abbot, more usually known as Canice or Canicus, who bore this name and, in C6, preached in Scotland

and throughout Ireland; he is the patron saint of the city of Kilkenny. Usual diminutive: *Ken.*

Kenny. An Irish diminutive of *Kean* and a British of *Kenneth.*

Kentigern, *m.* A Welsh name, from Celtic and meaning 'head chief'. Kentigern was a Pictish saint (C6), 'who recalled his countrymen from Pelagianism, and is regarded as the . . . patron of Glasgow. Persecution obliged him to take refuge in Wales, where he founded the church of Llandwy' (Yonge).

Keren, *f.*, is mostly a Jewish name, now rare in its entirety; *Kerenhappuch,* Heb. for 'horn of eyelash-paint', the name of one of Job's daughters. (*Jack and Jill.*)

Kerridwen. See *Ceiridwen.*

Kerrin. A variant of *Kieren.*

Kester. An English contraction of *Christopher*; now much less common than the delightful-manly *Kit* and the mere abbreviation, *Chris.*

Kevin. An Irish elaboration of *Kenneth,* it means 'handsome child'. A late C6–early 7 Kevin is one of the patron saints of Dublin. (Benedictines.)

Keziah, *f.* In Heb., 'cassia', it rested fittingly on the person of one of the three beauteous daughters of Job: the others, by the way, were Kerenhappuch (see *Keren*) and Jemima (q.v.). Now, despite its beauty, it is rare.

Kieren or *Kieron.* In Celtic, 'black' (? 'swarthy'), this Irish *m.* 'Christian' is probably identical with *Kiaran* (or *Kyran*), the name of that C6 saint who instituted the austere Church-rule called 'the Law of Kiaran (or Kieran)', and with

Kieran (or *Kyran*), that of 'The First-Born of Saints of Ireland' in C5. (Benedictines.)

KIRSTIN, *f.* A reduction of *Christian*; mostly among the Scots. Cf. the Scandinavian *Kirstine*. Cf.:

KIRSTY, *f.* A Scottish reduction of either *Christian* or *Christine*. Cf.:

KIT. As a diminutive of *Christopher*, it is older than *Chris*. See also *Kester*. Moreover, it forms a variant of:

KITTY. The prettiest diminutive of *Katharine*.

L

Lachlan, *m.* This very Scottish name, deriving from the Celtic, probably means 'warlike' (*laochail*), though some, less convincingly, have suggested Erse *lachtna*, 'green'. Weekley, whose opinion in these matters should always be respected, even when it is not shared, has stated (*Jack and Jill*) that *Lachlan* is of place-name origin: 'from Old Norse, apparently meaning "fjord-land" '.

LAETITIA. The etymologically more correct, but in practice unnecessary, form of *Letitia*.

LALAGE, a very Horatian name for a girl, comes straight from Greek, where it means 'Prattler', with a connotation of 'pretty prattler' or 'prettily prattling'; *lalagein*, 'to babble', is manifestly echoic. Diminutives: *Lal, Lally*.

LAMBERT. Old Ger. *Landberht*, 'land-bright' – hence, perhaps 'country's brightness' (? one who is the pride of the nation). This ambitious and encouraging *m.* name has spread, from Germany, not only to Holland and England as is natural enough, but also to France. In the English-speaking world, it is now more common as a sur- than as a font-name.

LANCE. Sometimes the diminutive of, now often a substitute for, by Withycombe treated as the original of *Lancelot* (not as I propose in the next entry, but from Old Ger. *Lanzo*, itself from *landa*, 'land').

LANCELOT; occ. LANCILOT; anciently LAUNCELOT, with *Launce* as a diminutive. From L. *ancillus* postulated from *ancilla*, 'a servant-maid,' via Fr. *ancel* or *ancelot*, *Lancelot* represents *l'ancelot*, '*the* man or (more properly) boy servant', the article and the noun soon becoming fused (cf. *newt*, from old '*an ewt*'); the Welsh supposed the name to be derived from *lance*. Weekley thinks it the product of a writer's fancy.

Ever since the medieval Arthurian cycle, coming to finest flower in Malory's *Morte d'Arthur*, Lancelot has been 'regarded as the type of penitence for misdirected love and chivalrous prowess, and in consequence Lancelot, and its contraction Lance, have never been entirely out of use in England; though not universal' (Yonge).

LANTY. An Irish diminutive of *Laurence*. Cf. the next two names.

LARKIN. An English diminutive of *Laurence*; cf., therefore:

LARRY. An Irish diminutive of *Laurence, Lawrence*. Cf. *Larkin* and *Lanty*.

LAUNCELOT. See *Lancelot*.

LAURA would appear to have been coined from L. *laurus*, the laurel-tree, as a *f.* of *Laurence* and its Continental equivalents (e.g., It. and Sp. *Lorenzo*). It was a favourite with English lyric and pastoral poets of mid C16–early 18, probably owing to the example of Petrarch, who in his sonnets to Laura made this name almost as famous poetically, as Dante did Beatrice. Diminutive: *Lolly*.

LAURENCE; occasionally LAWRENCE. Immediately from L. *Laurentius* ('boy of the city of Laurentium'), probably from *laurus*, 'the laurel,' itself related, back in some pre-Hellenic Mediterranean language, to the synonymous Greek *daphne*. *Laurentius* became a name of great note and the object of Christians' affection because of 'the gentle Roman deacon who, [in] 258, showed "the poor and the maimed, the halt and the blind", as the treasures of the Church, and was . . . roasted over a fire. . . . Constantine built a church on his tomb, and seven other churches at Rome are likewise dedicated to him' (Yonge). There are eight other Saints Laurence (Benedictines). For some obscure reason – but almost certainly nothing to do with any saint so named – *Laurence* (or

Lawrence) has become typical of sloth, esp. in *lazy Laurence* or *lazy as Laurence* and mainly in dialect (Apperson).

LAURETTA. A diminutive of *Laura* and now falling into disuse.

LAURIE. The usual diminutive of *Laurence.* Cf. *Lawrie* for *Lawrence.*

LAVINIA. Occurring notably in the Aeneid, it means, in L., 'a woman of Lavinium,' a city in Italy. The name figures in Shakespeare's *Titus Andronicus* and in a lovely episode (Lavinia and Palemon) in Thomson's *Seasons.*

LAWRENCE. See *Laurence.*

LAWRIE. The usual diminutive of *Lawrence*: cf. *Laurie.*

LAZARUS, *m.*, is the Latin shape of the Greek *Lazaros*, representing Heb. *Eleazar*, 'whom God assists'. Now rarely used except among the Jews, its employment has been prompted by the two New Testament characters: the Lazarus of Bethany (Mary and Martha's brother) whom Jesus restored to life; and that beggar in the parable of Dives and Lazarus who, in the Middle Ages, was the patron saint of lepers – whence archaic *lazar*, 'a leper,' and *lazaret*, 'a hospital for lepers'.

LEAH. Heb., 'wearied'; see also *Levi.* As Helena Swan, with unexpected tartness, remarks, 'This was the name of Laban's elder daughter, whom he palmed off on Jacob after Jacob's first seven years of service.' 'Dante,' says Charlotte Yonge, 'makes her the emblem of active and fruitful, as is her sister [Rachel] of meditative, love.'

LEANDER. Gr. 'lion-man'; for the first element, cf. *Leo*, and for the second, *Andrew*. Leander – cf. the famous Leander crew – was the Abydian youth that swam the Hellespont every night to visit Hero, a priestess of Aphrodite, and finally was drowned; a legend never more beautifully and vigorously treated than by Marlowe in *Hero and Leander*, never more tragically and impressively than by Grillparzer in his poetic drama.

LEAR. Now rare, its use owes much to the fame of Shakespeare's *King Lear*. A Welsh Llyr (Celtic *Lir*, 'the sea'), living about the time of the Roman conquest, was ill-treated by his daughter. *Lyr*, in connexion with unruly daughters or granddaughters, is common to both British and Irish legend. (Yonge.)

LEIGH; occasionally LEE. Apparently, as a British *m.*, it derives from the surname (*lea*, 'a meadow'): Weekley, *Surnames*. As an American *m.*, it usually commemorates the famous Southern general, Robert E. Lee (1807–70), brilliant strategist and fine man. As *f.*, it derives from *Letitia*; cf. *Letty*.

LEILA; occasionally LEILAH. Probably, through the Moors, from Arabic ('darkness' or 'night'), it has been to some extent popularized by Byron's Mohammedan child in *Don Juan* and by his unfortunate heroine in *The Giaour*. (Harvey.) Often Englished to *Lila*.

LELA. A variation of the preceding.

LEM; LEMMIE. Diminutives of:

LEMUEL, *m.* This once mainly Puritan and now mainly Jewish name is the 'Christian' of the hero of *Gulliver's Travels*. Heb., 'devoted to God'.

LEN. A pet-form of *Leonard*.

LENA. A reduction of *Eleanora* and *Leonora*, and a shortening of *Helena*; cf. *Lina*.

LENNIE. A familiar, affectionate diminutive of *Leonard*. Cf. *Len*.

LENORA. A Ger. and, derivatively, English contraction of *Leonora*.

LEO. L. (from Gr. *leōn*), 'a lion'. So 'thrilling' a name was certain to achieve popularity, but in common with most such names, it is rapidly becoming less frequent; it is still, however, something of a favourite with lovers of the occult, since Leo is the fifth sign of the Zodiac. Cf. *Lionel*, q.v.

LEOLINE, *m.* A derivative from *Llewellyn* and almost unknown to non-Celts.

LEON, *m*. From Gr. (see *Leo*), it is an Italian and Russian name that has made its way among English-speaking Jews. (Swan.)

LEONARD. 'Lion-hard,' i.e. 'lion-strong', it is a hybrid from Gr. and Teutonic. *Leonard* derives immediately from *Löwenhard*, the name of a C6 Frankish 'nobleman of the Court of King Clovis', who, 'like that monarch,' was 'converted to Christianity by St Remigius of Reims. . . . He was eminent for austerity of life and for the charitable help he never refused to those in trouble, more especially to poor prisoners. . . . His memory was throughout the Middle Ages venerated everywhere in Western Europe. In England, as elsewhere, many churches were dedicated in his honour' (Benedictines).

LEONIE adapts the Fr. *Léonie*, *f.* of *Léon* (see *Leon*).

LEONORA. An abbreviation of Ger. *Eleanora* or a more typically *f.* variation of *Leonor*, a Castilian form of Provençal *Aliénor* from It. *Elena*. The precise Ger. equivalent is *Lenore*, famous in Bürger's ballad.

'Lenore fuhr ums Morgenrot,
Empor aus schweren Träumen:
"Bist untreu, Wilhelm, oder tot?
Wie lange willst du säumen?" '

so stirringly translated, late in C18, by Scott. *Leonora* is falling into disuse.

LEOPOLD. Via Fr. *Léopold*, from Old Ger. *Leutbald*, 'people-bold'. 'Its introduction into England is quite recent,' says Helena Swan in 1905, 'and had, probably, some connexion with Leopold I [1790–1865], King of the Belgians, who was an uncle of Queen Victoria, and after whom she called her fourth son.' As the name of Kings and Emperors, it owes its prevalence to that Leopold who, styled 'The Pious', was Margrave of Austria and who, 'beloved of God and man,' died in 1136 (Benedictines).

LEOT. A Scottish transformation of *Loise*.

LES. The diminutive of *Leslie*.

LESBIA comes straight from the Latin poets. Literally 'girl of Lesbos', the name is commoner in Ireland than in England or Scotland or Wales; cf. the Lesbia Burke of two of Henry Kingsley's novels.

LESLIE, is, like *Howard* and *Percy*, derived from the surname, which may possibly be explained in the same way as the Lesly (more generally *Lesley*) of Scott's *Quentin Durward*, where we learn that 'the *Lesleys* claim descent from the hero who overthrew a Hungarian champion – "Between the *less lee* [lea] and the mair [greater]" ' (Weekley, *Romance of Names*). Occasionally it is bestowed on girls, usually in the form *Lesley*.

LESTER. (Cf. the preceding.) From the surname *Lester*, i.e. 'he of *Leicester*' (the city so named).

LETITIA. (See also *Laetitia.*) From L. *laetitia*, 'gladness,' 'happiness,' from *laetus*, 'gay,' 'glad,' 'joyful', apparently it had been prompted by *Lettice*; certainly it was much more general in C19 than it is now.

LETTICE. An English 'shape', made centuries ago (witness Lettice Knollys, wife of the Earl of Essex), of It. *Letizia*. See prec. entry.

LETTY. An English and Irish diminutive of *Letitia* and *Lettice*. Charlotte Yonge, however, holds that as an Irish name it derives from Teutonic and means 'truth'.

LEVI. Heb., 'joined'. It is now bestowed only by the Jews. The Biblical Leah thus named her third son, who, she hoped, would unite her husband more closely to her; Heb. *lawah*, 'hanging upon,' is the radical whence comes *Leah* itself.

LEW. The diminutive of *Lewis* as *Lou* is of *Louis*; also of *Llewellyn*.

LEWIS has a double origin, for on the one hand it constitutes an English adaptation of the Welsh *Llewellyn* and therefore, in Celtic, denotes 'lion-like', and on the other it is an Anglicism for Fr. *Louis*, which, in its earliest form *Hludowig* or *Hhlodowig* (sometimes spelt *Chlodowig*, *Chlodovech*), denotes, in Teutonic, 'famous' – lit., '*loud* war'. The second is much the more operative of the two lineages. The warlike Hludowig renounced his Teutonic gods, was baptized, and became the sole orthodox king in Europe: and his name was Latinized as *Chlodovisius*; this, retranslated into Fr., is *Clovis*, that Frankish sovereign of whom Oscar Browning has tersely said that, 'being greatly assisted by his orthodoxy, he succeeded, by either force or fraud, in gradually getting the greater part of Gaul under his sway, and when he died, in 511, left it to be divided between his four sons—a disastrous practice, which caused civil war and prevented unity'.

LEXY. A diminutive of *Alexandra, Alexandrina, Alexia* and (feminine) *Alexis.*

LIAM, *m.* An Irish name (*William*) that, like *Sean,* is making something of a stir in English rather than Irish literature.

LIBBY. A typically English derivation from 'Elizabeth'. Now exceedingly rare in any but rural districts and, even there, only in England.

LIDA, *f.* Originally and mainly Slavonic, it means 'people's love'.

LIDDY. The diminutive of *Lydia.*

LIL. The diminutive of all *Lil-* names. – Lila. See *Leila.*

LILIAS. 'A very popular Scottish form' (Swan) of:

LILIAN, which Charlotte Yonge thinks is, radically, the same as Neapolitan *Liliola,* Venetian *Ziliola* or *Zilia,* L. *Celia,* from *celum* (*coelum*), 'the heavens,' 'the sky'. This is probably so, but there was, at an early period in Christian symbolism, a confusion – or perhaps rather a fusion – with L. *lilium* (plural *lilia*), 'a lily,' for 'in Christian art the lily is the emblem of chastity, purity, and innocence' (Swan). Weekley, however, thinks that *Lilian, Lily,* etc., may derive ultimately, perhaps via some pet-form, from *Cecilia.*

LILITH, *f.,* is variously interpreted, from the Heb., to mean 'a serpent', 'a screech-owl' or, in the Revised Version, 'a night-monster,' i.e. a vampire. In Rabbinical literature, she, the first wife of Adam, was dispossessed by Eve; she took her revenge by becoming the serpent of the Tree of Knowledge: see D. G. Rossetti's *Eden Bower.* (Harvey.)

LILLA. This contraction of *Elizabeth* has perhaps been influenced by *Lilias* and:

LILLIAN. A spelling-variant of *Lilian*; perhaps on *Gillian.*

LILY; occasionally LILLY. Probably either a contraction or a shortening (*Lili*) of *Lilian*; yet it may come direct from English *lily*.

LIN. A diminutive of *Lionel.*

LINA. Short for *Adelina* or *Carolina* – or for *Adeline* or *Caroline.*

LINCOLN, a surname deriving from the place-name of the English cathedral-city, has, in the U.S.A., been frequently bestowed as a 'Christian' in honour of that great man, Abraham Lincoln (1809–65), President in 1861–65.

LINDA; familiarly LINDY. An abbreviation of *Belinda* – the obsolescent *Ethelinda* – *Melinda*, names formed with second element based on Ger. *-linde*, common in Ger. *f.* names and derived from *lind*, 'snake'; that *lind* probably refers to feminine guile, though perhaps to that restricted form of wisdom which we call prudence.

LIONEL. L., 'little lion,' from Gr. *λέων*, 'a lion,' should be compared with *Leo*, *Leon*, *Leonard*, and also with *Llewellyn.* It is an attractive name. Diminutive: *Li.*

LISA. A variant of *Liza.*

LISE. A shortening of *Elise*; and a variation of *Liza*; and also, more properly, a variation of *Louise.*

LIZ. A shortening and transformation of *Liza*, perhaps through a presumed *Lize*, or else directly from *Elizabeth.* Cf.:

LIZA. From *Eliza.* It is, as Somerset Maugham implies in his early and realistic novel, *Liza of Lambeth*, usually thought vulgar, as are *Liz* and *Lizzie.*

LIZZIE. Probably from *Liz* or *Elizabeth.*

LLEUEU. The Welsh form of *Lucy.*

LLEW. A Welsh *m.*; in Celtic, 'a lion' or, as some prefer, 'light'. Cf.:

LLEWELLYN, *m.* From Celtic, it means either 'lion-like' or 'lightning': see *Llew.* Llewellyn the Great of Wales, Llewellyn ap Iorwerth, who, after his many victories, finally yielded to Henry II, and Llewellyn ap Gryffydd, another mighty warrior (d. 1282), endeared the name to Welshmen.

LLWYD. The Welsh original and form of:

LLOYD, *m.* Celtic for 'grey', it is an Anglicization of *Llwyd.* Now both surname and 'Christian', it is an alternative name for *Lear*, which, as the sea, is fittingly called 'the grey' or 'the extended' (cf. the poetical 'grey wastes of ocean'). Yonge.

LLYR, *m.* This Welsh name is that of the sea-god of the ancient Britons and is perhaps identical with the *Lir* of Gaelic mythology. Cf. *Lear.* (Harvey.)

LODOWICK, *m.* A Scottish name corresponding to the English *Ludovick* and probably taken from the Northern form of the original word (*Hludowig*: see at *Lewis*), as Charlotte Yonge perspicaciously notes.

LOIS, *f.* A contraction of *Aloisia* (cf. Fr. *Loys* and Provençal *Aloys*, both being forms of *Louis*, however, and not of *Louise*), it is considerably more frequent in America than in Britain. *Lois*, from *Aloisia* or *Héloïse*, is properly *Loïs*; *Lois*, in one syllable, comes from the Heb. for 'better' and, in the U.S.A., is occasionally spelt *Loyce.* (Loughead.)

LOLA, *f.* Originally and mainly Spanish – it 'diminishes'

Dolores – it was popularized by the meretricious glitter of Lola Montez, who (1818–61), after dazzling London and the Continent with her dancing, became the regnant mistress of Ludwig I of Bavaria.

LOLLY. See *Laura*.

LORA. The pretty pet-name to *Leonora*. Not to be confused with *Laura*.

LORN, *m.* Irish and Scottish, this represents the *Loarn*, who with Aonghus (Angus) and Fergus led the migration from Ireland to Scotland. Etymology? 'The Dreaded'?

LORNA or LORNE, is a *f.* name of A.-S. origin. It has the same meaning as 'love-*lorn*', i.e. lost. The form *Lorna* owes its popularity – perhaps even its birth – to R. D. Blackmore's *Lorna Doone*, 1869. (Weekley.)

LOT. As an English name, less frequently from the Biblical person than from Celtic for 'a lion'. Now rare.

LOTHAIR. (See also *Lowther*.) From Frankish *Lothar*, from *Chlother*, from *Chlotachari* or *Hlodari*, 'famous warrior,' with which cf. the *Hlodowig* treated under *Lewis*. Always a royal or an aristocratic name – the Lothair of Disraeli's novel (published in 1870) is an extremely rich young nobleman – it has fallen into comparative neglect. (Yonge; Harvey.)

LOTHARIO. This is a doublet of *Lothair* (q.v. for etymology), and probably it represents a fanciful Italianate adaptation of *Lothar* (see *Lothair*). The use of this word for a gay and heartless libertine dates from that character as drawn by Nicholas Rowe in *The Fair Penitent*, a tragedy in blank verse, 1703.

LOTTIE, LOTTY. The pet-form of *Charlotte*; cf., therefore, *Chatty*, and see *Carrie*.

LOU. A diminutive of both *Louis* and *Louisa.* Cf. *Lew.*

LOUGHLAN, *m.* A variant of *Lachlan.*

LOUIE. An English diminutive of *Louisa* and contraction of *Louise.*

LOUIS. As an English name – for it is one of the three or four commonest Fr. 'Christians' – it is much less frequent than *Lewis,* q.v. for etymology.

LOUISA. The English (*à la* Latin) *f.* of the preceding. Cf.:

LOUISE. Properly, the Fr. *f.* of *Louis,* but now almost as general as *Louisa.*

LOVEDAY, *m.* and *f.* This Cornish, or mainly Cornish name, is probably from the surname; lit., 'a day appointed for reconciliations' (Weekley, *Romance of Names*).

LOWTHER. An English reshaping of *Lothario.*

LU. A diminutive – in most instances the only one – of all the *Lu*-names except *Luke.*

LUBIN. Now rare in England but tolerably common in Ireland (and, for that matter, France), it represents the A.-S. *Leofwine,* the name of one of King Harold's brothers; also, there is a St Lubin (otherwise Leobinus). In Teutonic, it means 'dear friend'.

LUCAN. A variant of *Lucius,* though immediately from L. *Lucanus,* a contraction of *Lucianus.*

LUCAS, *m.* See *Luke.*

LUCASTA. Either a variant of *Lucy* or formed on *Lucas*; in C20 deemed too poetical for everyday use.

LUCE. A pet-form of *Lucy* and its variants.

LUCETTA. A diminutive of *Lucy.* Cf. the preceding and *Lucilia.*

LUCIA. See *Lucy.*

LUCIAN. L. *Lucianus*, a transliteration of Gr. *Loukianos*, of obscure origin. Sometimes, however, the L. name may have been apprehended not as coming from the Greek Proper Name, but as a derivative of *Lucius.* Among the devout, the influence of the seven Saints Lucian has been considerable – but is lessening; among the ungodly (not necessarily the godless), that of the Greek satirist Lucian (born ca. 120 A.D.), whose *Dialogues* have been so admirably translated by the lexicographical Fowlers, is less, but not negligibly, noticeable.

LUCILIA. A somewhat prettified diminutive of *Lucy.* In L. there is the *m. Lucilius.*

LUCILLA. From St *Lucilla*, diminutive of *Lucia.*

LUCINA. This now rare variant of *Lucy* probably owes its English use to the three Saints Lucina (C1–3).

LUCINDA. A variant, influenced by the *-inda* names, of the preceding. See also *Lucy.*

LUCIUS. A very common L. name, denoting '(one) born at daylight' or, less probably, 'fair-complexioned' – from *lux* (genitive *lucis*), 'light' – it has been to a moderate extent popularized in England by the reverence due to the nineteen Saints Lucius, esp. to that chieftain of South Wales who, ca. 180, begged Christian missionaries from the Pope; Lucius Cary, Viscount Falkland, invested it with a fine lustre; and in Ireland it has been made to serve as the equivalent of the native *Lachtna* and *Loiseach.* (Benedictines; Yonge.)

LUCRETIA. This now rare original of the obsolete *Lucrece* derives either from L. *lucrum*, 'gain' or 'profit', or from *lux*, 'light'. Cf. *Lucius* and:

LUCY. Probably the English representation of Fr. *Lucie*, from L. *Lucia* (occasionally used in English), the *f.* of *Lucius*, q.v. It has never since been so popular as in C17, 'when many noble ladies were called Lucy, but poetry chose to celebrate them as *Lucinda*, or by some other fashionable variety [especially *Lucasta*] of this sweet and simple word,' Yonge; it is prominent, too, in martyrology. – Also the pet-form of *Lucian*, *Lucius*.

LUDO is the diminutive of:

LUDOVIC or LUDOVICK. See *Lodowick*.

LUDOWICK. A foolish fusion, or confusion, of *Ludovic(k)* with *Lodowick*.

LUISA. A variant of *Louisa*.

LUKE. Gr. *Loukas* becomes L. *Lucas*; the name signifies 'he of Lucania'. Thus the third Evangelist ('beloved physician and reputed painter') is *Loukas*, i.e. *Lucas*, which becomes Fr. *Luc* and English *Luke*. It is a manly 'Christian', which the C20 is returning to favour along with *Peter*. The variant *Lucas* is now mainly a surname.

LULU, *f.*; rarely *Lula*. Diminutive of *Louise* (*-sa*).

LUTHER. From the Ger. surname *Luther*, rendered impressive by Martin Luther (1483–1546). *Luther* is of the same origin as *Lothair*, q.v.

LYDIA. Gr., '(a woman) of Lydia,' that district of Asia Minor which, 'an early seat of Asiatic civilization,' exercised 'a very important influence on the Greeks' (Blakeney): cf.

'Lydian mode'. The name attracted the poets of mid C16–mid 18, in part because it figures rather prominently in L. lyric and satiric poetry.

LYNN; occasionally LYN. As in *Lynn O'Doyle*, the Irish short-story writer. (Of geographical origin? Or = *Lin*?)

LYONEL is an outmoded form of *Lionel*.

LYULF, *m.* This Scottish name merely re-shapes the Scandinavian *Leiul* or *Liedulf*, which, in terms of its Teutonic elements, signifies 'fierce wolf'.

M

MAB is a diminutive of *Mabel.* Shakespeare's Queen Mab may be that Irish heroine of romance who, from *Meadhbh* turning into the more 'human' *Meave,* became, 'like other favourite Irish heroines,' queen of the fairies. (Yonge.)

MABEL is short for *Amabel.* Helena Swan pertinently adds that 'it is a mistake to think that the name is derived from the French, *ma belle,* "my beautiful," or "my fair one", though often bestowed under that impression.' The name shows a – to some, disconcerting – tendency to fall below stairs.

MABLE. A variant of the preceding.

MABS. A pet-form of *Mab*: cf. *Babs.*

MAC. A diminutive of all the *Mac*-names.

MACAIRE. An Irish *m.*, it is probably an adaptation or a reduction of the Gr. name, *Makarios,* probably in its L. form, *Macarius,* especially as there were, in C4, two notable saints, Macarius the Younger and the Elder: in Classical Gr., *μακάριος* (makarios) is 'blessèd', 'happy', itself from *μάκαρ,* which is closer to our name but not its effective origin. In Fr., rather curiously, 'de bonne heure ce nom [*Macaire,* ou *Robert Macaire*] a été pris pour signifier un homme dangereux . . . le nom générique des fripons adroits et audacieux' (Littré): here, plainly, are the same semantics as in the two opposing senses of *blessèd* and Fr. *sacré.*

MACBEATH. The Gaelic original, now rare, of:

MACBETH, which is now more frequently a surname than a 'Christian'. Drawn from Celtic, it means 'son of life', perhaps with a connotation of liveliness or robust health.

The ill-fame of the Shakespearean Macbeth did his name no good.

MAC MARRY, *m.* '(The) son of bitterness,' *Mac* representing 'son' and *Marry* the L. *amarus* (cf. the Fr. *marri*, 'sorry,' 'penitent'). 'Also a Scottish derivative of *Mary*' (Swan).

MAC MURCHIE or MAC MURROCK. The same as for the preceding. There is some mystery here: may one suspect the influence of Old Norse *myrkr* (cf. A.-S. *mirce*), 'murk,' i.e. 'darkness'?

MADDIE. A diminutive of:

MADELINE. An English variant of *Magdalen(e)* – than which it is, in mid C19–20, far more general – on the model of other names in *-line*. Occasionally the Fr. form, *Madeleine*, occurs in English.

MADGE. A splendidly English re-shaping of *Margaret*. In C16–17, it was somewhat proletarian; in C20, it ranks with the best. Cf. the status of *Audrey*.

MADISON. See Note at end of Introduction. (Mostly in U.S.A.)

MADOC, *m.* Common in Wales and perhaps signifying 'son of fire; the impetuous' but far more probably a mere personification of Welsh *madawg* (adjective), 'advantaged; beneficiary; goodly; hence, strong and handsome': cf. the hero of Robert Southey's epic poem *Madoc* (1805), lit with Cymric fire.

MAE is an affected form (beloved by actresses) of *May*.

MAG. A diminutive – generally deemed rather vulgar – of *Margaret*. *Maggie* is more usual.

MAGDA is the diminutive of – though it is often bestowed without reference to – *Magdalene.* Adopted from German.

MAGDALEN; MAGDALENE (rare). Heb., '(the woman) of Magdala' or Dalmanutha, that city on the shores of Lake Gennesaret or Sea of Galilee which is famed as the birth-place of Mary Magdalene – at one time 'possessed by seven devils' and then, penitent, a thorough-going saint. The name is falling into disuse in both of its forms – forms 'reflected' in the Oxford college (*-en*) and the Cambridge (*-ene*).

MAGGIE, MAGGY. See *Mag.*

MAGNUS. See *Manus.*

MAHALAH, *f.* Heb., 'tenderness'. Now rare.

MAHON. In Celtic, 'a bear'. An Erse 'Christian' that is now mostly a surname.

MAIDA, *f.* From the battle of Maida (in Italy), 1806; whence also Maida Vale, the district in N.W. London. Cf. *Alma.*

MAIDIE. See *Maisie.* It is also a diminutive of *Maida.*

MAIDOC. An Irish form, somewhat unusual in these days, of Welsh *Madoc.*

MAIR. The Welsh form of *Maria* (and *Mary*). In English it is mostly a surname.

MAISIE, whence MYSIE; MAIDIE. Scottish diminutives, hence also independent variants, of *Margaret.*

MALACHI, -CHY. Usually *m.*, it is also, in late C19–20, occasionally *f.* In Heb., '(God's) messenger,' it is represented by two saints, Malachi the C5 prophet, and Malachy the early C12 bishop magnificently eulogized by St Bernard. (Benedictines.)

MALCOLM. Originally *Maolcolum*, 'a disciple of Columb,' it may, in the Celtic, be interpreted as 'servant of Colomba', the saint who, in C6, founded a hundred monasteries and, from Ireland, went to Scotland: 'the Apostle of Caledonia'. It is mostly a Scottish name. (See also *Colan* and *Colin*.)

MALISE, *m.* Also Scottish and also (in Celtic) 'a disciple' – of *Jesus*, the *-ise* corresponding to *Jes-*: cf. also *Joshua*, originally *Jehoshua*.

MALL. A sensible English contraction of *Matilda*.

MALVINA, MALVINE. *Malvina* is an invention (probably from *maol*, 'a handmaid': cf. *Malcolm*) of 'Ossian' Macpherson's, *Malvine* the Gallicism therefor. Both are rare in England.

MAMIE, mostly American, is strictly a diminutive of *Margaret*.

MANASSEH, grecized as *Manasses*. Heb. for 'he who causes forgetfulness'. (*Jack and Jill*.) A Puritan, now rare in England, less rare in U.S.A.

MANDY is the diminutive of *Amanda*.

MANFRED. Originally, in Old Ger., *Manifred*, 'man of peace,' whence, by contraction, *Manfred*. The name has had some slight currency, thanks to King Manfred of Sicily (C13) and to the 'hero' of Byron's dramatic poem, *Manfred*, 1817.

MANNY. This is a Jewish diminutive of *Manuel* and sometimes a mere nickname applied to Jewish youths, especially if they are lovers of boxing.

MANUEL. A shortening of *Immanuel* and *Emanuel*; see the latter. Now left mainly to the Spanish and the Portuguese.

MANUS, *m.* An Irish name, derived from L. *magnus*, 'great', is not to be derived from nor confused with Dutch *Manus*, 'public' (Teutonic). One seems to have heard of a Manus MacManus. *Magnus* itself is not uncommon in Scotland and the Scottish isles.

MARABEL. See *Mirabel*.

MARCELIA. A variant, somewhat fanciful, of

MARCELLA. The *f.*, mostly Irish and rather aristocratic, of *Marcellus*.

MARCELLINA, MARCELLINE. Diminutives (on L. and Fr. models) of *Marcella*.

MARCELLUS. The L. diminutive of *Marcus*. Now rare.

MARCH, *m.* In Celtic, 'a horse'; cf. A.-S. *mearg, mearh*. Become unusual as a baptismal, it is, in C20, usually a surname.

MARCHELL. Both *m.* and *f.* This Welsh equivalent of *March* may rather fuse Celtic *March* and L. *Marcella*, *Marcellus*. Now rare.

MARCIA. The *f.* of:

MARCIUS. A L. shape (from *Marcus*) of *Mark*, heard, now and then, in England.

MARCO. This It. equivalent of *Mark* is occasionally used in English as a pet-name.

MARCUS. This L. name, probably deriving from *Mars*, god

of war, is also a variant of *Mark*: from Gr. *Markos*. Fairly general in C19, it is rapidly losing ground.

MARGARET. This, one of the best of our English *f.* 'Christians', derives from Gr. *μαργαρίτης* (margaritēs) 'a pearl', from Persian *murvarid* or *murwari*, 'child of light,' hence 'a pearl'. The Persians 'imagined that oysters rose to the surface at night to worship the moon' – Dante's *la gran' Margherita* – 'and that as they opened their shells drops of congealed dew fell in, and became by the moon's rays transformed into pearls.' English variants are *Margaretta*, *Margery*, *Maggie*, *Meggie*, *Madge*, *Marget*, *Peggy*, *Greta*, *Gritty*, *Meta*; Scottish, *Marjorie* (now also English), *Maisie* and *Maidie* and *May* (likewise), and *Meg*. (Yonge; Swan.)

MARGARETA, MARGARITA. Respectively, near-Ger. and Sp. forms of *Margaret*, they are, in England, occasionally the alembicated or the fanciful expression of external affection. *Margaretta*, however, may fairly be adjudicated English.

MARGERY. An English spelling of *Marjorie*, *-y*: and in C20 rather fashionable. (For diminutives, see *Marjorie*.)

MARGET. An English contraction of *Margaret*. Cf. *Margot*.

MARGOT. A Fr. shortening of *Marguerite* adopted in England in latter half of C19 and popularized in English society by a certain witty lady.

MARGUERITE. Originally, and mainly, the Fr. form of *Margaret*. Less popular is the more English *Marigold*, another flower-name.

MARI. The Irish form of *Maria*, *Mary*.

MARIA. For the etymology, see *Mary*, its derivative. *Maria*, the It. and Sp. form, was once in England a royal name: but now it is regarded as 'ancillary'. Its associations with sanctity and religion appear to advantage in these verses forming the opening of a sonnet by Boccaccio:

O Regina degli angioli, o Maria,
　Ch' adorni il ciel co'tuo' lieti sembianti,
　E, stella in mar, dirizzi i naviganti
　A porto e segno di diretta via,
Per la gloria ove sei, Vergine pia,
　Ti prego guardi a' miei miseri pianti.

MARIAN. A variant, made in the Middle Ages, of *Marion*. Maid Marian appears in the later forms of the Robin Hood legend and as a personage in the morris-dance and the May-games.

MARIANA. A Spanish form of *Maria*; an English of *Mary* and (or via) *Maria*. It is out of favour, perhaps because too reminiscent of Tennyson's *Mariana* and *Mariana in the South*, themselves reminiscent of Shakespeare's Mariana, 'dejected, at the moated grange' (Harvey).

MARIANNE. Originally, a Fr. name. Lit., *Mary Anne*.

MARIBELLE, 'lovely Mary' (*la belle Marie*), is a fanciful American name, on the analogy of *Claribel*.

MARIE is properly the Fr. form of *Maria* and therefore the perfect equivalent of our English *Mary*, but its correct pronunciation (*Marë* and not, as too often, *Máree*) is so pleasant as to justify its adoption by the generous-minded Briton. (See also *Mary*.)

MARIETTE, *f.*, is a diminutive of Fr. *Marie*.

MARIGOLD. See *Marguerite*.

MARINA, an Italian name, the *f.* of L. *marinus*, 'of the sea,' was brought to England in 1934 by the Princess Marina and there popularized by her courtship and marriage with H.R.H. Prince George, the late Duke of Kent. Any girl so named will, ca. 1960–80, feel sorry that she was: parents should have more sense than to bestow these superannuating names, graceful as they admittedly are if viewed as compliments. *Marina*, according to some, 'has nothing to do with the sea. Hagia Marina is a popular saint of the Greek Church (6th century). Churches in her honour are numerous. There is one in Athens' (the Rev. J. C. Badcock); *Marina*, therefore, is a 'shape' of *Mary*, *Hagia Marina* being Holy Mary.

MARION. In mid C19–20, more general than *Marian*; a diminutive of Fr. *Marie*: cf. *Alison*. Also, occasionally *m.*, as in *Francis Marion Crawford*, the Italianate American novelist (1854–1909).

MARIS, *m.* A Scottish offshoot from *Mary*, says 'Swan'; but may it not be a contraction of:

MARIUS. L., 'of Mars,' it is an old Roman name: *Marius* was one of the most celebrated consuls (he held the office seven times), a great general, yet a rather foolish man, of whom a very shrewd character-sketch has been drawn by Oman in those ever-absorbing *Seven Roman Statesmen*.

MARJORIE, MARJORY. A Scottish (hence English) variant of *Margaret*. Diminutives: *Marge*, *Margie*.

MARK. Etymologists have not yet decided the origin of this crisply manly 'Christian': probably the word represents *Mavors* or *Mamers*, an important older L. deity from whom descends *Mars*; if this be correct, *Mark* is a cognate of *Martin* (q.v.). To the early Christian Church it was familiar as *Markos*, still a favourite Gr. name: see also *Marcius*, *Marco*, *Marcus*. The Church has, in fact, done much to spread the name in Europe and, hence, in U.K.; uncomparably, yet not negligibly, so has Marc Antony.

MARMADUKE, *m.* Now mostly a North Country name, it was in C13–16 frequently bestowed among the English nobility. Of Celtic origin, it may mean either 'sea leader' or 'a steward' (or 'chief officer of the Crown'). It is an impressive yet friendly name, with diminutive *Duke*.

MARR, *m.* Scottish, certainly; but is it, as Helena Swan asserts, a contraction of *Mary*, or is it, as I suspect, from *mair*, 'the greater'?

MARTA, MARTITA. Of these two *f.* names, perhaps the former is a variant, probably the latter is a diminutive, of *Martha*; cf. the pronunciation of the Fr. *Marthe.* If those are indeed the correct explanations (as I think they are), then the origin, as Miss Flora Loughead (*Given Names*, 1934) has suggested, lies in the Aramaean for 'lady': cf., therefore:

MARTHA. Aramaean, 'lady', is not, as formerly, to be compared with *Maria* and *Mary*. Now non-aristocratic in England, it has excellent Biblical and saintly precedence.

MARTIE, MARTY. A diminutive of *Martha.* (Contrast *Mattie.*) But *Mart* is the more usual diminutive of:

MARTIN. L. *Martinus*, from *Martius* (generally spelt *Marcius*), 'of Mars,' hence perhaps, 'a disciplinarian'. Whereas *Martinus* migrated to Germany, France changed it to *Martin*, a form adopted by the English, who, just to show their independence, gave it a variant, *Martyn.* The name has received an addition of reverence and respect from two saints: the first Pope Martin, who died of malnutrition (a euphemism foreign to his times) in 655; and, more especially, Martin of Tours, who, after many miraculous and natural good works, died in 401 to become the patron saint of tavern-keepers – to appear in art as 'a young soldier, mounted, dividing his cloak with a beggar' (Dawson) – and to grant to us the occasional blessing of a 'St Martin's summer' (ca. November 11) – not to be confused with a 'St Luke's summer' (ca. October 18).

MARTINA. The *f.* of *Martin*, *Marcus*, and *Mark*, it is bestowed only in England; yet it has a delightful variant in France: *Martine*. Cf. *Martita*, *Marta*.

MARTYN. A variant, now rare, of *Martin*.

MARV. The diminutive of *Marvin*, a variant of *Mervin*, q.v.

MARY. The English form of *Maria* (q.v.). The earliest form is *Miriam* (q.v.); either cognate or identical is the (? obsolete) Heb. *Marah*; *Miriam* is merely a variant of the Heb. *Mariam*(*ne*). *Miriam*, says Gesenius, the great C18 Ger. Orientalist, is Heb. *meri*, 'stubbornness' + the third person plural, thus, in all, 'their rebellion'; more probably, however, it represents Heb. *marah*, 'bitterness'; in the Middle Ages it was more poetically and irrelevantly explained as 'myrrh of the sea', 'lady of the sea', 'star of the sea' (cf. the quotation at *Maria*), all prompted by *mar*, which in one form or another means 'the sea' in L., Celtic, and Teutonic. From *Mariam*(*ne*) comes *Maria*, the first Occidental to bear the name being perhaps a Sp. maiden 'martyred by the Moors at Cordova in 851'; the name began to flourish in Europe ca. 1250, as a result of the Crusades. 'With us, the Blessed Virgin's name, having come through the French, was spelt in their fashion [*Marie*] till the translation of the Bible made our national Mary familiar. Mary II was the first of our Queens who dropped the *ie*. . . . Our Latin Maria is a late introduction, brought in by that taste which in [C18] made everything feminine end with an *a*,' though it was well known to the English aristocracy long before: was not Charles I's queen named Henrietta Maria? (Yonge.)

The two possible Heb. radicals of *Mary* and *Miriam* signify 'to be fat' and 'to be rebellious'. As Dr Cooke, former Regius Professor of Heb. at Oxford, remarks, 'No new-born child would be called "rebellious" by its mother. "Fat, plump" might well be a name bestowed by a gratified parent. In the East fatness was, and is, admired as an element of female beauty.' Diminutives: *May*, *Moll(y)*, *Poll(y)*.

MARYLYN, *f.*, is connected with *Mary*, of which it may be a diminutive. Cf. the Ger.-Jewish *Marialit*, the Ger. *Marlene* (dear to Dietrich-enthusiasts), and the Irish *Maureen*.

MAT. The usual diminutive of *Matthew*. Contrast *Matty*.

MATILDA. Teutonic, 'might of battle,' or 'mighty battle-maid,' it is, in Ger. and Fr., *Mathilde*: Ger. and Fr. *th* naturally becomes *t* in Anglicisms. It is still – despite its social *chute* – an impressive name to those who recall Matilda, wife of Henry the Fowler (at the head of the Holy Roman Empire in 913–36) and 'devoted to piety and good works', as Dawson remarks. Diminutives: *Matt(y)*, *Patty*, *Tilly*.

MATTHEW. The Heb. *Mattithyāh*, 'gift of the Lord,' became, in Gr., *Ματθαῖος* (Mat-thaios) and *Ματθίας* (Matthias), L. *Matthaeus* and *Matthias*: although *Matthew* and *Matthias* are doublets, it is more precise to derive the former from *Matthaeus*, the latter from L. *Matthias*. Although *Matthias* has generated a surname, as indeed has *Matthew* in the form of *Matthews* (? direct from L. or Ger. *Matthaeus*), *Matthias* has never been nearly so popular in England as in Austria and Germany, and even *Matthew* (contrast *John*, *Mark*, *Peter*) is fast losing ground here. (Yonge.)

MATTHIAS. An English variant, now rare, of the preceding (q.v.).

MATTIE; generally MATTY. The usual pet-form of the preceding (contrast *Mat*) and of *Matilda*.

MAUD, MAUDE. (See also *Alice*.) An English derivative, via Old Fr., of Ger. *Mahthildis*, modern *Mathilde*, English

Matilda, q.v., it has, for the cultured, been spoilt by Tennyson's too famous 'Come into the garden, Maud.'

MAUDIE. A diminutive of the preceding.

MAUDLIN. An English form, originally a contraction, of *Magdalen(e)*, as is:

MAUN, which, however, contracts also *Madeline.*

MAURA; variant, *Moira. Maura* derives from Late L. *Maria* – see *Mary.* Its diminutive is *Maureen* (q.v.). All three – *Maura, Moira, Maureen* – were originally and still are predominantly Irish, as is *Moragh,* pronounced Moira.

MAUREEN, MAURINE. The latter is rare before C20; and *Maureen* (note the typical Irish suffix *-een*) is an Irish name that Helena Swan says is a derivative of *Mary.* (Cf. *Marylyn.*) *Maureen* Anglicizes the Irish *Mairin,* a diminutive of Irish *Maire,* Mary.

MAURICE, *m.* See *Morrice, Morris.* As a font-name, *Maurice* is the more frequent form; as a surname, *Morrice* or *Morris* is rather the more general.

MAURINE. See *Maureen.*

MAVIS, *f.* From Fr. *mauvis,* it means – or rather *mavis* does, in poetical English – 'song thrush'. In one of Marie Corelli's novels, Mavis is the redoubtable Marie herself.

MAX. The usual diminutive of the next; *Maxie* is rare and childish. Whereas *Maxim* Anglicizes L. *maximus, Maximilian* is perhaps a blend. See:

MAXIM; MAXIMILIAN: L. *Maxim(us Aem)ilianus,* 'greatest Aemilianus,' i.e. the most important man in the *gens Aemilia.* It has for centuries been a favourite with Central

European royalty and aristocracy: cf. the Maximilian of the late Colonel T. F. Tweed's second and better novel.

MAXWELL. See Note at end of Introduction.

MAY. A contraction of both *Mary* and *Margaret*; not, as some have stated, a flower-name; nor yet, like *June*, a month-name.

MAYNARD. The Old Ger. *Meganhard* became *Meinhart*, 'main' – i.e. mighty – 'firmness'. It has become mostly a surname.

MEAGHAR (now rare), MEARA, *m.* From Celtic *mear*, 'merry'.

MEAVE. Perhaps an Irish variant – mostly among the peasantry – of *Mab*, q.v. The Irish spelling is *Meadhbh* (Withycombe).

MEG; MEGGIE or MEGGY. Diminutives of *Margaret*; or rather, *Meg* is such a diminutive, and *Meggie* is either an endearing, or a more familiar, form of *Meg*.

MEHETABEL or MEHITABEL. Heb., 'beneficent' or, literally, 'benefited by God!' Charlotte Yonge pertinently asks how comes it that this four-syllabled word – naming the wife of one of the princes of Edom – has been popular for three centuries or more, in England, though rare in C20 outside of English rural districts.

MELANIE. From the *f.* (*μέλαινα*: *melaina*) of the Gr. *μέλας* (*mĕlas*), 'black,' hence 'dark-complexioned': cf. the Melanesians. The more genuinely English form, *Melania*, is obsolete; the present form is adopted from the Fr. *Mélanie*. Diminutive, *Mel*, itself diminished to *Melly*. *Melanie* is sometimes spelt *Meloney* or *Mellon*(*e*)*y*, especially in the United States. However it may be spelt, it has the stress on the first syllable; the *a*, or the *o*, is therefore short.

MELCHIOR is an adoption of the Sp. and Ger. name, which derives from the Eastern *Melchi* or *Malek*, which signifies 'a king'. 'It is met with in Anglo-French families of Huguenot descent, but otherwise almost obsolete,' Swan. Originally, *Melchior* derived from the name of one of the Three Holy Kings in the Bible.

MELECENT; MELICENT. English variants of *Milicent.*

MELIA; MELIE. The former is a shortening of *Amelia*; the latter, a diminutive of *(A)melia.*

MELINA and MELINDA have sometimes been taken as variants; after some research and consideration, I have decided to distinguish.

Melina seems to be a Gr. name; *melina* (*μέλινα*) should mean 'of the ash-tree'. Perhaps, however, the name is the Latin form of Gr. *μελίνη* (*melinē*), Italian millet: a harvest-name. But there may have been confusion with *Melanie.*

Melinda demands quotation from the ever-delightful *Jack and Jill*: 'The later Stuarts had rather a craze for names in -inda, such as Clarinda, Dorinda, Florinda, Melinda, perhaps suggested by Ariosto's Belinda', itself 'possibly due to the many German names in -lind'. Now, *-lind* 'is usually Old German *lind*, snake . . . It is a common ending in German female names': if you are idealistic, you argue a connotation of 'wisdom'; if realistic, you speak of 'craftiness, guile'. – But what of the first element of *Melinda*? It is, I think, L. *mel*, 'honey': hence, the name would mean 'sweetly wise'.

MELISSA. Gr. *μέλισσα* (melissa), 'a bee,' hence 'honey' (generally *μέλι*, *meli*: L. *mel*). Perhaps Melissa was 'the nymph who first taught the use of honey'; in the It. poets of the Middle Ages, Melissa was a beneficent fairy. (Yonge.)

MELITTA. A variant of the preceding: the Attic *μέλιττα*, is exactly our name.

MELLIE or *-y*. Diminutive of *Melanie, Melinda.*

MELLONEY or *-ny*. See *Melanie.*

MELODY, *f.* An English rural name – and a beautiful. It occurs, for instance, in Beatrice Kean Seymour's *Daughter to Philip*, 1933.

MELONEY or *-ny*. See *Melanie.*

MELVA, *m.* Celtic, 'chief'. The original Melva (or Melvas) was king of the present Somersetshire; he lay ambushed amid green boughs to abduct King Arthur's wife. (Yonge.)

MELVIN, *m.* Very rare in Britain, fairly common in U.S.A. Perhaps formed from *Malvine* or *Melva.*

MENCE. An English shortening, now unusual, of *Clemence* (i.e. *Clement*). Cf.:

MENZIES. A Scottish shortening and re-shaping of *Clemence.* In C20 more common as sur- than as font-name, it is properly pronounced *Menggees* (hard *g*'s), for the *z* is the same as that in *Dalziel*(*l*), which is pronounced *Dee-ell.*

MERCEDES. This Sp. name arises from *Maria de las Mercedes*, (Virgin) Mary of the Mercies. Identical, therefore, with *Mercy.*

MERCIA. A.-S. origin and signifying 'woman from the border-lands'. (Loughead.)

MERCY. Popular in C17 among the Puritans, it has steadily lost favour until it has become the rarest of the abstract-virtue group of *f.* 'Christians': *Faith*, *Hope*, *Charity*, *Honor*, *Patience*, *Prudence*, etc.

MEREDITH, *m.* Welsh, 'sea-protector': cf., therefore, *Murphy* and *Murtagh*. Never very general as a baptismal, it is now mainly a surname.

MERIEL. As in *Meriel Bride – Secretary*: a novel by Douglas Sladen, 1935. A variant of *Muriel*.

MERLE, *f.* Modern, and more general in America than in England, it is Fr. *merle*, a blackbird. Madame Merle is a character – a cosmopolitan American – in Henry James's novel, *The Portrait of a Lady*, 1881 (Harvey). Cf. that other feathered songster, *Mavis*: q.v.

MERLIN. Welsh *Myrddin*, perhaps 'sea-hill'. Unusual in C20, it will, to the educated, for long recall the sage beguiled by Vivien in the Arthurian cycle: a story found in Nennius's history of the Britons and treated at length by Tennyson in the Idyll entitled *Merlin and Vivien*, 1859. To the Welsh, Merlin is a bard; perhaps originally he was an ancient British god. (Harvey.)

MERRY, *f.* A variant of *Mercy* so thorough in its transformation that when – as rarely – it is bestowed, it is usually in the belief that this name is the cheerful first cousin of *Felicity*.

MERVIN, MERVYN, *m.* (Diminutive: *Merv.*) An old Anglo-Saxon name: *Maerwine*, 'famous friend', the *-v-* being caused by Norman-French influence. (*Jack and Jill.*)

META. An occasional diminutive of *Margaret*; cf. the much more frequent *Meg*.

MEURIZ. The Welsh form of *Morris*, *Maurice*. Cf. the Ger. *Moritz*.

MEYRICK. From Teutonic, 'work-ruler,' and therefore to be compared with its doublet *Almeric(k)*, q.v. for further etymological detail.

MICAH seems, even in Heb., to have been a contraction of *Michael*; as a name, however, it has a wholly independent existence.

MICHAEL. In Heb., 'who (is) like to God?' As with *John* and *Mark*, so with *Michael*: we now think of it as an essentially British name, despite the fact that, in addition to being a favourite in Ireland, it is also a favourite in Germany, Spain, and Russia. Probably its popularity began in admiration for the Archangel Michael; moreover, knights received their spurs in the name of this chosen patron of Christian warriors: cf. the Order of St Michael and St George. (Swan.)

MICK, MICKIE or MICKY; MIKE. Diminutives of *Michael*.

MILCAH, *f.* Heb., 'queen'. In mid C19–20, rarely bestowed except among Jews – and none too common with them.

MILDRED; occasionally MILDRID. The A.-S. *Mildthryth* was the name of one of the three daughters of a King of Mercia and, in Teutonic radicals, it means either 'mild power' (Withycombe) or 'mild counsel' (Weekley). Less general now than in Victorian and Edwardian days.

MILDREDA. A variant of the preceding.

MILES is the English, *Myles* the Irish, form of a Gr. word meaning 'crusher': *μύλος* (mŭlos), 'a millstone'; cf. *μυλών* (mŭlōn), 'a mill,' whence the *Milon* of *The Golden Ass*, by Apuleius (delightfully translated by Jack Lindsay). More probable, however, is Weekley's statement that the name has now one, now another, origin: (1) *Michael*, in Fr. *Mihiel* or *Miel* (the variant *Michel* does not apply here), yields *Miles*, as the erudite Camden proposed; (2) 'Milo, the strong man of Crotona, was adopted very early in French . . . Its Old French nominative was Miles' – confirming my own etymology.

MILICENT. Teutonic, 'work-strong'. *Amalswinth* (cf. at *Almeric*) or, as some historians call her, *Amalasontha*, a most unfortunate Lombardic queen, became, with the Burgundians, *Melicerte*, *Melisende*, *Melisande*, *Melusine*. 'Melisende . . . was the princess who carried the uneasy crown of Jerusalem to the House of Anjou; and, perhaps from the Provençal connexions of the English court, Lady Melisent Stafford bore the name in [C13], whence Melicent has become known in England, and never quite disused, though often confounded with Melissa . . . and sometimes spelt Millicent' (Yonge). The modern Fr. form *Mélisande* occasionally appears in C20 English, with or without the accent.

MILLICENT. A spelling-variant of the preceding; now the usual form.

MILLIE or MILLY. A diminutive of *Aemilia*, *Emily*, and *Mil(l)icent.*

MINA. This is an English pet-form of *Wilhelmina*, whereas *Minella* is either a diminutive of *Mina* or a contraction and transposition of *Wilhelmina*, q.v. Cf. the Ger. *Mine*, *Minna*, and the Fr. *Mimi*. (Yonge.)

MINELLA. See the preceding.

MINERVA, *f.* Not often bestowed, *Minerva* was the Roman goddess of learning and of technical skill. The word is either of Etruscan origin (meaning unknown) or derivative from Gr. *menos*, 'purpose' – whence L. *mens*, 'mind'.

MINNA. A Scottish variant of:

MINNIE, *f.* Teutonic, 'love'. As Helena Swan neatly determines, 'This name, though generally used as a diminutive of Wilhelmina, or, in Ireland, of Mary, has a distinct . . . origin and meaning of its own. In Germany, Minna and Minne are still common names, dating back to the days of the troubadours, or, as they were then, in the twelfth and thirteenth [and fourteenth] centuries, called Minnesingers,' those persistent and insistent chanters of courtly love: inculcators of a rarefied, emasculated *ars amatoria*: why did not Landor or Traill write a dialogue between Ovid (*Tempora mutata, mutati mores!*) and Walther von der Vogelweide (*Unter den Linden mit mein Liebster . . .*)? But *Minnie*, as distinct from *Minna*, is sometimes a diminutive, or an independent name formed from that diminutive, of *Emmeline*, as Weekley reminds us in that charming book, *Jack and Jill* – a history, not a dictionary, of given-names.

Also a pet-form of *Minerva*.

MIRA. See *Myra*.

MIRABEL; occasionally elaborated to *Mirabella*. This *f.*, to be compared with the next, derives from L. *mirabilis*, 'wonderful'. In C17 comedy (e.g., Fletcher, Congreve) *Mirabell* was *m.* A 'French' variant is *Mirabelle*; a very English one, *Marabel*.

MIRANDA. L., 'worthy of admiration,' from *mirari*, 'to admire'. Its heyday was the late C16–17, and its survival in C19–20 (though it now verges on being a relic) must be, in part, attributed to the freshness and charm exhaled by the heroine of Shakespeare's *Tempest*.

MIRIAM is probably the earliest form of *Mary*. Miriam was the sister of Moses and Aaron, and her name vigorously survives. (For etymology, see *Mary*.)

MOGGY. A variant of *Molly*, hence a derivative of *Margaret*. Less general is *Moke*.

MOIRA, *f.* Celtic, 'soft,' is the probable etymology, but I suggest Gr. *Μοῖρα*, i.e. Moira, sole goddess of fate before the fateful trio (Clotho, Lachesis, Atropos), as a possible. Sometimes, however, it is a variant of *Maura.*

MOISSEY. The Manx form of *Maria, Mary.*

MOKE. See *Moggy.*

MOLL; MOLLY. Diminutives of *Mary.* The former is nowadays avoided because of its unpleasant associations in unconventional speech: see my Dictionaries *of Slang* and *of the Underworld.*

MONA, *f.* In Gr., *μόνα* is the Doric equivalent of the Attic *μονή* (monē): for which see *Monica.* Note, too, that *Mona* (here also from Gr.) is the ancient name of the Isle of Man and of the Isle of Anglesea: so perhaps, in some instances at least, the *f.* name may denote '(a girl) of or from Mona'. But note also that Withycombe states that *Mona,* with probable variant *Moyna,* comes from the Irish *Muadhnait,* diminutive of *muadh,* 'noble'.

MONCHA is the Erse form of:

MONICA, *f.* It may cast back to Gr. *μόνος* (monos), *f. μόνη,* 'alone' or 'unique'; both Weekley and Withycombe, very wisely, say that the origin is unknown. Its usage has been vivified by memories of St Monica, 'the saintly mother of St Augustine of Hippo, who owed his conversion . . . to Christianity and high sanctity to her prayers and tears' (Benedictines).

MONTAGU(E), *m.*, is a 'Christianizing' of the surname, which represents Fr. *mont aigu,* a (sharply) peaked hill. Shakespeare's *Montagues,* perhaps operative here, are the It. *Montecchi.*

MONTY. The diminutive of the preceding.

MORGAN, *m.* A Welsh and Irish (*Muirgen*) name, it derives from the Celtic and means 'a sea-dweller': cf. *Morvren*, *Morvryn*. *Morgwn*, the earlier form, was a heresiarch (ca. 400) who dubbed himself *Pelagius*, the Gr. equivalent: whence 'the Pelagian heresy'. In the Middle Ages, *Morgan* was also *f.*, as in *Morgan le Fay* (the fairy), who, sister to King Arthur, possessed magic powers.

MORGANA. The *f.* of *Morgan.* Cf. *fata Morgana*, which is, in Sicily, applied to a mirage seen on the Calabrian littoral and which results from Arthurian legends: see Sir E. K. Chambers, *Arthur of Britain.* (Harvey.)

MORGWN. The Welsh form of *Morgan*, itself mainly Welsh.

MORNA. An Anglicism for *Muirne*, a Gaelic name, it means either 'affection' or 'beloved'.

MORRICE, MORRIS, MAURICE (q.v.). As common now in England as it has long been in Ireland, and for centuries a surname also, it was originally *Muirgis*. Probably from L. *Mauritius*, a Proper Name formed from *Maurus*, 'a Moor'; the Gk. original, *Mauros*, is akin to Gk. *amauros*, 'dark' – here, in reference to complexion.

MORT; MORTIE or MORTY. Diminutives of *Mortimer*; in Ireland, *Morty* is also, though decreasingly, a derivative of *Murtagh*, q.v.

MORTIMER. (1) Celtic, 'sea-warrior,' and therefore to be compared with *Morgan*, *Murphy*, *Murtagh*, qq.v. Its employment as a surname indicates a prevalence that no longer holds good, though the name is vigorous enough. (2) As coming from Fr., it derives from a place-name *Mortemer*.

MORVREN, *m.* Celtic, 'sea-raven'. Or is it the same as:

MORVRYN, *m.* This Welsh name, from Celtic, is either 'sea-king' or, less probably, 'sea-hill' (cf. *Merlin*).

MOSES. This grand old Jewish name, for centuries now a surname too, 'probably came from the Coptic *mo*, water, and *usha*, saved; though the Hebrew, *mâshâh*, also presents a ready derivation: the great Law-giver'. The proposed 'drawn out (of the water)' is too anecdotal to be tenable. (Yonge.) ? Egyptian *mesu*, child (Webster). Diminutives: *Mose*, *Mo*, (Jewish) *Moysh*.

MOYNA. See *Mona* (at end).

MUIREADHACH, *m.* An Erse name and the original of *Murdoch* (common in Scotland). See *Murtagh*.

MUIRGEN. See *Morgan*.

MUIRNE. See *Morna*.

MUNGO, *m.* In Celtic, 'lovable; beloved'. 'This seems to have been originally not a name but a nickname given to St Kentigern, the Patron Saint of Glasgow, which is at the present day often called St Mungo' (Swan). The fame of Mungo Park, the British explorer of the African interior who died, young, in 1806, has done much to keep the name alive; nevertheless, it is now rare.

MUNGHU. The Gaelic form of the preceding.

MURCHISON, *m.* A Scottish derivative of *Mary*: i.e., 'Mary's son'.

MURDOCH, *m.* A Scottish variant of *Murtoch*, q.v. at *Murtagh*.

MURIEL. Probably from Old Irish *Muirgheal*, it means 'sea-white'; perhaps diminutive from Gr. *murrha*, myrrh. It occurs early in English parish registers, was long very common, and, after something of an eclipse in C17–18, it was revived in C19 with its variant *Meriel*. (Cf. *Myrtle*.)

MURPHY. From the obsolete *Murchada*, this widespread Irish name – now mostly a surname – derives from the Celtic, where the first element ('sea') is the same as that in *Murtagh*.

MURRAY, *m*. A 'Christianizing' of the surname, itself sometimes *Murrey*, 'dark red,' and sometimes Middle English *murie*, 'merry'. (Weekley, *Romance of Names*.)

MURTAGH; MURTOCH, *m*. The Irish and the Scottish forms of a name that, deriving from the Celtic, means 'sea-protector' – 'sea warrior' – 'sea man; seaman'.

[-MUS. See at *Erasmus*.]

MYFANWY, MYVANWY, *f*. From Celtic, either *mabanwy*, 'child of the water,' or *my-manwy*, 'my fine (or rare) one'. Yonge, in 1884, says that it is 'not yet extinct among families of strong emotional feeling, though in general Fanny' – very general ca. 1850–1900 – 'has been substituted for it.' That may be; certain it is that it remains something of a favourite in the present century.

MYLES. An Irish variant of *Miles*.

MYRA; less frequently, MIRA. Either variants of *Muriel* or, more probably, short for *Miranda*. This name is a favourite with the poet Crabbe.

MYRRHA; MYRRHENE (now rare). See *Myrtle*.

MYRTAH. A variant of *Myrtle*. Cf.:

MYRTILLA. A diminutive of *Myrtle*, it is often bestowed as an independent name.

MYRTLE. Gr. *μύῤῥα* (murrha), L. *murrha* and *myrrha*, Fr. *myrrhe*, 'the juice of the Arabian myrtle'; Gr. *μύρτος* (murtos), L. *myrtus*, Fr. *myrte*, 'myrtle'. (The common myrtle is a shrub sacred to Venus.) Now, *Myrtale* was a freed-woman, the friend of Horace: thence, our name, via Fr. *myrtille* (pronounced *mertil*), 'a bilberry'.

MYSIE. A Scottish contraction of, or endearment for, *Margaret*. In Scott's novel, *The Monastery*, 1820, Mysie Hopper is 'the miller's daughter . . . who marries Sir Piercie Shafton' (Harvey). See also *Maisie*.

N

NADINE, *f.* Russian *Nadezna*, 'Hope', becomes Fr. *Nadine*, adopted in Britain. (Withycombe.)

NAHUM, *m.* Heb., '(a source of) comfort'. Now rare, it was notorious, in the person of Nahum Tate, the mutilator of Shakespeare's *Lear* and Everyman's hymns.

NAN. A diminutive of *Anne* or *Hannah*, but, in late C19–20, often bestowed as a separate name.

NANCE. A diminutive (cf. *Nan*) of:

NANCY. Either a typically English metathesis of *Anne* or a variant of *Agnes*, perhaps influenced by the It. *Nanna*, a diminutive of *Anna*, and Ger. *Annchen*, likewise a diminutive (of *Anne*). 'A gipsy name,' remarks Charles Williams in his Tarot novel, *The Greater Trumps*, 1932.

NANNIE or NANNY. A Scottish diminutive, immediately, of *Nan*, but properly of *Anne* (or *Hannah*).

NANTY. A Scottish perversion of *Antony*. Contrast *Nancy*.

NAOMI. Heb., '(my) pleasant (one)'; cf., therefore, *Myfanwy*. The Biblical Naomi was the mother-in-law of Ruth: and with her she went from the Moabites on her return to Bethlehem.

NAP. The diminutive – very familiar – of:

NAPOLEON. It., 'one who belongs to the new city': Gr. *neapolis*: Naples. From an Alexandrian martyr (early C4), the name was adopted, in C12, by the noble Orsini family at Rome. Thence it spread to other parts of Italy and to Corsica. In late C18 Napoleon Bonaparte took it to France: on the great soldier-statesman's death in 1821, English pity and admiration caused the name to be adopted, in strict moderation, in Britain.

NARCISSUS. Gr., 'a daffodil'. Its adoption as a *m.* 'Christian' was caused, not in relation to that mythological youth who has given us 'Narcissism', but by the beauty and purity of the flower: five early saints are so named, and one of them was a miracle-working, vigorous old Bishop of Jerusalem in late C2–early 3. Rare in England.

NAT; occasionally NATTY. Diminutives of *Nathan* and *Nathaniel*; also of:

NATALIA, NATALIE, *f.* L. *natalis*, 'natal,' 'birth-,' from *nasci*, 'to be born', in especial reference to *natalis dies*, 'birthday' (of Christ): cf. the origin of the South African province of *Natal*. In C6 there was an abbot named *Natalis*; in late C3–early 4, a brave Christian woman, who, during the persecutions by Diocletian, ministered to those imprisoned: it is she who endeared *Natalia* to the devout. *Natalie* shows Fr. influence.

NATHAN. Heb., 'a gift': cf., therefore, the next. The word has something of the dignity that attaches to the Old Testament prophet who so sternly rebuked David.

NATHANIEL. Heb., 'gift of God'. The older form is *Nathanael*, *Nathaneel*. Since, in the list of apostles, Nathanael is called by his patronymic (*Bartholomaios*), *Nathanael* was neglected until the English adopted it. (Yonge.) Semantically cf. *Dorothy*.

NATTY. See *Nat*.

NEAL. In Celtic, *Niul*, 'a champion' (from *niadh*), this Irish *m.* name seems also to be a fusion of *Niale* and *Neill*, the former of legendary obscurity, the latter connected especially with Neill of the Nine Hostages, who, one of the last of Ireland's pagan kings, is also one of the greatest of the ancient Irish heroes. See also *Nial*.

NED; rarely NEDDY, which is mostly reserved for donkeys. Diminutives, like *Ed* and *Ted*, of *Edward*. Britons don't much care for *Ed* and *Eddie*; *Ted* is the most general of the three shorter forms, as *Teddy* is of the longer.

NEIL, NEILL. The former a mere spelling-variant of the latter, which parallels *Niul*, the original of *Neal*. See also *Nigel*.

NELL; NELLIE, NELLY. Diminutives of *Helen*, *Ellen* and *Eleanor(a)*, but occasionally used with no reference to those names, precisely as *Jack* is sometimes used independently of *John*.

NELSON. Its use as a baptismal name dates from 1798–1805, the period of the great English admiral's victories; especially in Norfolk, whence he hailed. 'More *Nelsons* are derived from Neil . . . than from Nell,' Weekley, *Romance of Names*; 'probably from Cornelleson, a Dutch variant of Cornelius' (Swan) may also be true of some.

NESSA, NESSIE. As these are respectively the Scottish and Manx diminutives of *Agnes*, so:

NEST, NESTA, are the Welsh.

NETTA. See *Nita* and cf. the Esthonian *f. Neto* of the same meaning. Pet-form: *Nettie* or *Netty*. Also, short for *Agneta*.

NEV is the usual diminutive of:

NEVILLE. This aristocratic surname of Fr. origin (*Neuville*; lit., the new city) was introduced by the Normans, as were *Percy* and *Lascelles*; only in C19 did it become at all general as a 'Christian'. (A. H. Smith, *Early Northern Nick-Names and Surnames*, a brochure published in 1934.)

NIAL or *Niall* is a Celtic *m.* name; especially Irish and Scottish. Literally, it means 'a champion'. See also *Neal* and *Neil*.

NICHOLAS. In Scotland, *m.* and *f.*; elsewhere, only *m.* As in *Nicodemus*, the first element is Gr. *νίκη* (nikë), 'victory'; both *λαός* (laŏs) and *δῆμος* (dēmos) mean 'the people'. Hence 'victory of the people'. Whereas Nicodemus was a scribe, a Pharisee, and a secret disciple of Jesus, Nicholas – reputed bishop, ca. 300, of Myra in Asia Minor – is 'the patron saint of Russia, and of children, scholars, sailors, virgins, and thieves' – in short, of simple folk – 'in consequence of various legends relating to benefits conferred by him on these' (Harvey). His chief title to fame is as Santa Claus (*Claus*=*Klaas*=*Nicolaas*).

NICK; NICKY. Diminutives of *Nicholas* and *Nicodemus*. The fact that *Old Nick* is the devil has not much checked its prevalence.

NICODEMUS. An English 'virtual doublet' of *Nicholas*.

NICOL. A Scottish shortening of *Nicholas*. Cf. *Nick*.

NIEL. A Scottish form of *Neal*. See also *Nial*.

NIGEL. From L. *niger*, 'black,' perhaps with a reminiscence of pre-Classical L. *nigellus*, 'somewhat black,' 'dark'; *Nigellus*, moreover, was a Roman surname, probably at first the nickname of some swarthy fellow. As a Scottish name, which it still is in the main, it occurs in Domesday Book, 'and in even earlier documents. It is also the English form of Neal,' q.v. (Swan). – Several modern philologists say that *Nigel* derives from *Nicholas*: an opinion to which I do not subscribe.

NINA. Originally a pet-form of *Anna* (or *Anne*), via *Nanine*, a Fr. pet-form of *Anne*. (*Jack and Jill*.)

NINIAN, *m.* A Scottish name of Celtic origin and problematic etymology, it is falling into disuse. There died, in 432, Bishop Ninian, 'the Apostle of Cumberland and of the Southern Picts of Scotland' (Benedictines): whence its adoption.

NITA. A charming girl's name of L. origin, for ultimately it derives from *nitidus*, bright, neat, pure: *puella nitida. Netta* is a doublet showing French influence. Often, however, it shortens either *Anita* or Sp. *Juanita.*

NOAH. Heb., 'rest'. Mankind has retained a pleasant memory of him who invented the Noah's ark still dear to children.

NOB. An occasional, mainly rural diminutive of *Robert*: cf. *Bob*, *Rob*, and the obsolete *Hob*.

NOEL; also NOWELL (q.v.). Cf. the C16 *Christmas*, bestowed on a male child born on Christmas Day or during Christmastide, as, originally, *Noel* was. Adopted from Fr. *Noël*, *noël* being Christmas, it is a derivative of L. *natalis* (cf. St Natalis), 'natal,' 'birth-,' from *nasci*, 'to be born'. Cf. *Natalia*.

NOLL. The usual diminutive of *Oliver*. Cf. *Ollie*.

NONA. L. *nona*, 'the ninth (female child)'. Formerly, only in large families, but now without the slightest etymological fitness.

NORA, NORAH. A mainly Irish name, earlier *Onora*, a Hibernicism for *Honor* – or perhaps rather *Honora* or *Honoria*, q.v. Also short for *Eleanora* and *Leonora*.

NORBERT. Teutonic, 'Niord's brightness': cf., therefore, *Norman*. It is under a cloud, not yet opaque.

NOREEN. A diminutive, originally Irish (*Noirin*), of *Nora.* Outside of Eire, it is usually bestowed as a name in its own right. (Withycombe.)

NORM is, so far as I know, the only diminutive of *Norman.*

NORMA, *f.* This name, more general in U.S.A. than in the British Empire, comes from the L. *norma*, a square, hence a pattern, a norm, but via 'Bellini's famous opera (1830)', as I learn from *Jack and Jill.*

NORMAN. Lit., 'a Northman' – i.e., a Norwegian; hence, from the settlement in N.W. France, a Norman. The name was in use in England before the Norman Conquest. In C13, 'English nobles carried Norman to Scotland, where it was adopted in the Leslie family, and, like Nigel, became exclusively Scottish.' Not exclusively, Miss Yonge; for in mid C19–20, it has been frequently given to non-Scottish boys.

NORRIE is a diminutive of *Nora(h)* and *Eleanor.*

NOWELL. A very English form of *Noel*, q.v. To many cultured persons it is associated with an anthologist and editor of fine taste and great ability.

NULLIE. A diminutive – older than *Ursy* – of *Ursula.* For the form, cf. *Noll* for *Oliver.*

NUMPS. See *Humps.*

O

OBADIAH. This Heb.-derived *m.* font-name (lit., 'servant of the Lord') is now very rare except in the U.S.A. Obadiah was a prophet at the Court of Ahab: the Book of Obadiah foretells the destruction of Edom (the low-lying region south of the Dead Sea).

OBIE. A diminutive of the preceding.

OCTAVIA, OCTAVIUS. In L., 'the eighth daughter, son,' respectively: L. *octavus*, 'eighth'. Some presumable Octavius founded the *gens Octavia* (Octavian clan); an Octavius married the sister of Julius Caesar, and their son Octavianus became the emperor Augustus; the Emperor's sister was Octavia, the second wife of Mark Antony: their joint renown firmly established both names, which have, in common with most lengthy Latinities, been rarely bestowed since ca. 1880. Cf. *Septimus*.

ODETTE. A diminutive of *Odile*, but in Britain frequently bestowed as an independent name.

ODILE, *f.* Properly and mainly Fr., but like the Ger. form, *Odila*, it is of Teutonic origin: '(she of) the fatherland'. Given its correct pronunciation (*o-dēl*), it is attractive. Cf.:

ODO, *m.* A Ger., hence English, name, it derives ultimately from Old High Ger. *anda*, akin to O.E. *ead*, 'rich'. (See especially *Jack and Jill*.)

OLGA, *f.* A Slavonic name of disputed origin: it is probably from Russian *Oleg*, 'holy' and therefore parallel to the Scandinavian *Helga*.

OLIVE. (See *Olivia* and *Oliver*.) This *f.* should be compared with *Daisy*, *Lily*, *Myrtle*, *Poppy*, *Rhoda*, *Rose*, *Rosemary*, *Violet*.

OLIVER, *m.* The Anglicism of Fr. *Olivier*, It. *Oliviero*, from L. *oliva*, 'the olive'. 'But it is much to be suspected that it would never have blossomed into use, but for the Teutonic Olaf (forefather's relic). . . . The paladin of Charlemagne' – whence *a Roland for an Oliver* – is 'almost certainly a transmogrified Anlaf, or Olaf' (Yonge); 'There can be little doubt that Oliver was adapted from the famous Old Norse *Olafr*' (Weekley); the origin is, in short, obscure (see especially Withycombe). The name fell into disrepute with Loyalists when Oliver Cromwell rose to pre-eminence.

OLIVIA. The Italianate original of *Olive*; for etymology, see *Oliver*.

OLLIE. An occasional diminutive of *Olive* and *Oliver*. Cf. *Noll*.

OPHELIA. Gr., either from the word for 'a serpent' (wisdom) or from *ōphĕlia*, 'assistance'. It is now bestowed only by the romantic and is something of a burden for any girl not a wild-wan beauty. The influence of Shakespeare's heroine, once considerable, is lessening in the realms of nomenclature, though not in those of literature: Guillermo Valencia, in his exquisite poem, *Leyendo a Silva*, likens a girl 'en su lecho de gasas et de blondas' to 'Ofelia mecida por los ondas'.

ORIANA. This Tennysonian heroine's name means 'resurgent (girl)'.

ORLANDO. Originally and mainly It., this is a doublet of Fr. *Roland*: the Sp. *Roldan* and the Portuguese *Rolando* afford an interesting sidelight on philological chop-and-change. Lit. 'fame of the land', it is famous in It. romance; notably in Ariosto's *Orlando Furioso* and Boiardo's *Orlando Innamorato*; Orlando is also the lover of Shakespeare's Rosalind and the title of Virginia Woolf's strangest novel (Harvey). See also *Roland*.

ORSON, *m.* An English variation of It. *Orso*, 'a bear,' from L. *ursus*, it is now seldom used. Cf. Ursus Major as a nickname for Dr Samuel Johnson.

OS. A familiar diminutive of all the names in *Os-*.

OSBERT, *m.*, like the Ger. *f. Osberta*, derives from the Teutonic and means 'divinely bright'; names in *ans*, *as*, and *os* testify to 'the idea of deity', those in *bert* to 'brightness' (A.-S. *beorhtnis*). *Osbert* is now rare, but it is notable as the 'Christian' of a brilliant member of a brilliant literary family. For the first element, cf.:

OSBORN. In Teutonic languages, it is 'divine man (*born* of woman)'. It is 'an old English name, which occurs as early as the *Domesday Book*' (Swan). Its former prevalence led to its adoption as a surname.

OSCAR. This is the O.E. *Osgar*, 'divine spear', doubtless with reference to a superlative warrior. See especially Macpherson's *Ossian* and, derivatively, Byron's *Oscar of Alva*.

OSMOND; OSMUND, the earlier form. This *m.* name – in the Teutonic it signifies 'divine protection' – represents the Norwegian *Asmundr*. St Osmund was a Norman noble: he became Chancellor of England and, later, Bishop of Salisbury – a model prelate until his death in 1099. (Benedictines.) Like all the *Os-* names except perhaps *Oscar*, it is falling into disuse.

OSRED, *m.* This very old English name derives from Teutonic, in which it represents 'divine counsel'.

OSRIC, *m.* Another very old name, it means, in Teutonic, 'divine rule or power'. The *-ric* is cognate with L. *rex*, a king: cf., therefore, *Rex*.

OSSIE. A diminutive of names in *Os-*, as *Os* itself is.

OSWALD. 'Aasvalldr, divine power, was in Germany Ansvalt . . . Asvald; but the Anglo-Saxon Oswald was the glory of the name in the Northumbrian monarch [d. 642], "free of hand," as even his Welsh foes called him' (Yonge); he has been canonized by the Catholic Church.

OSWELL, *m.* The first element is that of *Oswald*, but I am not sure about *-well*: it may be a thinning of *wald* (as in *Oswald*) or, less probably, a corruption of Teutonic *welf*, 'a wolf,' or a variant of the word forming the surname *Weld* ('a weald' or 'wold').

OTTO. As a Ger. name, probably a Teutonic word, meaning 'rich' (see *Odo*); but, as an It. name, it may possibly be a contraction of *Ottavio*, 'the eighth' (see *Octavia*, *Octavius*); as an English name, it draws on both Italy and Germany. It is famous for its frequent occurrence in the royal lines of the Holy Roman Empire and of Bavaria.

OWAIN. The specifically Welsh form of:

OWEN, which is now almost as English as it is Welsh, and a surname as well as a 'Christian'. 'The notable Owen Glendower, as Shakespeare has taught us to call him, was really Owain ap Gruffydd of Glendfrdwy, his estate in Merionethshire, where he kept a grand household. It was he who made Owen the most common of Welsh names. Owain is so like [Welsh] *oen* . . . a sheep or lamb, that it is generally so translated; but it is most likely that . . . Owen ought to be carried much further back to the same source as the Erse Eoghan, which comes from *eoghunn*, youth, from *og*, young, and is translated, young warrior,' Yonge. Weekley, however, in *Jack and Jill* states that *Owen* is borrowed from Greco-Latin *Eugenius*: cf., therefore, *Eugene*.

P

PADDY. A familiar form, general since the late C18, of *Patrick*. Cf. *Pat* and *Patsy*.

PADRAIC. As in *Padraic Colum*, a notable Irish writer much better known in the U.S.A. than in Britain – more's the pity for Britain. A more 'national' form of *Patrick*.

PAGAN. See:

PAIN, PAYNE, *m.* Lit., 'a countryman,' it comes from Fr. *payen* (the same) and thus from L. *paganus*, 'rustic,' lit. 'of a canton or district'. It is now comparatively rare as a 'Christian', frequent as a surname. Even *Pagan* is occasionally found, whether as *m.* or as *f.*

PALEY. An English variant of *Pauley*; now rather rare as a baptismal name.

PAM. The diminutive of:

PAMELA. Adopted by Richardson, for his *Pamela, or Virtue Rewarded*, 1741, from Sidney's *Arcadia*. In Richardson, as now, it was *Pámela*, but in Sidney it was *Paméla* (i.e. *Pa-mēl-a* in contrast to *Pám-ĕ-la*) and probably derived from Gr. *πᾶν μέλι* (pan meli), 'all honey,' i.e. 'all sweetness'. From being lower-class, as it still was, in the main, as late as the 1880's, it has become fashionable among the upper classes once more.

PASCAL. This *m.* name, originally an adjective (cf. *Paschal*), is formed from Gr. *Πάσχα* (Pascha), 'sufferings,' i.e. the Passion of Christ. Properly applied to a child born at Easter, it is now rare in England. Cf.:

PASCOE. An English transformation, especially Cornish, of the preceding; now mostly a surname.

PAT. The most used diminutive of *Patrick*; the sole (?) diminutive of *Patricia*. Cf. *Patsy* and *Paddy*.

PATIENCE. Either L. *patiens*, 'long-suffering,' or *patientia*, 'patience,' it achieved a vogue among the Puritans and is still fairly common in English rural districts. It is of the *Prudence*, *Hope*, *Faith*, *Mercy*, *Charity* group of *f.* baptismal names. Diminutive: *Patty*.

PATRICIA. The *f.* of *Patrick* has, to an amusing extent, been influenced, socially, by its etymological sense ('patrician'), whereas *Patrick* is as wide as the air. It is said to be of Scottish coinage.

PATRICK. L. *patricius*, 'a patrician, a nobleman,' the *patricii* being the three hundred ruling families of Rome; *patricius* comes from *pater*. The name was 'as a title given half in jest to the young Roman-British Calpurnius, who was stolen by Irish pirates in his youth and, when ransomed, returned again to be the apostle of his captors, and left a name passionately revered in that warm-hearted land. The earlier Irish, however, were far too respectful to their apostle to call themselves by his name,' Yonge; that we do not know the exact dates of his birth (late C4) and death (ca. 464) need not render us sceptical of his authenticity. *Patrick* has, in C18–20, been by far the commonest *m.* 'Christian' in Ireland: see also *Paddy* and *Pat*.

PATE, PATIE. A Scottish diminutive of *Patrick*. Cf.:

PATSY, PATTY. Diminutives of *Martha*; the former, also of *Patrick*; the latter, also of *Patience*.

PAUL. 'The cognomen Paullus, or Paulus, the contraction of Pauxillus, originated with one of the Aemilian gens [or clan], who was small in stature,' L. *paul(l)us*, 'little,' 'small'. The activities of the Apostle, who had, it is too often but very conveniently forgotten, persecuted the Christians until he was converted by a vision, popularized his name throughout the Continent, where it has always been more general than in England, 'in spite of . . . the dedication of our great cathedral' (Yonge). It is very prominent among the saints (there were thirty-eight of them), among kings and princes, and in our own literature: see especially Harvey.

PAULA. The *f.* of *Paul.* It came to England from the Continental forms: It. *Paola*, Port. *Paula.* Of the five Saints Paula, much the most important is she who, dying in 404, after twenty years of 'eminent sanctity,' had been the contemporary of St Jerome, her spiritual adviser and biographer (Benedictines.)

PAULET, *m.* An English diminutive (becoming rare) of *Paul.*

PAULINA (now rare); PAULINE. The diminutive of *Paula.* The second form is the later, and probably adopted direct from the Fr.

PAWLEY. An English re-shaping of *Paul.* Cf. *Paley.*

PAYNE. See *Pain.*

PEARL, *f.* Another jewel-name. Cf. *Beryl* (p. 55). The diminutive is *Pearlie.*

PEEVLIN. The Welsh form of *Paul.*

PEG. A shortened form of:

PEGGOTY and PEGGY, which are diminutives of *Margaret. Peggoty* is less usual and less aristocratic than *Peggy.*

PELHAM. See Note at end of Introduction.

PEN. A diminutive of:

PENELOPE. Gr., 'a weaver,' such being the name applied, legend-wise after the event, to her whom we know as Penelope, that wife of Ulysses who, with a guile worthy of her errant lord ('evil communications . . .'), span in the day and unravelled at night the large robe that she was dutifully and conveniently making for her aged father-in-law. (It is pleasant to ignore the aspersions cast by the more slanderous of gossipy chroniclers.) The name, owing to its 'visual' difficulties, has been avoided by the illiterate; I once heard a charwoman pronounce it as *Penny-lope*.

PENNY. The predominant diminutive of *Penelope*. So named is the adorable heroine of Denis Mackail's delightful novel *Chelbury Abbey*. Cf. *Pen*.

PEPPI. See *Perpetua*.

PERCE. A non-aristocratic diminutive of *Percy* and *Percival*. Cf. *Cec*, *Gus*, *Lou*.

PERCEVAL; in C19–20, generally PERCIVAL. (Cf. the next.) 'The *Pierce*- [sur]names are very curious, and it is hard to say exactly what the verb meant in these compounds. The much discussed *Perceval*, *Percival* is simply what it appears to be, viz. "pierce vale" ' (Weekley, *Surnames*). 'Yonge' cites some very odd etymologies, she herself preferring a Celtic one, 'companion of the chalice,' which 'Swan' repeats with the alternative, 'finder of the Holy Grail'. Diminutive: *Percy*.

PERCY. Like *Howard* and *Stanley*, it 'Christianizes' a fine old aristocratic surname, although in C19–20 it has belonged to the masses as well as the classes. *Percy* was extremely popular in mid C19 and is still employed in the U.S.A. for 'a typical young Englishman' (Weekley, *W. & N.*). 'One origin of *Percy, Pearcey, Pursey*, etc., is [Fr.] *perce-haie*, pierce hedge,' recorded in the *Hundred Rolls*, 1273, as (*William*) *Percehaye*: Weekley, *Surnames*. (Cf. *Perceval.*) Another is the village of *Perci* in Normandy (Withycombe).

PEREGRINE, *m.*, is the L. *peregrinus*, 'a wanderer,' whence, via Fr., our *pilgrim*. It is 'a name sometimes given in honour of St Peregrinus, or Pellegrino, an Irish prince, who dwelt as a hermit on the Apennines, and sometimes to commemorate a birth that has taken place when the parents have been wandering in a foreign land' (Swan). Cf. Smollett's novel, *Peregrine Pickle*, 1751.

PERPETUA (L., 'everlasting, enduring') is a Catholic *f.*, commemorating the C3 virgin martyr. Diminutive *Peppi.*

PERRY. The diminutive of *Peregrine.*

PETE. A mainly American shortening of:

PETER. Gr. πέτρος, 'a stone,' perhaps influenced by πέτρα, (and not in the American sense of the word) 'a rock,' with the implication 'firm as a rock': 'Thou art *Petros* (a stone), and on this *Petra* (a rock) I will build my Church,' said Christ. In his lifetime, the apostle was called by the Heb. or Syriac equivalent *Cephas*; but as Gr. *Petros* or as L. *Petrus* he descended to Biblical and manly fame. The name did not – *Peter's pence* may have hindered it – become general in England before C18; Peter the Great, who visited England in 1698, may have caused, certainly he promoted, a certain measure of popularity. In late C19–20, it has been very popular indeed; many post-War Peters owe 'nominal' paternity to *Joan and Peter*, a much-read novel by H. G. Wells (1918).

PETRINA and PETRONELLA or -ILLA. The former is the direct *f.* of *Peter*; the latter, a diminutive of *Petronia*, the *f.* of L. *Petronius*, perhaps from *petra*, 'a stone' (Withycombe).

Both are now uncommon, especially the latter – despite the canonization of the Roman virgin, who, 'converted to Christianity by . . . St Peter,' then 'ministered to him until her death at an early age' (Benedictines).

PHEBE. (One syllable only.) The diminutive of *Phoebe*.

PHELIM. An Irish *m.* name (Celtic, 'the ever good') originally *Feidlim* or *Feiolim*, which became *Felim* or *Felimy* and finally (? in C16) and Grecizingly (*Φ* for *f*) *Phelim*. 'Felim once had a feminine Fedlimi, now either forgotten or transmuted into Felicia,' Young. See also at *Felix*.

PHEMIE. A contraction of *Euphemia*. Cf. *Effie* and:

PHENIE. A transformed contraction of *Euphemia*.

PHIL. A diminutive of *Philip*, and of *Phyllis*; the latter is more properly contracted as *Phyl*. Also of *Philippa*.

PHILANDER, *m.* Long dead in the British Empire, but still not more than moribund in the U.S.A. Gr., 'man-loving'. See also *Philetus*.

PHILEMON, *m.* Gr., 'loving, friendly'. It has fallen, though not irretrievably, into disuse. Two Philemons were saints and martyrs (C1, C4), but to most cultured Englishmen the name evokes the pleasant figure of Philemon Holland, doctor-scholar and accurate, vivid translator of Livy, Pliny, Plutarch, and other Classics as well as of our native, Latinizing Camden.

PHILETUS, *m.* Gr. for 'love', says 'Yonge'; 'lover,' says 'Swan': the original is *Φιλότης* (philotēs), 'love,' affection,' 'friendship'. 'Whether Philadelphia set the fashion, or whether the length of the name is the allurement, Americans have a decided turn for all these commencements with "Phile"; and Philetus, Philander, &c., are to be found continually among the roughest inhabitants of the back-woods and far-west. With us they are at a discount,' Yonge; they are no longer so general in America.

PHILIBERT, *m.* Teutonic, 'exceeding bright'. Somewhat obsolescent, it merits survival if only in honour of the C7 Fr. Philibert, founder of two abbeys, reclaimer of waste lands, and hero in the face of exile imposed more than once 'by the lawless potentates of his age' (Benedictines). See *Fulbert.*

PHILIDA. A variant of *Phyllida*, q.v.

PHILIP. Gr. Φίλιππος (Philippos), 'fond of horses' (cf. Persian *Aspamistras*, 'horse-lover'), became general in the Near East colonized by Macedon, so many of whose kings and princes bore this name. The Apostle Philip and Philip the Deacon (one of seven deacons appointed by the Apostles); French and Spanish kings; noblemen innumerable: they all contributed to spread *Philip* (etc.) throughout Europe.

PHILIPPA. The English *f.* of the preceding. Cf. It. *Filippa*, whence the lovesome maid in Browning's *Pippa Passes.*

PHILLADA (rare); PHILLIDA. Variations of *Phyllida.*

PHILLIPP. The Scottish form of *Philip.*

PHILLIS. See *Phyllis.*

PHINEAS, *m.* Is this from the Celtic *finn*, 'white' + *-as*, 'house,' as it often is in proper-name suffixes? The Phineas Finn of Trollope's Parliamentary tetralogy is 'an irresistible but penniless young Irishman' (Harvey). Or is it *phoenix*, Middle English *fenice* or *phenes* (Weekley, *Surnames*)? Sometimes it is the Biblical *Phinehas* (*Numbers*, xxv, 7–9), perhaps with the lit. meaning, 'brazen mouth': ? speaking words that are boastful.

PHIP. A diminutive of *Philip*. Cf. *Phil.*

PHOEBE. As Phoebus is the sun-god (Apollo), so Phoebe is the moon-goddess (Artemis; Roman Diana); they are the *m.* and *f.* of the Gr. adjective for 'radiant' or 'bright', deriving from φώς (phōs), 'light' (cf. *phosphorus*, 'that which brings light'). As Charlotte Yonge briefly summarizes it, 'Phoebe was a good deal in use among the women of Greek birth in the early Roman empire; and "Phoebe, our sister," the deaconess of Cenchrea, is commended by St Paul to the Romans; but she has had few namesakes, except in England; the Italian Febe only being used as a synonym for the moon.'

PHYL. See *Phil.*

PHYLLIDA. A variant of *Phyllis*. 'Phyllida . . . The name had stuck in his mind as an unusual, somewhat highfalutin one,' Richard Blaker (in his excellent novel, *Night-Shift*), 1934.

PHYLLIS; occasionally PHILLIS. From Gr. *phullis*, genitive *phullidis*, 'a green leaf' or 'bough'. In old myth she was a Thalian who, because her lover so tarried that she thought herself forgotten, committed suicide by hanging: whereupon 'she was metamorphosed into a tree' (Blakeney). The name has been much used by lyric and pastoral poets. Robert Greene,

> Their love begun and ended both in one;
> Phillis was loved, and she liked Corydon.

Sir Charles Sedley,

> Phillis, men say that all my vows,
> Are to thy fortune paid;
> Alas, my heart he little knows
> Who thinks my love a trade.

PIERCE. A Fr., thence an English and, more frequently, Irish form of *Peter*; see:

PIERS. An early English contraction – from the Fr. – of *Peter* (Gr. *Πέτρος*). Cf. the preceding.

PIP. An occasional diminutive of *Philip*, as Ian Hay's delightful *Pip, a Romance of Youth* makes abundantly clear.

PLAXY. This Cornish *f.* is of considerable antiquity, and one cannot help but wonder how – if it really did – it came to be derived, unless it were through those influential Phoenicians, from a Gr. word meaning 'active'; 'Swan' (? from 'Yonge') doesn't say which word, but I presume she intends *πρακτική*, praktikë, '(a) busy (woman)', probably with a glance at Gr. *πρᾶξις* (praxis), 'busyness' or 'business': perhaps cf. Theocritus's Praxinoa.

POLLOCK. An English *m.* derivative from *Paul*, it is now mostly a surname.

POLLY. A diminutive of *Mary*, just as *Molly* is. The further diminutive, *Poll*, is now reserved for parrots.

POLSON. An English derivative of *Paul*: 'Paul's son'.

POMPEY. L. *Pompeius*, '(a man) of Pompeii'. The name owes much to Cn. Pompeius Magnus, Pompey the Great, the Triumvir: scourge of pirates, conqueror of Mithridates, conquered by Julius Caesar in 48 B.C. (The man is brilliantly portrayed in Oman's *Seven Roman Statesmen.*) In C18, appeared Coventry's satirical novel, the *Life of Pompey the Little* (1751): for some odd reason, Pompey was already a name for lap-dogs. Yet it has maintained something of its dignity and is still heard occasionally.

POPPY is a *f.* flower-name that is little favoured by the cultured.

PORTIA. This *f.*, of pretty Shakespearean memory, is of

ugly origin, for in L. (*porcus*, *-a*) it signifies a hog, a sow; though via *Porcia*, originally 'a female member of the great Porcian clan (*gens Porcia*)'.

PREU, PREW. Variants of *Pru*, *Prue*.

PRIMROSE, *f.* A flower-name, lit. 'first, or early, bloom'; it arose late in C19.

PRISCILLA. The diminutive of L. *prisca*, the *f.* of *priscus*, 'olden,' 'ancient,' 'of antique time'. It is going out of fashion; has been so going since the late C19. Its heyday was in C17, chiefly among the Puritans, who revered the memory of Priscilla, 'a noble Roman matron . . . grandmother of SS. Praxedes and Pudentiana . . . [and] the hostess in Rome of St Peter the Apostle, by whom she had been converted to Christianity' (Benedictines).

PROSPER. L. *prosper* or *prosperus*, 'fortunate,' 'prosperous,' from *spero*, 'I hope,' became medieval It. *prospero*, a name which Shakespeare 'must have heard through the famous condottiere, *Prospero Colonna*, when he bestowed it upon his wondrous magician, Duke of Milan' (Yonge). It is, however, worth noting that in C5 there lived two – or was it three? – bishops named Prosper, one of whom was a very great controversialist.

PRU, PRUE. Diminutive of:

PRUDENCE. Cf. L. *Prudentia*, *f.* of *Prudentius*, from *prudens*, 'discreet,' 'prudent'. It became popular among the Puritans late in C16: not from a St Prudentia, for there wasn't – and, except unofficially, isn't – such a saint, but from the abstract 'prudence' (L. *prudentia*). It is thus one with *Faith*, *Mercy*, *Patience*. It has, in C19–20, been more general in the U.S.A. than in England.

PRUE. See *Pru.*

PUGH. This Celtic *m.* 'Christian' (whence the surname) contracts '*Ap Hu*, a Welsh patronymic' (Swan).

Q

QUEENIE. This *f.* probably derives from *queen.* It is also, especially among Cockneys, a nickname for all girls named *Victoria,* as Julian Franklyn tells me.

QUENTIN. In L., *Quintus,* 'the fifth,' was a very common fore-name; there was, moreover, a Quintian 'gens' or clan. In 287 one Quintinus – now canonized as St Quentin – was martyred on the Somme. (He wasn't the only one.) Thence the name spread to Scotland: witness Quentin Durward in C15. And to Ireland. But in Ireland it generally represents *Cu-mhaighe* ('hound of the plain'), pronounced *Cooey.* (Charlotte Yonge has a very interesting section on numeral 'Christians': cf. *Sextus, Septimus, Otto, Nona.*)

QUINTIN. A variant of the preceding.

R

RAB. The Scottish equivalent to *Rob*. Whence *Rabbie*, as in affectionate allusions to Rabbie Burns.

RACHEL. (See also at *Leah*.) Heb., 'a ewe,' emblematic of gentleness. The favourite wife of Jacob has always been a favourite among Biblical women, and the name received additional lustre from the magnificent tragic parts of Rachel, the Jewish-French actress, who, in 1858, died young and whose last illness forms the subject of a poem by Matthew Arnold.

RAFE is merely the phonetic representation of the fashionable pronunciation of:

RALF; usually RALPH. The O.E. *raedwulf*, lit. 'counsel (of) wolf', became *Radulf*, which became *Ralf*; it corresponds to the Fr. *Raoul*. A notable Ralph was Ralph Sherwin, that excellent classical scholar (Oxon.) who was, in 1581 with Edmund Campion, martyred for refusing to abjure the Catholic faith. (Benedictines.)

RAN. The diminutive of *Randal*.

RANALD. A variant of *Ronald*.

RANDAL; occasionally RANDLE, the more general form in C13–18. It is a derivative of *Randolf* (or *Randolph*), q.v. for etymology; and, though now rather uncommon, is bestowed especially by those who prefer 'Saxon' to Greek or Latin names. It graced two C17 lexicographers of decided character and very considerable merit: Cotgrave of the French-English Dictionary, and Holme of the *Armoury*.

RANDO. A diminutive – cf. *Randy*, q.v. – of:

RANDOLF; now always RANDOLPH. *Rand*, 'a northern prefix' is 'best referred to the Gothic *razn*, a house, and likewise a shield, from the protection both afford'; the second element is *wulf*, 'a wolf,' which 'was highly popular as a name-root,' Yonge. The early form is *Randulf*; and the sense is 'shield-wolf' or 'house-wolf', presumably a fierce defender of home-comforts. The spelling *Randolph* results from the Latinized *Radulphus* and the surname-form, *Randolph*.

RANDY. An 'endearment' for *Randolph*: but, because of its meaning in dialect and slang, to be avoided. Preferably, *Rando*.

RAONMILL. A Gaelic form of *Reginald*.

RAPHAEL. Heb., 'the medicine of God; God's healing', Raphael was therefore a very suitable angel to guide Tobias and heal his father: see *Tobias*, *Tobit*. The *-ph-* spelling, which results from Gr. influence, is that current in England, France and Germany; but in Italy and Spain, where the name is more general, the spelling is respectively *Raffaelle* and *Rafael*. (Yonge.)

RASTUS. This American *m.* abounds more among the negroes than among the whites. Yonge and Swan omit this name, which I surmise to be sometimes a shortening of *Adrastus* (one of the heroes of the celebrated war of 'The Seven against Thebes', which forms the subject of a tragedy by Aeschylus): which is perhaps Gr. ἄδραστος (adrastos), 'not running away,' i.e. 'staunch,' 'courageous'. More often, however, it shortens the Gr. name *Erastus* ('beloved'), itself almost obsolete.

RAY. As *m.*, it was originally the diminutive of *Raymond*; but I confess that as *f.*, *Ray* baffles me, unless it is simply the *Ra-* of *Rachel* or short for the Fr. *f. Raymonde*. Cf. the problem offered by the *f.* of *Kay*.

RAYMOND; RAYMUND, an old spelling, now extremely rare. Old Frankish *Raginmund*, 'wise protection,' is its ancestor. The three Saints (C5–13) are spelt *Raymund*, but the modern Fr. spelling has usually been *Raimond*, whence ours: for this name abounds in the records of the chivalry of France.

REBA. A diminutive of *Rebecca*. Cf. *Becky*.

REBECCA, REBEKAH. Heb., 'a snare' (lit., 'a noosed cord'), from *rabak*, 'to bind'; the former spelling derives from the New Testament Gr., as *Jack and Jill* reminds us. The Heb. origin (*ribka*) is probably intended to intimate the firmness of the marriage-bond; utter loyalty to family is recognized by Gentiles to be one of the Jews' most distinctive badges, just as generosity is, by those who know, admitted to be another, as indeed it is for the Scot. Both Jews and Scots have a marked sense of humour: hence the best stories about meanness and avarice are invented and spread by East-Enders and Aberdonians. Diminutives: *Reba* and *Becky*.

REDMOND. Teutonic, 'counsel- or council-protection': for the second element, cf. the *-mond* of *Raymond*. This Irish *m*. derives 'most likely from the Irish and Danish names Hromunt or Romund' (Swan).

REECE. The English form of *Rhys*, q.v. Cf. *Rice*.

REG, REGGIE. Diminutives of *Reginald* and:

REGINA. Direct from L., where it means 'queen', as some of those born since the death of Victoria Regina may need reminding. It shows signs of incipient decay.

REGINALD. Teutonic, 'judgement-power' or 'counsel-power or ruler' is usually taken to mean 'powerful judgement'; *-ald* is a combining form of Teutonic *wald*, 'power' (cf. *Waldo*, q.v.). The Scandinavian original is *Ragnwold* or *Rognwald*. '*Ragn*, or judgement, . . . is connected with the

Latin *rego*, to rule . . . Reginald Pole' – the great early C16 cardinal devoted to the restoration of Catholicism in England – 'was in his own time known as Reynold. We get the longer name from his Latinism as Reginaldus' (Yonge). Withycombe, however, derives *Reginald* from O.E. *Regenweald*, both elements (*regen* and *weald*) meaning power: hence, 'the exceeding powerful One'. It has always been a favourite with the upper classes, but, owing to their example, by no means confined to them. Diminutives: *Reg*, *Reggie*, *Rex*.

RENE. A shortening of *Irene*.

RENFRED is not so obsolescent as the ignorant have supposed. A very old English *m.* name, it signifies 'judgement of peace': for the first element, cf. *Reginald* (q.v.); for the second, *Frieda*.

REUBEN. Heb., "'behold, a son!" cries the mother in her first pride' (Yonge). It was Reuben, the eldest son of Jacob and Leah, who founded one of the twelve tribes of Israel. In the U.S.A., fairly general; in the British Empire, now mainly among Jews. Diminutive: *Rube*.

REX is not always L. *rex*, 'a king,' but sometimes an English 'telescoping' of *Reginald*. Occasionally, however, it is heard as a diminutive of *Eric*.

REYNOLD. Though usually thought of as *Reynolds*, a surname, *Reynold* is still occasionally bestowed as a font-name. It constitutes the early form of *Reginald* and probably shows the influence of Fr. *Renaud*, It. *Rinaldo*, Polish *Raynold*.

RHO is a diminutive of *Rhoda* and also of *Roland* (p. 240); the more correct spelling of this diminutive of *Roland* is *Ro*.

RHODA; RHODE (rare). Gr. *ῥόδον* (rhodon), 'a rose,' pl. *ῥόδα* (rhoda); *ῥοδῆ* (rhodë), 'a rose-bush': of these, the last seems to be the origin, though one cannot rule out another possibility – ‘Ῥόδια (Rhodia), ‘a woman of (the island of) Rhodes’. Diminutives: *Rho* and: –

RHODY. The diminutive of *Rhoda*, and none the less so that the obsolescent *Rhode* is pronounced in the same way.

RHYS. This very general Welsh *m.* (cf. Rhys Davies, who may go further than any other living Welsh writer) is pronounced *Reece* (q.v.). *Rhys*, in Welsh, is ‘a rushing – i.e. impetuous – man or warrior’ and may, ultimately, be cognate with that very widespread radical which is seen in Teutonic *rik*, A.-S. *rice*, L. *rex*, and *raj*, *rajah*. (Yonge.) Cf. *Rice*.

RIA. A mainly lower-class diminutive of *Maria*. (J. Redding Ware, *Passing English*, 1909.)

RICE. An English form of *Rhys*: from an incorrect pronunciation thereof.

RICHARD. From O.E. *richeard*, ‘rule hard,’ i.e. ‘stern ruler or king’. ‘The name owed its frequency . . . to Ricehard, . . . an Anglo-Saxon monarch of Kent, who left his throne to become a monk at Lucca.’ (Both Weekley and Withycombe regard him rather as fable than as fact; the former says, ‘Old Fr. from Teutonic’ *Ricohard*.) ‘The third Norman duke bore the name, and transmitted it to two successors, whence we obtained as many as twenty Richards at the conquest, and have used it as a favourite national name ever since. Two more [truly noble] saints bore it,’ the excellent bishop of Chichester, ‘who, dying in 1253, was canonized only nine years later, and a hermit, who,’ late in C12, ‘was made bishop of Andria, in Apulia’ (Yonge). Whence the diminutives *Diccon* (obsolete), *Rick* (obsolescent), *Ritchie* (q.v.), and *Dick* (q.v.).

RICKY. See *Eric*.

RINA. This is one of the diminutives of *Katharine*: in its variant *Katharina*.

RITA is a diminutive, either of *Margarita* or of It. *Margherita*. See therefore *Margaret*.

RITCHIE. A Scottish diminutive (now also a frequent surname) of *Richard*.

RO. See *Roland*.

ROB. Properly the original of *Robin*, *Rob* was at first, and sometimes even now, a diminution of *Robert*: qq.v. Cf. *Rab*.

ROBBIE. A Scottish pet-name for a *Robert*.

ROBERT. 'Hruadperaht, or bright fame, was the original form, the property of a bishop, who [ca. 700] founded the first Christian church at Wurms. [Usually *Hrodebert*: *hrod* or *hrothi*, fame+*berhta*, bright: cf. the A.-S. name, *Hreodbeorht*. (Withycombe.)] Honoured alike in France and Germany, he became Ruprecht in the latter, and Robert in the former. . . . *Red* was long supposed to be the origin of the name, which some made Redbert, or bright speech, others Redbeard! The German form, however, disproves both of these,' Yonge. *Robert*, adopted from France, was soon thoroughly Anglicized. In France, it was, in the Middle Ages, a Royal name; throughout Europe, it was revered, still is revered, as the name of seven saints, of whom the most important are the founder (d. 1098), in France, of the Cistercian Order, a branch of the Benedictine, and Robert of Newminster, a Yorkshire priest (d. 1159), who 'was united in spiritual friendship with St Bernard of Clairvaux, the great Saint of the Age, and with St Godric, the holy hermit of Durham' (Benedictines). Whence *Robin* (q.v.), *Rob*, *Hob* (obsolete), *Bob*, and *Rupert* (q.v.). – Cf. *Roger*.

ROBERTA is the *f.* form of *Robert*, q.v. for etymology.

ROBIN. Originally a diminutive of *Rob*; but, ever since C12, predominantly an independent name. The Irish form is

Roibin. The *-in* connotes the diminution that is prompted by affection, and the name owes some of its popularity to the legends of *Robin Goodfellow* and *Robin Hood* (Apperson).

ROBINA; rarely, ROBINIA. The *f.* of *Robin*, they are virtually unknown outside of Scotland.

ROBINETTE. A fanciful elaboration of *Robina*.

ROD. A diminutive, as is the affectionate *Roddy*, of *Roderic* and *Rodney*.

RODERIC, RODERICK. Northern *Hrothrekr*, Old Ger. *Hrodric*, lit. 'fame rule' – hence 'famous ruler'. Part of its English use must be attributed to the fame of various bearers of Sp. *Rodrigo*; 'in Wales, Scotland, and Ireland, Roderick has a sort of false honour, being adopted as the equivalent of the native Keltic names, the Welsh Rhydderc and the Gadhaelic Ruadh,' as Charlotte Yonge, always scornful of such 'honour rooted (*more philologico*) in dishonour', remarks.

RODNEY, *m.*, is a 'Christianizing' of the surname, which may be a degeneration from *Rodnight*, O.E. *radcniht*, lit. 'road-servant,' i.e. 'a tenant who held his land on condition of accompanying his lord as a mounted servitor' (Weekley, *Surnames*). Sometimes *Rodney* arises in a Somersetshire place-name (Weekley, *Jack and Jill*).

RODOLPH; occ. RODOLF (cf. *Randolf*, *Randolph*). Teutonic, 'wolf-fame,' it is a contraction of the Norse *Hrothwulf* [lit., 'fame (of) wolf'], which soon became *Hrolfr*, which finally became *Rolf* (or *Rolph*). Likewise, *Rudolf* is a variant, properly and mainly Ger., as is *Rudolph*, from the Fr. form, *Rodolphe*.

ROGER. In Teutonic, 'spear of fame,' it is lit. 'fame-spear' and its earliest form is O.E. *Hrothgar* or, as in the *Nibelungenlied*, *Hruodger* or *Hrodgar*. In the Middle Ages a knightly name, it had, by C17 or even earlier, become a general one, especially in the 'truly rural' districts: witness the obsolete diminutive *Hodge*, which has long been generic for a rustic. There are even three Saints Roger, though none before C12 and none after C16. Cf. *Robert*. The diminutive is *Rog*, pronounced *Rodge*.

ROIBIN. See *Robin*.

ROLAND. The first element is that of *Robert*, *Roderic(k)*, *Rodolph*, and *Roger*; the second, the general Teutonic radical, *land*: 'famous land': the whole, therefore, may be '(one who is – or is hoped to be – the) fame of the land'. A certain prefect slain at Roncesvalles in the days of Charlemagne was called *Rotolando*, a punning name 'from his rolling himself on the ground' (Yonge) or '*Rotlandus*' (Swan): from his name and fame there have been evolved those of *Roland* and the Chanson de Roland. The Sp. *Roldan* and the It. *Orlando* are the same person: a fact obvious only to students of language, for they are conversant with the almost innumerable metatheses of words; the transposition here is a frequent one. Diminutives: *R(h)o* and *Rolly*.

ROLF, ROLPH, occasionally ROLFE. See *Rodolph*.

ROLLO. This transformation of *Rudolph* exhibits two linguistic 'habits': contraction of two syllables into one; addition of *o*, which is common both to the Romance languages (Portuguese *Rolando* for *Roland*) and to the Germanic (*Bruno*, *Waldo*).

ROLLY or ROLY: a pet-form of *Roland*.

ROMA; whence (?) ROMER. It is either a contraction of *Romola* or, more probably, a direct personification of *Roma*, the L. of *Rome*, a word apparently cognate with that Teutonic radical *hruod*, 'fame,' which forms the basis alike of so many 'Christians' (see at *Romulus*) and of that strange cant word, *rum*; for *rum*, see my *Underworld*.

ROMEO. 'O Romeo, Romeo, wherefore are thou Romeo?' cried despairing Juliet in a somewhat different context. He is, because of *Romulus*, by way of It. *Romolo*, of which it is an attractive reduction. Despite the Shakespearean lover, the name has not gained much hold.

ROMOLA. The *f.* of *Romolo*, from L. *Romulus*, it is originally and mainly an It. name.

ROMULUS. Never at all general among the English-speaking peoples, it owes its employment solely to the myth of Romulus and Remus, the founders of Rome. The *-ulus* is the L. diminutive suffix; the *m.*, at that early date, was probably a euphonic convenience (though the Ger. *Ruhm*, 'fame,' perhaps disproves this); *Ro-* is the ancient Teutonic *hruod*, 'fame,' as in *Robert*, *Roderick*, *Roger*, *Roland*, etc. Or, to put it in another way, *Romulus* is the L. equivalent of Frankish L. *Chrodomarus*, Teutonic *Hruodmar*, which, lit. 'famed renown', is but a reduplication of 'fame', i.e. of *hruod*.

RON. A diminutive of *Ronald*.

RONA appears to be the *f.* of – and derived from – *Ronald*.

RONALD, like the English *Reynold*, is a variation of *Reginald*. *Ronald* and its variant *Ranald* are Scottish.

RONNIE. A diminutive of *Ronald*.

ROOSEVELT, a surname of Dutch extraction (*roos*, a rose +*veld*, a field: compare *veld roos*, a wild rose), has, since ca. 1905, graced many a young American hopeful: did not Theodore ('Teddy Bear') Roosevelt (1858–1919), author, hunter, astute politician and, in 1901–09, President, start the impulse, and did not his distant cousin, Franklin Delano

Roosevelt (1882–1945), idealistic statesman and true democrat, one of the U.S.A.'s four greatest men (Washington, Jefferson, Lincoln, 'F.D.R.'), President from 1933 until his death, did not he corroborate and notably augment that impulse? (For the guidance of Britons: both branches of the Roosevelt family pronounce their name *Rō′-zĕ-velt.*)

RORIE, RORY. This Irish *m.*, from a Celtic radical means ing 'red' or 'ruddy', and therefore corresponding to the old Irish names *Ruadvi*, *Ruad an*, *Ruadhaic* (cf. the Scottish *Ruaridh* and the Welsh *Rhydderch*), is often abandoned for *Roderic*(*k*), q.v.

ROSA. See *Rose*.

ROSABEL, ROSABELLA. The latter is merely *rosa bella*, 'pretty rose,' with *Rosabel* as a shortening or an Anglicism. On the analogy of *Isabel*.

ROSALIA, now rare; ROSALIE. (See also at *Rosemary*.) The latter has been adopted from France, *Rosalie* being the Fr. of *Rosalia*, which Charlotte Yonge treats as a mere elaboration of *Rosa* (or *Rose*); which Helena Swan boldly declares to be 'rose and lily' (? 'lilies'), L. *rosa et lilium*, pl. *lilia* (? *rosa*[*et li*]*lia!*); and which I hesitantly explain as *Rosalia*, 'the ceremony of hanging up the garlands,' at the *Rosales Escae*, 'the feast of the roses,' with which cf. the U.S. Decoration Day (May 30th), on which the tombs of those who fell in the Civil War are strewn, or garlanded, with flowers, as 'Lewis and Short' mentions.

ROSALIND, from Sp. ROSALINDA (now rare); ROSALINE or, rarely, ROSELINE. 'Fair as a rose': *Rosa*+*linda*, as in Sp. *linda*, '(a) fair or pretty (woman)'. (I find it difficult to accept Withycombe's Old Ger. *Roslindis*: *hros*, 'a horse' +*lindi*, 'a serpent'.) It is improbable that Shakespeare invented it, but the name appears first in *As You Like It*, as Charlotte Yonge has noted.

ROSAMOND, ROSAMUND. The former varies the latter, which occurs first as *Rosamunda*, 'horse-protection'; the 'poetical' derivation from L. *rosa* ('a rose'), almost certainly erroneous, 'gave rise to the Latin epigram, *Rosa mundi, sed non Rosa munda* (the rose of the world, but not a pure rose)', Yonge.

ROSANNA, ROSANNE; ROSEANNA. Combinations of *Rosa*, or *Rose*, and *Anna* or *Anne*.

ROSA; ROSE. Charlotte Yonge maintains that 'the first use of *hrôs* among the Teutons was a meaning sometimes fame,' – cf. the *hruod* in *Robert* and *Romulus*, qq.v. – 'sometimes a horse': this theory is supported by *Rosamond*, q.v. She notes that *Rohais* and *Roesia* were current as aristocratic *f.* names among the Fr. in C12–13, and thinks that they should be so derived. Nevertheless, as she freely admits, there was an Italian St Rosa or Rose, who died ca. 1250, and she herself mentions the Sicilian St Rosalia, 'the darling of each heart and eye,' who died in 1160, and that 'Rosel and Rosette both occur at Cambrai between 900 and 1200'. Certainly, the C15–20 *Rosa* and *Rose*, whatever their dim-distant origin, are to be referred to the burgeoning and the full-blown rose, the latter so often symbolic and 'nominal' of a ruddy-cheeked country wench. In short, the very old L.-from-Gr. flower-name has absorbed several Teutonic names of 'fame' or 'nobility' origin.

ROSELINE. See *Rosalind*.

ROSEMARY. The writer hopes that he may, without being condemned as either pretentious or 'sloppy', be allowed to repeat the text of the Christmas card he issued in 1933: – 'In no way related to Rosalia, austere and penitential Sicilian, nor to Rosalie, the patron saint of the "Poilus", nor to Rosy Lee, the goddess of Cockneys and other Englishmen, Rosemary yet has – though her parents, "herbae gemmantes rore recenti," may occasionally doubt it – a saintly association ("odi profanos . . .") with the Virgin Mary and a poetic with "Le Roman de la Rose", for it was owing to their pure and floral influence that *rosmarine* (Latin *ros marinus*, dew of the sea, by way of Old French *rosmarin*, now *romarin*) became *rosemary*, the fragrant evergreen, no less restorative and emblematic than our dainty Rosemary, who already promises to fulfil the unwilling prophecy of the sage and merry Skelton: "the soverayne rosemary."' (Perhaps it should be added that *Rosalie* is French soldiers' slang for a bayonet; *Rosy Lee* is rhyming slang for tea.)

ROSEANNA. See *Rosanna*.

ROSETTA, ROSINA. The English and the Italian-become-English pet-form of *Rose*. Contrast:

ROSIA, *f.* In Teutonic, 'fame'. 'Not commonly met with,' notes Helena Swan.

ROSIE. A diminutive of *Rosa*, *Rose*, *Rosalind*, *Rosamund*, *Rosetta*, *Rosina*, *Rosita* (Sp.), *Rosemary*.

ROSS. See Note at end of Introduction.

ROWENA. Originally *Rhonwen*, which in Welsh signifies 'white skirt' – a startlingly early anticipation of 'a bit of skirt', for the first Rowena was 'a daughter of Hengist the Saxon, the unwitting cause of the invasion of England', ca. 450. The name received fresh life from the Rowena of Scott's *Ivanhoe*, 1819, but it is drooping again.

ROWLAND. An English variant of *Roland*.

ROY. (See also *Rory*.) Probably Celtic 'red': Gaelic has *ruadh*, Cymric has *r(h)ud*, O.E. has *rudig* (Teutonic *rudu*), English has *ruddy*, Gr. has *ῥόδος* (rhŏdos), L. has *ravus*: the Celtic word is prominent in Irish and Scottish nomenclature, for in Ireland and Scotland 'the true undiluted Gaels are divided between the black and the red'. Thence, certainly, the surnames *Roe* and *Roy*; thence, again, the 'Christian'. This is a more convincing derivation than that from *roy*, old Fr. for *roi*, 'king.'

RUBE. A familiar pet-name for a Reuben. In American slang, a *rube* is a rustic: cf. *hick* from *Richard*. See *Underworld*.

RUBY. Often said to be a contraction of *Robina* (q.v.), it is, nevertheless, more probably a 'jewel-name' like *Beryl*, *Emerald* and *Pearl*. It has, in the main, failed to attract the upper classes.

RUDOLF, RUDOLPH. See *Rodolph*.

RUDY. The diminutive of *Rudolph*.

RUE. See *Ruth*.

RUFUS. L. *rufus*, 'red-haired,' as in Plautus's *rufus quidam*, 'a certain red-headed fellow'; this adjective is cognate with L. *ruber*, 'red' (cf. our 'rubrics'). Popularized in England as the nickname of William II (d. 1100), but in C19–20 it has been the prerogative – rarely usurped in the British Empire – of Americans.

RUPERT was originally, and still is, a Ger. *m.* name, *Ruprecht* or *Rupprecht*, earlier (and obsoletely) *Hruodebert* or, better, *Hrodebert*, which in Teutonic designates '(one for whom) bright, i.e. brilliant, fame (is expected – or hoped)': it is, then, a doublet of *Robert*, q.v. The name arrived dashingly in England with Charles the First's nephew, Prince Rupert, the erratically brilliant, too rash deviser and leader of cavalry charges against the Roundheads. 'The Rupert of Debate' was a name given either by Lord Lytton in his poem *The New Timon*, 1846, or by Disraeli, in 1844, to Edward Stanley, 14th Earl of Derby, statesman and magnificent orator (1799–1866).

RUPERTA. The *f.*, more or less restricted to Scotland, of *Rupert*, itself a variant of *Robert*: cf., therefore, *Robina*.

RUSSELL, *m.* More common as a surname, *Russell* Anglicizes the Old French *Roussel*, 'the Red-Head' (cf. *Rufus*): from *roux*, 'red' – a doublet of *rouge*.

RUTH. Heb., but whether 'trembling' or 'uniting' or 'friend' or, better, 'beauty' (or 'vision of beauty') we know not. 'In spite of the touching sweetness of her history, Ruth's name has never been in vogue, except' – but it is an important exception – 'under the influence of our English version of the Bible.' In later literature *Ruth* appears in Mrs Gaskell's novel of that name, which has, except in its allegory, nothing to do with the Biblical person; in one of Keats's finest poems ('. . . amid the alien corn'); and in one of Victor Hugo's finest, *Booz Endormi* ('Pendant qu'il sommeillait, Ruth, une moabite, S'était couchée aux pieds de Booz, le sein nu, Espérant on ne sait quel rayon inconnu, Quand viendrait du réveil la lumière subite'). The pet form is *Rue*.

S

SABINA, *f.*, 'is often found among the peasantry about Gloucester, but it is possible that this may be [not in honour of the two more important of the three Saints Sabina, but] a corruption of Sabrina (the Severn),' Yonge. The origin of the Saints' name is L. *Sabina*, 'a Sabine woman'.

SABRIN (now very rare), SABRINA (in C20, unusual). It is, as *Sabrina* – for *Sabrin* is a curtailment – a Latinized and poetical name for the river Severn; but its employment as a *f.* 'Christian' seems to have, at least in the main, sprung from Milton's *Comus*, in which, presented at Ludlow Castle, Sabrina is the nymph haunting the Severn. The invocation in Milton ('Sabrina fair, Listen where thou art sitting Under the glassy, cool, translucent wave. . . . Listen and save') of a lucid loveliness, forms the opening piece in that fascinating volume of translations into Greek and Latin verse which, written by various Victorian scholars, is entitled *Sabrinae Corolla*.

SACHEVERELL, *m.* This uncommon 'Christian', which is borne by a talented post-1918 writer and occurs in Beatrice Kean Seymour's novel, *Daughter to Philip*, is obviously from the surname, which probably derives from the Fr. village of Saint-Chevreuil-du-Tronchet (Weekley, *Romance of Names*).

SACHIE. A diminutive of the preceding.

SADIE. A pet-name for *Sarah* and, in the Dominions, occasionally bestowed as an independent font-name.

SAL; SALLY. The former is short for the latter, which familiarizes the Hebraic *Sarah* to English use and usage.

SALOME. Heb., 'peace,' which does not closely fit the Biblical Salome, for she asked for – and got – John the

Baptist's head on a charger: a theme on which Oscar Wilde wrote, in French, *Salomé*, the English ban on which was removed only in 1931. Now rare.

SAM; SAMMY or SAMMIE. Familiar forms of *Samuel.*

SAMPSON, SAMSON. Heb., 'like the sun; resplendent', which fits very closely with the Biblical Samson. There were, in C6, two future saints – a priest at Constantinople and a monk of Caldey (in Wales); in the same century lived, also at Constantinople, a Samson Xenodochius, who, founding an important hospital for the sick poor, himself was welcomed into the asylum of saints.

SAMUEL is a particularly apt name, for, as Charlotte Yonge phrases it with pardonable sentiment, ' "Asked of God" is the import of Samuel, a name so endeared by the beautiful history of the call to the child in the temple, that it could not be quite forgotten. . . . The reading of the Holy Scriptures was . . . the cause of its use here . . ., since we scarcely find it before the Reformation.' Rather: 'heard of God' or 'name of God' (*Jack and Jill*).

SANCHIA. Provençal and Sp. *Sanchia* or *Sancha*, from L. *sanctus*, 'holy, saintly'. (Withycombe.) A pleasant, encourageable *f.* name.

SANDERS. A Scottish re-shaping of *Alexander*. Cf. *Saunders* and *Sandy*.

SANDRA. This pretty *f.* name is now less used than it might be. It is of It. origin. Popularized in England by Meredith's *Sandra Belloni* (1864). From *Alexandra* (p. 33).

SANDY. A diminutive of *Sanders*, hence ultimately of *Alexander*. Often used in generic address to a Scot, though during and since the war of 1914–18 *Jock* has been more usual in this connexion.

Sapphira. Gr. σάπφειρος (sap-pheiros), 'the lapis lazuli or sapphire'. Charlotte Yonge errs when she states that it 'was erased for ever from the nomenclature of Christians by the fate of the unhappy Sapphira', who, along with her husband Ananias, was struck dead after being sternly rebuked by Peter for lying: which nemesis seems dangerously near to being supererogatory, or else the rebuke was. Perhaps, however, the name means 'the beautiful one': Heb. *saphir*, 'beautiful'.

Sara, Sarah. The former is, in C19–20, usually regarded as the Continental, the latter as the British and American form of the name. *Sarah* and its contraction *Sally* were not in common use until after the Reformation. In Ireland it has been adopted for *Sadhbh* (pronounced 'Soyv'), *Sorcha*, and *Saraid*, of which the first two are extant; by Highlanders it is often employed as a rendering of their native *More* ('great'). The Heb. *Sarai*, 'the quarrelsome,' became *Sarah*, 'the princess' (from *sar*, 'a prince'). In Genesis we are told 'how Jehovah, in token of his love, took the last letter of his name and added it to Sara . . . "God said unto Abraham, As for Sarai thy wife, thou shalt not call her name Sarai, but Sarah shall her name be" ' (Swan).

Saul. Heb. 'asked for' (cf. *Samuel*), this name, that of the first king of Israel, has become both a 'Christian' and a surname – as the former, rather commoner in U.S.A. than in Britain.

Saunders. A Scottish transformation of *Alexander* and a variant, therefore, of *Sanders*.

Savy. An Irish diminutive of *Xavier* through Latinized *Saverius*.

Sawny. A diminutive of *Sanders* and *Alexander*, and a variant of *Sandy*. It is, now, pretty generally avoided because of its slang and colloquial senses.

SEAFORTH is the English form of *Siegfried* (q.v.) and now more frequent as a surname than as a 'Christian'.

SEAMUS, *m.* Incorrect spelling of *Seumas.* See also *Shamus.*

SEAN. (Pronounced *Shawn.*) An Irish form of *John.* The more correct Erse 'shape' is *Eoin,* with which cf. the Gaelic *Iain.*

SEBA, *m.* Rare in England; not uncommon in U.S.A. In origin, probably a shortening of:

SEBASTIAN. L. *Sebastianus,* a discreet derivative of *Sebastos* (*Sebastoi* or *Augusti* was Diocletian's designation of the joint emperors), 'the venerated; majestic' from Gr. *σέβας* (sĕbas), 'awe' or 'veneration'. It has become somewhat rare among the British, excepting always among Catholics, who revere the memory of the Roman martyr: as is so often represented in medieval art, he was 'tied to a tree' and his body 'made a target for the Roman archers, after which, it being discovered that he was still breathing, he was clubbed to death (A.D. 288),' Benedictines.

SELINA. Not used in England until C18, when, probably in mistake for the Fr. *Céline,* it belonged to the Countess of Huntingdon of Wesleyan fame. It derives from Gr. *Selēnē,* a name for the moon-goddess and, later, for one of the Cleopatras. From a radical (*elé*) meaning 'heat' or 'light'. (Yonge.) Cf. *Helen.*

SEONAID. A Gaelic form of *Jo(h)anna.*

SEP. The diminutive of:

SEPTIMUS. L., 'the seventh (boy)', as the obsolete *Septima* is 'the seventh girl'; but the name, when, as rarely, it is still bestowed, now shows, in general, a fine disregard for numerical accuracy.

SERENA is a *f.* name that, though rare in the British Empire, is not uncommon in the U.S.A.; it derives from L. *serenus*, calm or untroubled.

SETH. Heb., 'appointed'; perhaps 'compensation'. This manly and agreeable name is – though slowly in rural districts – dying out in Britain; America has wisely retained it. It is also a surname brilliant in the realms of philosophy.

SEUMAS, SEUMUIS. An Irish *m.* name, from Heb. ('supplanter') through Erse. It is therefore the Irish companion to Scottish *Hamish* and English *James*, q.v.

SEXTUS. L., 'the sixth (boy)'. This and its variant *Sixtus* are even more moribund than *Septimus*.

SHAMUS. An Anglicized form of *Seumas*, as

SHAN or SHANE is of *Séan*. But both names remain essentially Irish.

SHAR; SHARLIE. Diminutives of *Charlotte*. Cf. *Lottie*.

SHAWN. An Irish form of *John*. See *Séan*.

SHEELAH, SHE(E)LAGH. This Irish *f.* contracts trisyllabic *Sighile*, q.v.

SHEILA. The English form of the preceding. For its unconventional sense, see *Slang*, p. 420. Diminutive: *She*.

SHENA. 'Gaelic form of *Jane*' (Withycombe).

SHIR. The diminutive of:

SHIRLEY. A girl's name not much used before the late C19. From the surname, itself from an English place-name. In *Jack and Jill*, Weekley attributes its given-name popularity to Charlotte Brontë's *Shirley*, a semi-autobiographical novel published in 1849.

SHOLTO was adopted as a name in the Douglas family, and crept from thence to others. I have found no instance of it before the C17, 'and the probable derivation . . . would be Celtic *sioltaich*, a sewer' (Yonge). Probable?

SI. Short for *Simon* (contrast *Sim*) and for *Silas*.

SIB; SIBBIE. Respectively short and diminutive for *Sibyl* and:

SIBILA, SIBILLA, SIBILLE. Variants, on L. and Fr. models, of:

SIBYL; SYBIL. Gr. σίβυλλα (sibŭlla), 'a Sybil,' 'a prophetess,' and, derivatively, L. *sibylla*, show the correct spelling; cf. the equation *Silvester*, *Silvanus*: *Sylvanus*, *Sylvester*. The origin of this important word is problematic, but 'Doric Σιοβόλλα (Siobolla) for Attic Θεοβούλη (Theoboulē) divine wish' (Weekley) seems a happy guess, despite its ancientry and despite Charlotte Yonge's 'wise old woman' from *sab(i)us*, an old It., though not a Roman word. It became popular among English ladies of Norman blood; in Scotland and Ireland it may have been adopted for the Gaelic *Selbhflaith*, 'lady of possessions' (Yonge).

SID. The diminutive of:

SIDNEY, SYDNEY. Both *m.* and, though less often, *f.* Like *Howard* and *Percy*, it is a surname adopted for sweeter uses. *Sidney* probably telescopes *St Denis*: cf. 'the educated pronunciation of *St John*' as *Sinjun*. (Weekley, *Romance of Names*.)

SIEGFRIED is, in Teutonic, 'victorious peace,' which sounds ambiguous. This is, properly, the Ger. form, but the English *Sigefrid* is obsolete: and since Wagner's opera, *Sieg-*

fried, the Ger. form has had some small success in England and America; the Wars of 1914–18 and 1939–45 have somewhat damaged it in England. Diminutives: *Zig*, *Zig(g)ie*.

SIG. The pet-name for any Siegfried.

SIGHILE. 'In Ireland, the Norman settlers introduced [*Cecilia*], and it became Sighile,' Yonge.

SILAS. '[Sylvanus] had become a Roman name just before the Christian era, and belonged to the companion of St Paul . . . Sylvanus in the Epistles, and, by the contraction, Silas in the Acts . . . Silas has been revived in England,' Yonge; and George Eliot may have further revived it by her novel, *Silas Marner*, 1861. Diminutive: *Si*.

SILE. An Irish (Erse) variant of *Sheelah*. Pronounced Seelay.

SILVAN; SILVANUS. For the latter, see *Sylvanus*; *Silvan* is a shortening of *Silvanus*. In L., the more Classical spelling of *Sylvanus*, *Sylvester*, *Sylvia* is that in *sil-*, as basically in *silva*, 'a forest'.

SILVERIUS. A variant of (*Sil-* or) *Sylvanus*. Is there a confusion of L. *silvester* (a variant of *silvestris*) and *silvosus*, of almost exactly the same meaning? The English use, never general, of *Silverius* owes much to the martyr pope who died in 538.

SILVESTER. (See also *Sylvester*.) From the L. *silvestris*, 'belonging to wood or forest,' it is thus of a more general origin than is *Sylvanus*. 'Not uncommon in English rural districts and in Ireland,' Swan in 1905.

SILVIA. See *Sylvia*.

SILVIE. A pet-name for any *Sylvia*.

SIM. The 'endearment' of the next. Contrast *Si*.

SIMEON. Heb., 'obedient; hearkening' (n. or adj.), derives from *schama*, 'to hear': cf., therefore, *Samuel*. Already in C1 A.D. had *Simeon* been confused with *Simon* (q.v.); it is, then, noteworthy that the Heb. name should have been retained for nine saints, the Gr. for only three.

SIMON. In Gr., *Σίμων* is 'the snub-nose', but as a New-Testament name it seems to have been a mere Grecism for *Simeon*, q.v. So complete is the identification of the two names that *Simon* is often dismissed as a contraction of *Simeon*. Diminutive: *Si*.

SINTY. The diminutive of *Hyacinth*.

SIS; SISSIE. Variants of *Cis*, *Cissie*, q.v. In slang, a 'Sissie' is an effeminate male; in colloquialism, *Sis* is, in address, a pet-form of *sister*.

SISLEY. An English variant of *Cicely* and, rarely, of *Cecil*.

SIXTUS. See *Sextus*.

SOL, SOLLY. Diminutives of:

SOLOMON. The Heb. name *Salomo(n)* or *Solomon* means 'the peaceable': cf. the Ger. *Friedrich* (Frederick) and the Gr. *Eirēnaios* (and our *Irene*). The fame of King Solomon (C10 B.C.) has ensured its survival, especially among the Jews, who have made it a surname, as in Solomon J. Solomon, the witty painter of portraits and 'historicals'.

SONIA is a rather aristocratic *f*. 'Christian'. From Slavonic, it means 'wise one'. (Loughead.)

SOPHIA, SOPHY. Gr. *σοφία* (sophia), 'wisdom'. Ecclesiasticus speaks of 'Wisdom . . . the mother of fair Love and

Hope and holy Fear'; there was, in C2, St Sophia, the mother of the Virgin-Saints, Faith, Hope, and Charity; Justinian I (483–565), emperor of the Eastern Roman Empire, built at Constantinople the Church of St Sophia, dedicated to Christ as the Wisdom of God, thus (he declared) surpassing Solomon; whence its adoption by the Slavonic peoples, from whom *Sophia* spread to Germany, thence to France as *Sophie* and to England, where, under the Hanoverian Kings, it became very fashionable. 'Though its reign has passed with the taste for ornamental nomenclature, yet the soft and easy sound of Sophy still makes her hold her own,' Yonge.

SOPHIE. A diminutive of *Sophia*. Perhaps adopted from Fr. Contrast:

SOPHY. See *Sophia*.

SORCHA, *f.* An Irish name, from a Celtic term meaning 'bright' (? 'dazzling-fair').

SPASH. See *Aspasia*.

STACEY, STACY, *f.* and *m.* Anglicizations, by contraction, of *Anastasia* and *Anastasius*.

STAN. The diminutive of *Stanley* and:

STANISLAS, STANISLAUS. The latter is the usual English form, *Stanislas* being originally and properly Fr.; they represent Slavonic *Stanislav*, 'camp' – i.e. martial – 'glory'. There were, thus named, two famous Polish saints: Bishop Stanislaus of C11 and Stanislaus Kostka of late C16.

STANDISH. As in *Standish O'Grady*, that masterly Irish writer of short stories. Probably from the surname *Standish*, with which cf. the surnames *Standaloft*, *Standeven*, *Standfast* (Weekley's *Surnames*).

STANLEY, which, like *Howard*, *Percy*, and *Sidney*, was originally a very aristocratic surname. Professor Ernest Weekley mentions a Ricardus le Nouthird (neat-herd] de Stanley Porter, occurring ca. 1300, in the Register of the Freemen of York. The name does not appear in Searle, who, however, has *Stanburgh* and *Stangrim*; whence I deduce that *Stanley* was originally '(he who lives by the [? great] stone in the lea' or meadow, although it may derive from the English place-name Stanley ('stony meadow').

STELLA. From L. *stella*, 'a star,' and therefore a doublet of *Esther*. In English literature there are three famous Stellas: the Stella, i.e. Penelope Devereux, in Sidney's sonnets, punningly titled Astrophel and Stella, 1591; she of Waller's poems, Lady Dorothy Sidney; Swift's friend, Esther Johnson. (Harvey.)

STEPHANA, STEPHANIE. The *f.* of *Stephen*. *Stephanie*, which is the later, was probably influenced by the Fr. forms of the name. *Stephana* is obsolescent.

STEPHEN. Gr. Στέφανος, the first Stephanos (cf. Ger. *Stephan*; Fr. *Stéphan*, much more frequently *Etienne*) was probably 'so called by an exulting family whose father had returned with the parsley as crown [στεφάνη, stephanë] upon his brow. For Stephanos was an old Greek name . . . before it came to that Hellenist deacon who first of all achieved the greatest of all the [Christian] victories, and won the crown,' Yonge. Its use in England dates from ca. 1100: a use accelerated by its prevalence among kings, especially Stephen of England (1105–54) and Stephen the First of Hungary (977–1038), who, for his defeat of the pagan nobles and his admirable Kingship, was canonized. Moreover, there are sixteen other Saints, for the 'Hellenist deacon' was naturally one, being known to religious fame as 'the First Christian Martyr' (Benedictines). The usual diminutive is *Steve*, but *Steevie* does survive.

STEVE. The diminutive – perhaps via the next, with which cf. the Dutch *Steven* – of the preceding.

STEVEN. This very English form of *Stephen* is borne, e.g., by the 'fatherless bairn' in Francis Brett Young's novel, *Portrait of Clare*, 1927.

SUE is the pet-form of *Susan* and *Susanna(h)*. Cf.:

SUKEY. An English contraction, now considered non-aristocratic, of *Susanna(h)*. Cf.:

SUSAN. The English shortening of *Susanna*, but in C20 much more frequently bestowed as an independent name.

SUSANNA (properly, the German form); SUSANNAH. In Heb., it is 'graceful white lily': a combination of *shush*, 'a white lily,' and *hannah*, 'grace' – cf. *Hannah*. 'Shushan, the royal city of Assyria, the city among lilies, has thus acquired its name. As a woman's name it is very ancient, and long before the city existed there were Assyrian princesses who bore it,' Swan. The *History of Susannah* is an apocryphal book of the Old Testament; Victor Hugo has an arrestingly beautiful Susannah. Moreover, there were, in C2–4, three Saints Susanna, all martyrs; two virgins.

SUSIE. The diminutive of *Susan* and *Susanna(h)*. Cf. the 1914–1918 War-time 'Sister Susie's sewing shirts for soldiers'.

SUZANNE, the Fr. shape of *Susanna*, occurs now and then in Britain; especially since ca. 1910, in honour of that great French lawn-tennis player, Suzanne Lenglen.

SWAIN or SWAYN, *m*. '*Svinn*, which is wise in the northern tongues, is in those of central Europe, strong. . . . Whether this be the root or not, Svein is in the north a strong youth . . . but [as] Svend becoming a favourite name of the kings of Denmark, belonging to him whom Etheldred's treachery brought down on England, where it was called Swayn' (Yonge). It is very common in Norse: witness E. H. Lind's admirably painstaking *Norsk-Isländska Dopnamn*, 1905–31.

SYBIL. See *Sibyl.*

SYDNEY. See *Sidney.*

SYLVAN. See *Silvan.*

SYLVANUS; SILVANUS, which is, when any L. allusion is intended, or association implied, the correct spelling; otherwise, *Sylvanus* is usual. It was adopted in England when, in C16, the Latin classics became widely read. Silvanus, a divinity of the fields and forests, is also the protector of field-boundaries. 'In connexion with woods (*sylvestris deus*), he especially presided over plantations, and delighted in trees growing wild' (Blakeney). 'Sylvanus Urban' was Edward Cave, who (1691–1754) founded *The Gentleman's Magazine*, over which, thus urbanely, he efficiently watched from 1731 till his death. Cf.:

SYLVESTER. Like the preceding and like the obsolete *Sylvius*, it is a *m.* equivalent of *Sylvia.* See also *Silvester.*

SYLVIA, SILVIA. 'Who is Sylvia, what is she?' as the song goes in *The Two Gentlemen of Verona*. Apparently, one who lives in a wood (L. *silva*): not necessarily a dryad, but equally delightful and more accessible. A frequent name for a shepherdess in pastoral romance, *Sylvia* 'turned into a poetical name for a country maid, and has since been used as a village Christian name', says Charlotte Yonge in the early eighties; in this our century, it has become almost aristocratic. A Sylvia should, whatever her age, be charming, and in her youth, a compendium of youth's charms.

T

TABITHA. In C20, it is regarded as very 'Victorian,' this, one of the names of the widow of Joppa. It derives either from Aramaic ('a gazelle') or from Syriac ('clear-sighted'), as Yonge has mentioned.

TAD. An American diminutive of *Thady* (or *Thaddeus*) and, only among Irish-Americans, of:

TADHGH. Celtic for 'poet', this Irish *m.* has, except among the cultured, 'degenerated into Teague, Teige, or Thady, and then has been translated into Timothy, Thaddeus, Theodore, Theodosius, according to the fancy of the owner, though Tim is perhaps the most usual' (Yonge).

TAFFY. A Welsh diminutive of *David* and hence, among non-Welshmen, a nickname for any Welsh man or woman: see *David* for the full significance of such a nickname.

TAFLINE. The Welsh *f.* of *David*; cf. the preceding.

TALBOT. See Note at end of the Introduction.

TAM, TAMMIE. A Scottish diminutive of *Thomas*. Cf. *Tom.*

TAMSIN, TAMZINE. This is a feminine form – via *Thomasina* – of *Thomas* and rare except in Devon and, especially, Cornwall. (F. Tennyson Jesse, *Many Latitudes*, 1928.) Also, intermediately, *Tamasine.*

TANCRED; occasionally **TANKRED.** 'In the *Nibelungenlied* the father of Chriemhilt . . . was "hight Dankrat". . . . The first syllable of the name is the same as our word *thank* . . . [He] was thus Thank-rade, or grateful speech, and from him the Northmen seem to have taken their Thakraad, which in Normandy became Tancred, the knight of Hauteville, whose twelve gallant sons chased the Saracens from Apulia, and were the founders of the only brave dynasty that ever ruled in the enervating realms of the Two Sicilies' (Yonge). It has always been emblematic of chivalry; for instance, Disraeli, to his Zionistic novel *Tancred*, published in 1847, appended the sub-title, The New Crusade. Weekley, however, says that, lit., the name means 'thought-strong'; Withycombe, 'think counsel' (hence 'thoughtful counsellor'?).

TATE. In Scandinavia, its phonetic equivalent is *m.*, in O.E. the word appears only as *f.*; but when, as seldom, it is used in modern English, it is *m.* In Teutonic it signifies 'cheerful'.

TEAGUE, *m.* As an Irish 'Christian', it is a degeneration from *Tadhgh*, q.v. But in C17–18 it occupied the position that, in C19–20, has fallen to *Paddy*: that of a, indeed the most general, nickname for an Irishman. In the very odd *Dictionary of the Canting Crew*, by one B. E., Gent., published in 1698, we find these two entries: '*Teague-land*, Ireland' and '*Teague-landers*, Irishmen'.

TED, TEDDY. Transformations of *Edward*; the latter, also a diminutive of *Theodore*. Cf. *Ned*.

TEENA. See *Tina*.

TEENIE or TEENY. A diminutive of *Christina*.

TEIGE. See *Tadhgh*.

TERENCE. The Englishing of L. *Terentius*, the name of a celebrated writer of comedy and of the Terentian Clan (*gens Terentia*): from *terenus*, 'soft' or 'tender,' says Charlotte Yonge; but is there such a word? Probably the adjective in *gens Terentia* derives from *teres*, 'smooth,' with which cf. Gr. τέρην (terēn: 'tender'), which has, by metathesis, led to L. *tener*, 'tender'. Common only among the Irish, it was adopted by them as a supposed rendering of *Turlough* (see *Turlozgh*).

TERESA. Described by Helena Swan as 'the Italian and Spanish form of Theresa', it is now the usual form of a *f.* which, in its Gr. original, indicates 'a reaper' (lit. 'carrying ears of corn') and connotes the bad old days when, as still on the Continent, women worked in the fields. (Withycombe dislikes this etymology and tentatively proposes that *Theresa* derives from one or other of the two Mediterranean islands named *Thérasia*; Weekley, however, leans towards my opinion by saying, 'Probably from Gr. *theros*, summer, harvest'.) The name leapt into popularity simultaneously with the spreading of the fame of St Teresa, who reformed the Carmelite Order, wrote significantly on the nature, procedure and value of mystical prayer, founded over thirty convents, died in 1582, and left an autobiography 'written with charming candour, and, from the literary point of view, a Spanish classic' (Benedictines). Also see *Tess*.

TERRY. A diminutive of both *Terence* and *Teresa* (*Theresa*).

TESS; TESSA; TESSIE. Diminutives of *Teresa*.

TEWDUR, TEWDWR. The Welsh spelling of *Tudor*, q.v.

THADDEUS; formerly, often THADDAEUS. This *m.* 'Christian' may be a Latinized version of *Judah* (or *Jude*), 'but though Ireland swarms with Thadys, who write themselves Thaddeus, this is only as a supposed English version of their ancient Erse, Tadhgh (a poet),' as Charlotte Yonge so sweetly remarks. But Weekley, concerning *Thaddaeus*, says: 'Greek form of Theudas (? = praise)'.

THADY. The usual variant of the preceding.

THECLA, THEKLA. In Gr., 'divine fame,' hence 'glory of God'. It is strange that the name has not become more general in England, for it is that of 'one of the most celebrated of the Saints of the early Church. . . . She was converted . . . by St Paul . . . and she afterwards attached herself to the service of the Apostle, attending him on several of his missionary journeys' (Benedictines); 'said to have . . . followed him about everywhere dressed as a boy,' adds Dawson. Did Paul insist on this to prevent slander? And, in any event, how did these young women 'get away with it', for the difficulties in the way of impersonation—see, e.g., my *Dictionary of Slang and Unconventional English* at *cunny-thumbed* – are very considerable?

THEO. A diminutive of all the names in *Theo-*.

THEOBALD. In C19–20, mainly a surname, *Theobald*; in Teutonic it signifies 'folk-bold'. In 1247 there died a French nobleman turned Cistercian monk of whom Alban Butler, in his *Lives of the Saints* (published in C18), nobly wrote that 'he lived in the midst of his brethren as the servant of every one, and surpassed all others in his love of poverty, silence and holy prayer'.

THEODORA. A *f.*, now – except among the old-fashioned – deemed too dignified, of :

THEODORE. Gr. *Theodoros*, L. *Theodorus*, Portuguese *Theodoro*, Fr. *Théodore*, Ger. *Theodor*, it means 'God's gift'; in *Dorothea(-y)*, the order is reversed to 'gift of God'. (Cf. the uncompounded *Dora*.) There were numerous saints to spread its use and popularity in Europe; in fact, twenty-eight of them, 'the favourite of the west being he of Heraclea, a young soldier, who [in 318] burnt the temple of Cybele, and was martyred in consequence. The Venetians brought home his legend, and made him their champion and one of their patron saints' (Yonge).

THEODORIC; often contracted to THEODRIC. In Teutonic, 'people's ruler' (Old Ger. *Thiudoricus* – cf. O.E. *Theo-*

dric); therefore not to be confused with the 'gift' names in *Theo-*. Once it was a notability among 'Christians', but its very sonority has led to its present decrepitude.

THEODOSIA. Like *Theodora*, 'divine gift,' it is, though less directly, a *f.* of *Theodore*, q.v., its immediate counterpart being the obsolete *Theodosius*, 'divinely given'. It came to England largely because of the fame attached to the various Saints Theodosia.

THEOPHILUS. The dedicatee of the Gospel of St Luke – *Θεόφιλος* (Theophilos) – must have been thus named ('beloved of God') before his conversion to Christianity; but it soon became a favourite with Christians – though more so in England than on the Continent, despite the many saints proud to be so called. It is now rarely bestowed except traditionally or among the learned: for the sake of one's son – a boy among boys – it should be avoided unless pugilistic ability is fairly predictable.

THERESA. This is the more traditional, but in late C19–20 less usual, English form of the name that is now generally written *Teresa* (q.v.), than which it sounds much less euphonious.

THIRZAH, TIRZAH, *f.* Heb., 'pleasantness'. Gessner's *Death of Abel* (a 'narrative idyl', as Laurie Magnus describes it) was, in translation (late C18), very popular 'among the lower classes in England, whence Thyrza has become rather a favourite in English cottages', Yonge. *Thyrza* may sometimes be used for *Theresa*, as Weekley has noted.

THOMAS. (See also towards the end of the notice on *William*.) Its popularity may be attributed to the prevalence, of *Thomas* among the saints; that prevalence, to the fame of the Apostle 'whom we know by the Aramaic and Greek epithets Thomas and Didymus, both meaning a twin. Tradition declares that his fellow-twin was a sister called Lysia'

(Yonge). 'An ancient Syriac work, the *Acta Thomae*, describes him as having laboured as a missionary in India and having suffered martyrdom there. The shrine . . . commemorating his death still stands near Madras. The ancient churches of Southern India are often known as "Christians of St Thomas" ' (Harvey).

THOMASINA (or -SSINA); THOMAS(S)INE. The *f.* of the preceding. Cf. *Tamsin*, q.v.

THORALD. See *Thorold.*

THORBURN. (Cf. the next two names.) Like Thurlow, it is now more general as a surname than as a baptismal name. Teutonic, 'Thor's bear,' its direct antecedent is the Norse *Thorbjorn.* (Swan.)

THOROLD is a Norwegian *m.* name (*Thorald*) naturalized, though never popular, in England. In Teutonic, it connotes 'Thor's rule or power': 'like the Danish Thorwaldsen, and the German Thorwald, [it] is the direct descendant of the Norse Thorvalldr' (Swan). Its most distinguished English representative is Thorold Rogers (in full, James Edward Thorold Rogers), who, the first under the Act of 1870, relinquished holy orders and wrote the valuable *History of Agriculture* and *Six Centuries of Work and Wages*; he died in 1890.

THURLOW. Etymologically comparable with *Thorold*, for in Teutonic it means 'Thor's sport'. Now mainly a surname, it probably derives, immediately, from the Norse *Thorleik.* Cf. *Thorburn.*

THYRZA. See *Thirzah.*

TIBAL, TIBBLE. Pleasant English derivatives of *Theobald*, generally pronounced *Tibbald.*

TIBBIE. A Scottish pet-name for *Isabel.*

TIBBLE. See *Tibal.*

TIERNAN. From Celtic, it means 'kingly' (*tighearn*, a king), and because several Irish princes were thus named, so were many of their subjects. Those princes adopted it in honour of Bishop (later Saint) Tigernach or Tigernake, who, losing his sight, strove for celestial vision, to which he may have attained ca. 550.

TIERNAY, TIERNEY. A variant of the preceding.

TILDA, TILLY. The former is a shortening of *Matilda* and the second an endearing of *Tilda.*

TIM. The diminutive of the next. (See also at *Tadhgh.*)

TIMOTHY. Gr. *Timotheos*, L. *Timotheus*, Fr. *Timothée*, means, lit., 'honour God,' (hence, 'honouring God'); and like other providential pre-Christian names (e.g. *Theophilus*) it was welcomed by the Church, especially when Timotheos, 'the beloved disciple of the Apostle St Paul, who ordained him Bishop of Ephesus in Asia Minor and addressed to him two of the New Testament Epistles,' was, ca. 97, stoned to death by 'the infuriated worshippers of the great idol, "Diana of the Ephesians" ' (Benedictines). See also *Tadhgh.*

TINA. A diminutive of *Albertina*, *Christina*, *Ernestine* and *Justina.* Variant: *Teena.*

TIRCONNEL, *m.* The *connel* is presumably identical with *Connel*, *Con(n)al*, q.v.; it is tempting to equate the *Tir* with *Thor* – cf. *Tyrrell*, O.E. *Thurweald* – but a mongrel compound of Teutonic and Celtic is somewhat rare. It is a Celtic name: and *Tirconaill* is the original of *Donegal.* 'Lord of the hand'?

TIRZAH. See *Thirzah.*

TITUS. Either from L. *tutus*, 'safe' or, more probably, from Gr. τίω (tiō: 'I honour'). 'It was one of the most common praenomina from the earliest times, and belonged to both father and son of the two emperors connected with the fall of Jerusalem,' Yonge. It is becoming rare.

TOBIAS. Heb., 'God is good'. The apocryphal Book of Tobit is, when one examines it, no more – but also, no less – than an historical romance dealing with the Jewish captivity; the atmosphere of the marvellous investing Tobit and his son Tobias contributed to the accretion of awed respect for the name *Tobias*; scenes from this Book appear frequently in medieval art. (Yonge.)

TOBIT. Heb., 'son of Tobias,' perhaps via *Tobides*. But, as an English name, it is simply a variant of *Tobias*. The confusion or the variation of the names – for which, see preceding notice – occurred in the Gr. version.

TOBY. An Anglicization of *Tobias*. In Ireland 'it has enjoyed the honour, together with Thaddeus and Timothy, of figuring as an equivalent for [Erse] Tadhgh, a poet,' Yonge.

TOM. The usual, more adult pet-form of *Thomas*. Its transferred uses, like those of *Jack*, are numerous. 'In the 16th century we find Tom [as a nickname for a man-servant] . . . and *Tom* and *Tib* (i.e. *Isabel*) were rival personifications of *Jack* and *Jill*. *Tomboy* was an unruly boy before becoming a boisterous girl, and the wandering lunatic was *Tom o' Bedlam*,' Weekley, *W. & N.* For slang and colloquial senses, see my *Slang*.

TOMMY. A further endearing of *Thomas*; immediately, a diminutive of *Tom*. Its chief transferred sense is that of an English private soldier: cf. *Sammy*, an American one (1914–1918). See also *George*, near end.

TONY. The pet-form of *Antony*, q.v.

TOOLE. This very Irish *m.* 'Christian' was originally *Tuathal*, which may, in the Celtic, be rendered 'lordly' or 'majestic'. One seems to have heard of 'the great O'Toole'.

TOTTIE. See entry at *Bunty*.

TRACE. A diminutive of:

TRACY. An English re-shaping (how thorough we are, linguistically!) of *Theresa*, q.v. 'In rural districts, and in Wales, [it] is still [in 1905] given as a girl's name, but is far more common now as a surname,' Swan; as *m.*, for it is occasionally *m.*, it is, I suggest, a corruption of *Terence*: for does not *Terry* abridge both *Terence* and *T(h)eresa*?

TREFOR. The Welsh form and original of *Trevor*.

TREV. The diminutive of:

TREVOR. A 'Christianizing' of the surname, which is of obscure origin and distinguished tenancy.

TRICKSIE or -Y. See *Trix*.

TRIFFIE, TRIFFY. A diminutive of *Tryphaena*.

TRISSIE or TRISSY. See *Beatie*.

TRISTRAM. 'A herald' from Celtic, says Charlotte Yonge, equating it to *Trwst* (q.v.); she continues, 'The influence of Latin upon Welsh, however, made *trist* really mean sad [L. *tristis*, Fr. *triste*] . . . ; and Tristram, or sad face, became identified with the notion of sorrow.' Helena Swan subscribes to this transition in the meaning of *Trist-*, yet (and, mark you, she was no fool) she has defined the O.E. *Thurstan* (of which Searle gives sixteen authentic examples) as 'Thor's stone' (or 'jewel') and derived it from the Norse *Thorstein*: it is this 'Thor' etymology which Professor Weekley supports.

Cf. therefore *Thorold*, *Thorburn*, and *Thurlow*. Though now rare in English – it is fairly vigorous in Fr. as *Tristan* – it still conveys something of the glamour attaching to that pre-Arthurian, and Arthurian, hero of romance who is a central figure in Malory's *Morte d'Arthur*, in Matthew Arnold's *Tristram and Iseult*, and in Swinburne's *Tristram of Lyonnesse*. *Tristram* is intimately connected with Cornwall: the tomb of the legendary hero can be seen near Lostwithiel; it bears his name in the form *Drustagni*.

TRIX, TRIXY. Occasionally spelt *Tricks*, *Tricksie*. See *Beatie*.

TRUDA, TRUDE, strictly pet-forms of *Gertrude*, are occasionally bestowed as an independent name.

TRUTH or TROTH. *f.* 'Not very often used' (Swan), it is to be related to such abstract virtue names as *Alethea* (likewise 'truth'), *Charity*, *Faith*, *Hope*, *Mercy*.

TRWST. A Celtic name (*m*)., it derives from a word meaning 'a proclaimer'; it became mixed up with L. *tristis* ('sad') and is now seldom heard. See also *Tristram*.

TRYPHAENA, now generally TRYPHENA. Gr., 'delicious (female),' 'dainty (girl)'. Strangely, this at first not very puritanical name was given English currency by the Puritans, impressed perhaps by the worth of St Tryphen(n)a.

TUDOR. A mere transcription of the correct Welsh form of *Theodore* (q.v. for etymology). 'The ancient Britons must have known and used this name [*Theodorus*]; for among their host of obscure saints of princely birth appears Tewdwr; and the Welsh made so much use of this form that when the handsome Owen ap Tewdwr won the heart of the widow of Harry of Monmouth, Tudor was an acknowledged surname, and in two generations more it became a royal one,' Yonge. Mostly a Welsh 'Christian'.

Turlozgh. (Pronounced *Turlough.*) This Irish *m.* font-name is now somewhat rare. The Irish *Toirdhealbhac* means 'tower-like': a tower of strength and, one hopes, a very present help. (Withycombe.) See also at end of *Terence.*

U

UCHTRED. In Teutonic, it signifies 'mind-council' or '-counsel': with the *Ucht-*, cf. the *Hu-* of *Hugh* and *Hubert*; but Weekley (*Jack and Jill*) thinks the first element to represent O.E. *uht*, 'spirit, sprite' (cf., therefore, *Alfred*); with the *-red*, cf. almost any name with that ending. It is confined, for by far the most part, to the family of Shuttleworth. See also *Hugh* (and *Hugo*) and *Hubert*.

ULICK. This mainly Irish name comes from the Danish, where it signifies 'mind-reward': does this connote peace of mind, content, inner happiness, or merely a monetary compensation for the toils and figments of one's brain?

ULRIC or ULRICK, the latter being much the more usual, though neither is, in C20, common. This is a Norman spelling of O.E. *Wulfric*, 'wolf-rule' (Withycombe).

ULRICA. A *f.* derivative, Latin-fashion and, in fact, originally Roman, of the preceding, than which, in C20 at least, it is rather more frequent.

ULRICK. See *Ulric*.

ULYSSES. Rare except in Ireland, where it has, in C20, become considerably less general than in C19, when it was used less in a direct descent from the crafty Greek adventurer (lit., 'the hater' – though *he* was not a particularly good hater), than as a Classical manipulation of *Ulick*. Whether, among 'highbrows', the use of the name by James Joyce in his slow-motion, rather desperately and sombrely brilliant masterpiece, has caused many little precocities to be thus christened, it is perhaps a little too early to say.

UNA. Originally Irish (*Oonagh*), it may, as Celtic, mean 'famine'; it may even mean 'born in famine' (Swan): but, as

Charlotte Yonge remarked nearly a century ago, this seems doubtful. Spenser was probably right, etymologically as well as semantically, when, in *The Faerie Queene*, he made Una represent the *one* undivided Church, or the one truth (in contrast to Duessa or falsehood), for L. *unus*, f. *una*, one, corresponds to Old Irish *óen*, and the *w*- pronunciation, originally dialectal, became general only ca. 1700 (Weekley).

URBAN. L., 'of the town'. Its use as a 'Christian' (now seldom heard) is the natural result of its prevalence in the early and medieval Church, which numbers ten full saints, and two saints beatified but not yet canonized: of these twelve, three were Popes and at least two were famous bishops; moreover, five other Urbans have been Popes. (Benedictines.)

URIAH. Now rare and never very common, *Uriah* – from the name of the unfortunate Hittite for whose wife David had an all-consuming infatuation – is remembered chiefly for Uriah Heep, that subsidiary character in Dickens's *David Copperfield* who is now symbolic of hypocritical sanctimoniousness and humility. In Heb., 'the Lord is (my) light'.

URSE. An occasional diminutive of *Ursula*, as also is *Ursie* (q.v. at *Ursy*).

URSLEY. A typical English re-shaping, now seldom heard of:

URSULA. In the L., 'little bear,' from *ursa* (cf. *Ursa Major*), a she-bear. The name sprang into popularity as a result of the merging of the old myth of the little bear and the stars with the legend of Ursula, that Breton maiden who, on the way to marry a British husband, was wrecked on the German coast and slain by the terrible Alaric in company with her virgin companions. (Yonge.)

URSY, URSIE. The diminutive of the preceding. See also *Nullie* and cf. *Urse*.

UZZIAH. Now rare, it derives from Heb., 'might of the Lord'. Uzziah (or Azariah) was the Jewish king who, in C8 B.C., was visited with leprosy for having tried to burn incense on the altar: which makes one think of Gilbert's 'making the punishment fit the crime'.

V

Val. A diminutive of the next four names.

VALENTINE. From L. *Valentinus*, a diminutive from *valens*, 'strong': for the etymology, cf. *Valerius*. 'Valentinus,' says Charlotte Yonge, 'was a Roman priest, who is said to have endeavoured to give a Christian signification to the old [pagan] custom of drawing lots in favour of Juno Februata, and thus fixed his own name and festival' – 'Benedictines' categorically denies this – 'to the curious fashion prevailing all over England' (but now general only in rural districts) 'of either the choice of a "true Valentine", or of receiving as such the first person of the opposite sex encountered in that morning' (February the 14th). It is now also a surname.

VALERIAN, *m.* The Anglicization of L. *Valerianus*, the adjective corresponding to *Valerius*, q.v. Although euphonious, it is, I fear, doomed as an English name.

VALERIE. Adopted from the Fr. (*Valérie*), itself from L. *Valeria*, in which form the name does not appear in England – despite the undeniable charm of Shakespeare's Valeria in *Coriolanus* and despite three Saints Valeria. It is the *f.* of:

VALERIUS. L., 'healthy'. It derives from *valēre*, to be strong, to be (so much) worth, and *valor*, value and courage. It is falling into disuse. Cf. the preceding trio of names.

VAN. The usual diminutive of the next two names.

VANESSA is not recorded by 'Swan'; and 'Yonge' barely touches on it. As Swift's name (see especially his journal and letters) for Esther Vanhomrigh, it is obviously a Latinization of *Van-* + *Esther*; Swift – again obviously – knew something of Heb. and therefore presumably knew that the It. *m. Vanni* was, in Heb., 'grace of God': the Dean, who was passionately attached to this lady, may even have known that the Dutch *Vanjuscha* has the same derivation (see too *John*); I question Charlotte Yonge's 'the generic title of our finest English butterflies, Vanessa'. The name, never general, was, in a mild way, popularized by Hugh Walpole as the title of the fourth and last volume (1934) of the Herries chronicle.

VANORA. Celtic, 'white wave'. It is the Scottish equivalent to *Guinevere*; like *Guinevere*, however, it is becoming rather rare.

VASHTI. This *f.* name (diminutive: *Vassy*) is mostly Cornish and it derives from the Persian for 'star': cf., therefore, *Esther* (p. 109).

VENETIA. In Celtic, 'blessed'; or, as a variant of *Beatrix*, more probably 'joy-giver'. One suspects that *Venetia*, as a L. locality-name, may have been slightly operative; also (*Jack and Jill*) that, like C17 *Venice*, it sometimes euphemizes *Venus*. Now rather rare, after having been fairly common, among the upper classes, in late C18–19. *Venetia*, a novel by Benjamin Disraeli, appeared in 1837.

VERA. In Serbia, this *f.* 'Christian' derives from a Slavonic word signifying 'faith', but in England it usually derives from the L., '(a) true (woman)'.

VERE, *m.* An aristocratic name, probably direct from the *de Vere's*: cf. 'Vere de Vere'. As a surname, *Vere*, originally Fr., may derive, not from L. *verus* but from Fr. *vair* (cf. the aristocratic *Grey*); more probably from a French place-name: *Ver*. Charles Montague, Lord Halifax, wrote in 1703, as a toast to the Duchess of St Albans:

> The line of Vere, so long renown'd in arms,
> Concludes with lustre in St Alban's charms.
> Her conq'ring eyes have made their race complete.
> They rose in valour and in beauty set.

VERENA. A rather uncommon *f.* name (as in Robert Hichens's subtle novel, *The Paradine Case*) not suggested by *verbena* and *Veronica*, but adopted from the Ger. and meaning 'true picture'.

VERNON is a happy name, for it signifies 'flourishing'. From a L. word meaning 'to be strong', it is cognate with *vernal*, spring-like.

VERONICA. Originally a mongrel word from L. *verus*, 'true,' 'real,' and Gr. *εἰκών* (eikōn), 'an image,' which were 'jumbled together by the popular tongue in the name of a crucifix at Lucca [in Italy], which was called the *Veraiconica*', soon shortened to *Veronica*, 'and was that Holy Face of Lucca by which William Rufus . . . was wont to swear,' Yonge. Somewhere about the year 1300 there arose a legendary patron saint so named; moreover, Veronica of Binasco, canonized in C18, was 'an Augustinian nun at Milan who lived a life of wonderful penance and high prayer, passing away in universal repute of sanctity . . . [in] 1497,' Benedictines. In *Jack and Jill*, however, Weekley writes, that it 'is more probably a distortion of Berenice, a Macedonian form of Gr. Pherenike, bringer of victory, the Bernice of Acts xxv'.

VERRA. A variant of *Vera*.

VESTA, *f.* L., 'a hearth'; *Vesta*, goddess of the hearth.

VI. The diminutive of *Viola* and *Violet*.

VIC, VICKY. Diminutives of the next two names, *Vic* being the more general for the former, *Vicky* for the latter.

VICTOR. L. 'victorious', 'the conqueror' (cf. *Vincent*, q.v.), from *vincere*, to defeat; Cicero speaks of *victor omnium gentium*, a world-conqueror, and the term was applied as an epithet to Jupiter and Hercules. This splendid name, which has appealed as much to the religious as to the worldly, was rarely bestowed outside of Italy until the French Revolution, when Victor became fashionable in France (Victor Hugo, the greatest French lyrist, was born in 1802); thence it passed to England. It has been hopefully attached to three Italian kings (Victor Emmanuel), three Italian dukes (Victor Amadeus, likewise 'serving two gods'), three popes and two antipopes, three canonized bishops, thirty-five saints in all (Benedictines), and others, less famous perhaps but hardly less deserving; among these latter is a Roman historian (C4 A.D.). As a name, it goes from strength to strength, by warlike to peaceable victory. But if the schools speak of a *victor ludorum* (perhaps on the analogy of *victor bellorum*), why do they not have also a *victor studiorum*?

VICTORIA. Popularized in the British Empire by the accession of a queen so youthful that she captured the hearts, as well as the imagination of an outwardly stolid, inwardly sentimental nation. The earliest Victoria was the Roman goddess of victory (for etymology, see *Victor*), but the first historical Victoria was a Roman virgin stabbed to death in 250 for refusing to accept either a heathen husband or a heathen idol (Benedictines).

VICTORINE. Originally and mainly a Fr. diminutive of the preceding.

VIDA. A Welsh *f.* of *David*, as also is *Tafline* (q.v.). In some instances, the name may represent Sp. *vida* (cf. It. *vita*, itself direct from L. *vita*), 'life'.

VIN; VINCE; VINNY. Diminutives of *Vincent*. Cf. *Fran* and *France*. *Vinny* (or *Viney*) also pet-forms *Lavinia*.

VINCENT. L. *vincens*, 'conquering': cf., therefore, *Victor*. *Vincentius* adorned three 'martyrs of the tenth persecution' (under Diocletian in 303–4), and several other early martyrs as well; as it did St Vincent of Lerins, the C5 author of the

Commonitorium – the great Dominican scholar of Beauvais (C13) – the even greater C14–15 Dominican preacher, Vincent Ferrer – and St Vincent de Paul (1576–1660), a noted divine and a splendid, practical social worker. (Yonge; Benedictines.)

VINEY, VINNY. See *Vin.*

VIOLA. Originally, as still mainly, the It. form of *Violet*, from L. *viola*, the violet. It is, however, possible that, at first, in the form of *Violante*, it was a corruption of a L. proper name, e.g. *Valentinus* (Yonge). It is much less general than, and rather superior socially to:

VIOLET. The It. *viola* (see *Viola*) has diminutive *violetta*, which became *violete* in Old Fr., the Mod. Fr. being *violette*. Into Scotland, which has always been fond of this name (now somewhat degraded socially in England, though a few aristocrats still bear it), it entered, ca. 1570, in its present shape: 'the Scottish love of floral names took hold of it' (Yonge).

VIRGIE, VIRGY. A diminutive, generally for *Virginia*, rarely for:

VIRGIL. In L., the original is frequently spelt *Vergilius*, but that fact need not obscure the radical, which is present in *virēre*, to flourish, and *virga*, a green bough, as well as in *ver*, the Spring. Though rare in late C19–20, *Virgil* was not infrequent in C16–mid 19, when the fame of that other 'poets' poet', Publius Vergilius Maro (70–19 B.C.), meant rather more to Englishmen than it does now; in U.S.A., less rare.

VIRGINIA. A name that, like its non-adopted *m.* counterpart (*Virginius*), was at first spelt *Ver-*; like *Virgil* (q.v.), it relates to Spring and all fair growing things. Only incurably romantic and obstinate people persist in deriving *Virginia* from L. *virgo*, a virgin: that Raleigh named the American colony in honour of the Virgin Queen does not prove that he was unaware of the Classical *Virginia*.

VIRGY. See *Virgie*.

VIV. The usual diminutive of the next four names.

VIVIAN, rarely *f.* From L. *Vivianus*, and *Viviana*, from *vivus*, 'alive' – akin to *vita*, 'life', via *Vivia Perpetua*, the noble young matron and martyr (203) canonized as St Perpetua. For the etymology, cf. both *Virgil* and *Virginia*.

VIVIEN; mostly *f.* This was originally a French form of *Vivian*, of which the *f.* is *Vivienne*. She notably occurs in Tennyson's *Merlin and Vivien*, 1859, but as an unscrupulous wench and 'designing hussy'; there, however, 'the name probably originated in misreading of MS *Ninian*, a Celt name' (Withycombe).

VIVYAN. A mainly C19–20 variant of *Vivian*. Cf.:

VYVIAN, VYVYAN. Somewhat alembicated variations of the preceding.

W

WAL. An occasional diminutive of *Walter*. Cf. *Wally*.

WALBURGA, *f.* From A.-S. *Waldburga*, 'powerful protection' in olden Teutonic. Now very aristocratic and somewhat rare, this is the name (canonized as *Walburga*) of 'one of the English nun princesses in Germany', daughter of 'a Saxon prince in Wessex'. Dying, in 776, as Abbess of Heidenheim, she 'strangely became connected with the witches' sabbath' and 'patroness of the celebrated Valpurgisnacht' (see Goethe's *Faust*, Part I). Yonge; Benedictines.

WALDO, *m.* A Frankish name from Norse *vald*, 'power'. It is thus cognate with *Walter*. For the *-o*, cf. *Bruno* and *Rollo*.

WALLACE. See Note at end of Introduction.

WALLY. The usual pet-form of *Walter*, though before the present century the more general diminutive was *Wat* or:

WALT. Cf. *Wal*.

WALTER. This is the most notable of, the predominant among, the names (mostly *m.*) based on a Teutonic word denoting power or rule. In Frankish, it means 'ruling the folk'; it came to England via France, from Old German *Waldhar*, *har* being short for *harja*, 'folk'. Its first great representative was Waldheri, a young Aquitanian prince in the Chanson de Roland; it attained glorious sanctity, ca. 990, through a monk of the dukedom of Aquitaine, and as he was followed by two other Saints so named, he and they caused it to be spread far and wide; it was common in both Normandy and England at the time of the Conquest. Its Ger. form is *Waltier* or *Gualtier*; its Fr., *Gautier*. (Yonge; Swan: Weekley; Withycombe.)

WANDA, *f.* Is this a corruption, via a presumed *Wander*, of the next? More probably from Teutonic: 'shepherdess'. Still more probably (Withycombe) from Old Ger. *vand*, 'stem, stock'.

WANDERS, *f.* Scottish from Celtic, in which language it means 'white wave', hence perhaps 'wave-crest'. See also *Winifred*.

WARNER. In the Teutonic, it is 'protect-army', hence 'protecting warrior': cf. Ger. *Warno* and *Werner*. The *-er* is cognate with A.-S. *here*, an army, especially an invading army, and therefore of the same radical as (*to*) *harry*. Withycombe, however, states the origin to reside in Old Ger. *Warinhari*: folk-name *Warin* or *Varin* + *harja*, 'folk'. It is now more general as a surname than as a font-name.

WARREN. Teutonic, lit. 'a protecting friend'. Its first element is that of *Warner*; a defender is, in A.-S., *weard* (ward). Yonge notes that the whole name *Warren* may come direct from Ger. *Warand*, a participle name, 'unless there was a Warewine to account for it'. 'A shortening of one of the Old German names in *Warin*, protection' (Weekley). Like *Warner*, it is now mostly a surname.

WASHINGTON, properly a surname derived from an English place-name, has, ever since 1776 or so, been a fairly common American given name, in honour of George Washington (1732–99), American General, statesman and first President (1789–97) of the U.S.A., a very great man.

WAT. A diminutive, now rare, of *Walter*. Cf. *Wally* and *Walt*. Still more familiar is:

WATTIE, WATTY. A pet-form of *Walter*.

WEBSTER. See note at end of Introduction.

WENDA, WENDY. From the rare *Wendla*, which in Teutonic is 'wanderer': cf. the outworn *wend one's way*. The latter form (*Wendy*) was popularized by Barrie in 1904.

WENEFREDE, WENEFRIDE. Now rare for *Winifred*, of which it is the original.

WILF; WILFIE or WILFY. Diminutives – the latter is fatuous when not, lit., childish – of:

WILFRED, WILFRID, From the A.-S. *Wilfrith*, which, as in the parent Teutonic, means 'will-peace', i.e. 'resolute peace'. The first element (*wil*) is thus the same as in *William*, q.v. The 'earnest but turbulent Wilfrith, the Yorkshire bishop', who died in 709 and was canonized, 'hardly deserved to be' so named: though several times banished from England, 'he sacrificed himself utterly for the good of his flock.' Mainly from him came the now obsolete *Wilfroy*, especially frequent in registers of Yorkshire; operative, too, was Wilfrid the Younger, who was closely associated with Whitby, York, and Ripon – who died in 744 – and who is often confused, because he too was a bishop and has likewise been canonized, with his more famous predecessor. (Yonge; Benedictines.) *Wilfred* is the commoner form among Protestants, *Wilfrid* among Catholics.

WILHELMINA. A *f.* derivative from *William*: cf. the Ger. *Wilhelmine*. Cf. also:

WILHEMINA. A careless variant of *Wilhelmina*, or perhaps a fusion of the obsolete *Williamina* with *Wilhelmina*.

WILL. A pleasant diminutive – in late C19–20, more general among women than among men – of *William*.

WILLA is a girl's name, more general in the U.S.A. than in the British Isles. Cognate with *Wilhelmina*, q.v., it is of Teutonic origin and it means 'resolute'. Its diminutive is *Will.* (Loughead.)

WILLIAM. The *Will* part of the name represents the Teutonic for 'resolution' (cf. *Wilfred*, *Wilfrid*); *-iam*, Teutonic *helm* as 'helmet': therefore, the whole represents either 'a stout helmet' or 'helmet of resolution' (cf. 'garment of, robed in, righteousness'), and the name was originally Ger. – as, of course, it still is in the form *Wilhelm* – before it spread to all the other European countries. In England, whither it came from France, it is almost as popular now as ever it was, its most glorious period being from 1066 to ca. 1300; it graces a palace or a mansion as comfortably as it does a semi-detached house or a hovel. It is the second commonest of all 'Christians' in England, only *John* beating it, though *Thomas* must run it very close. (In slang, a 'William' is a *bill* of exchange.)

WILLIE, WILLY. Except in Scotland, it is now rather avoided by men as a diminutive of *William*; *Bill* has, since ca. 1880, been, among men, by far the most popular pet-name form, as in C20 it is among women of the middle and upper classes; *Willie* is now reserved mainly for children. During the war of 1914–18, *Big Willie* and *Little Willie* were, in the wake of a series of cartoons in *The Daily Mirror*, the British soldiers' names for the Kaiser and the Crown Prince.

WILLIS. Originally and, for the most part, still a surname. The *Will-* is probably that of *William*, and the name may represent *Will's* (son): cf. *Wilson*, q.v.

WILMER, *m.* Mostly American – in England it is a surname. Either from Ger. *Wilmar*, 'willing fame,' or, in Common Teutonic, 'willing warrior' (cf. *Warner*).

WILMETT, *f.* An occasional variant of *Wilmot*: q.v. for origin. See also *Mina*.

WILMOT. Both *f.* and, now mainly, *m.* As *f.*, it is a very English transformation of *Wilhelmina*; but, as *m.*, it is an Anglicizing of Ger. *Wilmod*, 'resolute mood,' i.e. 'unwavering courage'. In both instances, however, it may simply be 'little William', *-ot* being very common in M.E.

WILSON. A comparatively little used *m.* 'Christian', coming direct from the surname; that surname obviously simplifies *Will's son.*

WIN. The usual diminutive of the next two names.

WINFRED. Now seldom used for:

WINIFRED, WINIFRID. Earlier *Wenefrede*, *-fride*, it means, in Celtic 'white wave *or* stream', and is therefore a doublet of *Wanders* (q.v.). By many it is regarded as typically English but, in 1794, Mrs A. M. Bennett in her novel, *Ellen*, could, of a girl so named, write that it 'had such a welchy vulgar sound, she chose to be called Maria' (*O.E.D.*). It has some interesting forms: the Welsh *Gwenfrewi*, the English *Jennifer*, the Breton *Jenovefa*, the Fr. *Geneviève*, the Russian *Zenevieva* (Yonge). See also *Winnie.*

WINNE, *f.* A Celtic name of Celtic origin ('white'). Perhaps a contraction of the obsolete *Wenefride* influenced by the English 'shape' thereof. See also *Wyn.*

WINNIE or WINNY. A diminutive, disliked by most girls over ten years of age, of *Winifred*; very much to be preferred is *Win.* Among the Irish, however, *Winny* pet-forms *Una.*

WINSTON. See Note at end of Introduction.

WYN. An affected variant of *Win*; a natural but rare variant of *Winne.* Occasionally used as *m.*

X

XAVIER. This male name – from Arabic *ga'afar*, 'splendid' (cf. the Giafar of *The Arabian Nights*) – is obsolescent except among Catholics, who, in using it, commemorate St Francis Xavier, a noble Spaniard famed for his missions in the middle of the 16th Century to India, Ceylon, the East Indies, Japan and China. Xavier thus appears to have originally been, in Europe, a Spanish surname.

XENOPHON, *m.* There has never been a fashion in, nor much popularity for, Xenophon; but it isn't obsolete. Its most celebrated C20 tenant has been that South African cricketer who specialized in well-spun guile. The name comes from that of the Athenian general and historian of mid C5–early 4, B.C., and, lit., it seems to mean 'speaking a foreign language', from the Greek *xenophōnein*, 'to speak like a foreigner'.

XINA. An occasional diminutive of *Christina* (*-e*). Cf. *Chris* and *Chrissie*.

Y

YDA is a 'literary' variant of *Ida* and should not be encouraged.

YNYR, *f.* The Welsh form of *Honor*.

YSOBEL. See *Isabel*.

YSOLT, YSEULT; ISOLD, ISOLDA, ISOLDE; Anglicized as *Izod*. From the Fr. *Yseulte*, perhaps from *Adsalutta*, a Celtic goddess; apparently the word means 'spectacle'. Though rapidly growing rarer, *Ysolt* is still bestowed by the cultured on a baby girl for whom even a feckless 'highbrow' would wish a less tragic 'life-story' than that which befell Ysolt of the white hands, she who, in medieval romance and beautiful, haunting Swinburnian embroidery, is linked, in deathless story after despairing death, with *Tristram*.

YVETTE, YVONNE, *f.* Mostly Fr.; whence, occasionally, in English use. 'Of all Breton names Yves is the commonest. It is the Old French nominative of Yvain, identical with Evan and John. . . . From it are derived the female names Yvette and Yvonne' (*Jack and Jill*): *Yvette* from *Yves*, *Yvonne* from *Yvain*. These two names are occasionally bestowed upon girl twins.

Z

ZACHARIAH. In Heb., 'God has remembered'. *Zacharias*, a variant, is obsolete except among Jews and Puritans. One of its pet-forms is *Zach* or *Zack*.

ZACHARY. This is a typical English simplification of *Zachariah* and *Zacharias*; in C19–20, it has been more common than those two names, but it, too, is becoming rare. The only notable Englishman thus named or, rather, the only one with whom memory claims acquaintance at the moment–is the early C19 philanthropist, Zachary Macaulay, the wealthy merchant who, not content with fathering the eminent historian, opposed the slave-traffic.

ZACKY. A diminutive of *Zachariah* and *Zachary*, via *Zack*.

ZED. The diminutive of:

ZEDEKIAH, *m.* Now very rare except among the Jews and, less, among the rural labouring class, and they are much less fond of it than they were. Lit. (in Heb.), 'God is righteousness', it is the name of that king whom direfully prophetic Jeremiah saw led into captivity.

ZENOBIA. Now rare, and apt to excite derision, this was once a favourite 'literary' and fashionable name after that of 'the brilliant queen of Palmyra', who, after annexing Egypt, was defeated and captured by Aurelian in 272 A.D. Of Arabian birth, she probably bore, originally, 'the true Arabic name of Zeenab (ornament of the father),' Yonge.

ZERAH, *m.* Heb., 'rising of light'. From, or akin to, the name of the Biblical prophet Ezra. At one time used by Puritans, it is now, except among Jews, very, very rare.

ZILLA, ZILLAH. In Heb., 'shade, shadow,' *Zillah* (the

correct, more usual form) was the name of one of Biblical Lamech's two wives; in C19–20, it has been almost confined to Gypsy women. (Yonge.)

ZOE, *f.* There are two Saints so named; one a Roman lady cruelly done to death late in C3 (Benedictines). Its radical (*zōë*, 'life') is Greek and at the base of such words as *zoology*. As a proper name, it arose thus: – ' "The mother of all living" [Eve] received from the lips of Adam a name signifying life [or life-giving], sounding in the original like *Chavva*. . . . It was not copied by any of her daughters for a long time, and when first the Alexandrian Jews came on it in their translation, they rendered it by *Zoe* . . . , in order to show that connexion of the name with the prophecy,' Yonge.

ZONA; its pet-form being ZONE. An American *f.* name, apparently from the Gr. for 'a girdle'.

ZORA is known to Australians chiefly as adorning a passionate poetess of the present century. Arabic, 'dawn'.

ZOROASTER. Probably of Persian origin and traditionally meaning 'golden star'; his name and renown link him, semantically, with *Cyrus* (q.v.). The Zoroaster (Zarathushtra) who popularized the name, which is falling into disuse, was the founder, ca. 1000 B.C., of a great Persian religion that 'was at its best in the period of the Achaemenian Kings (558–330 B.C.). During the Mohammedan invasions,' which began in C7 (A.D.), 'Zoroastrianism was completely crushed. Many Zoroastrians fled to India, where they have continued as the Parsees.' The *ad hoc* of this is that 'Fire is held sacred by the Zoroastrians as being the source of all things', R. B. Ince, *A Dictionary of Religion*, 1936 (dated 1935).

SOME GIVEN NAMES EITHER OBSOLETE OR EXTREMELY OBSOLESCENT

SOME GIVEN NAMES[1] EITHER OBSOLETE OR EXTREMELY OBSOLESCENT

I. MASCULINE

Abacuck
Abdiel
Abimelech
Abishalom
Adelgar
Adelgard
Aelfric
Aella
Aethelbald
Aethelbright
Aethelred
Aethelric
Aethelwulf
Ahasuerus
Aidan
Alharic
Almroth
Alured
Alysander
Amyntas
Ananias
Angel
Armine (-myn)
Ascelin
Athalaric
Aurelian
Aylward
Aymar
Azariah

Baldred
Baldric
Balthazar
Banquo
Baptist
Bardolf, -ph
Barnabas
Barret(t)
Beavois
Bees
Benoni
Beorn
Berengar
Berenger
Bernal
Bertel
Bonte
Brockwell
Bruin

Cadfer
Cahir
Cain
Caligula
Calisto
Calixtus
Ceadwalla
Cenred
Charlet
Christmas
Clairmond
Clovis
Cnut
Colbrand
Columb
Constantine
Cutha
Cyriack

Dagobert
Dallas
Diccon
Donnet
Dorian
Drogo

Eadgar
Eadmund
Eadward
Edelmar
Eldred
Eldrid
Eliakim
Elkanah
Elle
Erastus
Ernold
Ernulf
Esdras
Ethelbald
Ethelweld
Ethelwine
Ethert

[1] For a much fuller list, see Yonge and, for A.-S. names, Searle. A few—e.g., *Dallas*, *Lovell*—survive as surnames.

Eudo
Eusebius

Fabricius
Faramond
Feargus
Fe(i)dlim
Florentinus
Florian
Florentius
Frewen
Frith
Fulk(e)

Galahad
Galfrid
Gamaliel
Garnet
Garnier
Garrath
German
Giffard
Gillet
Gisborne
Giselhar
Godric
Goldwin
Grimbald
Guelf
Gurth
Guthlac
Guthrum

Habbabuk
Hagtar
Halkin
Hamlet
Hananeel
Hanani
Hananiah
Harald
Hardiknut
Hardwig
Hardwin
Haymon
Helmut
Hengist
Hereward
Heriot
Herod
Herodias
Herodotus
Hierom
Hildebrand
Hob
Hodaiah
Hodge
Hosanna
Hutchin

Ichabod
Ilbert
Imbert
Ingelbrand
Isaiah
Isambart
Isombard
Issachar
Izod

Jaddua
Jaga
Japhet
Jared
Jareth
Jarrath
Jeconiah
Jehoiada
Jehoiachin
Jehoram
Jephthah
Jerram
Jeshua
Jethro
Joab
Jotham
Judah
Judas
Junius

Kenrick
Kenward
Kitto
Knut

Ladislas
Lamech
Landfranc
Laurentius
Leger
Leofric
Leofwin
Leonidas
Liebhard
Lovell
Lucifer
Lucretius
Lycidas

Maddis
Maginfred
Magnus
Malaleel
Maldred

Marioth
Martinus
Martius
Maryath
Mathaniah
Mauger
Mayne
Melchisedec, -sadek
Merewine
Methusalem
Murtagh

Naphthali
Nehemiah
Neot
Norval

Oberon
Offa
Ogier
Olaf
Olave
Oswy

Palafox
Pancras
Paulin
Peleg
Pentecost
Peredur
Pharamond
Philologus
Pilgrim
Polycarp
Polydore
Polydorus
Postumus
Prochorus

Radolf
Rainer
Ranulf
Rayner
Redwald
Reynard
Ricehard
Ronwen

Saebert
Saemuad
Saher
Sampol
Sayres
Scipio
Seabert
Seawald
Seaward
Sibbald
Sigismund
Sigurd
Siward
Sophron
Stigand

Tamlane
Tancard
Telemachus
Theodoric
Thias
Thurstan
Torquil
Tostain
Tostig
Traherne
Tunstan
Tunstell
Turcetyl
Tybal(t)
Tycho

Ulfac
Ulfilas
Ulfric
Ulphilas
Uric

Vercingetorix
Victorian
Vigheard
Viglaf
Virdumarus
Virginius
Vortigern
Vulfgar
Vulfherc
Vulfmar
Vulfnot
Vulfstan

Waldemar
Walan
Walstan
Waltheof
Walwine
Walwyn
Water
Wattles
Wayland
Wawyn
Werner
Weland
Wig
Wigram

Wilfrith
Wilfroy
Wilkin
Willibald
Winfred
Winfrith

Winibald
Wulfstan
Wystan

Ybel
Ywaine

Zaccheus
Zacharias
Zebulon
Zephaniah
Zerubabel

II. FEMININE

Adelgis
Adelhilda
Adeliz
Adeliza
Adosinda
Aelgifu
Agape
Aglaia
Ala
Alatea
Albina
Albinia
Alida
Amanda
Amata
Amice
Amoret
Anchoret
Arethusa
Ariadne
Armine
Arminel
Astarte
Asteria
Athene
Aveline

Basilia
Bathilda

Bega
Begga
Belphoebe
Benedicta
Bera
Berchta
Berengaria
Beret
Berinthia
Berghild
Berwine
Bertwine
Bibania
Birget
Blancheflour
Boadicea
Brilliona
Britomart
Britomartis
Brunahaut
Brunehilda
Brunilla
Brynhild

Calista
Ceara
Chloris
Chriemhilda
Christophera

Chrysogon
Clairmond
Clarona
Clemency
Clorinda
Clothilda
Clothilde
Clotilda
Columba
Comfort
Corisande
Creirdyddlydd
Custance
Cuthburh
Cwen

Davina
Decima
Dennet
Desdemona
Dionetta
Dionysia
Diot
Dodo
Doralicia
Dowsabel
Dymphna

Eadgith

Edana
Eden
Edaena
Ed(d)eva
Eddid
Edgith
Edgytha
Eglantine
Eglentyne
Elfleda
Eldfrida
Elgiva
Elissa
Ermengard(e)
Ethelburg
Ethelgiva
Ethelwine
Eulalia
Euphame
Eustachia or -cia
Everilda
Eweline

Felicitas
Fidelia
Florentia
Florentina
Fredegonde
Frideswide
Frithswith
Frusannah

Ganivra
Gerda
Gillet
Godiva
Goodeth
Gracilia
Gudrun
Gunilda

Hadassah
Hardwina
Helewise
Hephzibah
Hermine
Hildegarde
Hildegonda
Hildelildis
Hildiridur
Hippolyta
Hodierna
Hosanna
Huldah

Ib
Ibbot(h)
Idonea
Ismay
Ismenia

Jacoba
Jacquenetta
Jacquetta
Jacuita
Jaculin
Jael
Jocosa
Jocunda
Joletta
Juletta
Julitte
Justa

Katren
Katty
Kerenhappuch
Keturah

Laurana
Laurentia
Libby
Linnet
Linot
Lisbet(h)
Luciana
Lucippe

Malkin
Marah
Mariel
Mariamne
Melior, -ra
Milborough
Milburga
Mildgyth
Mildthyrth
Miliora

Nib

Olympius
Oriel
Osyth

Parnel
Parthenope
Perahta
Perchta
Percis
Pernel
Philomena
Prisca

Quenburga

Rhodeia
Rhodocella
Roesia
Rosalba
Rosaura
Roseclear

Sacharissa
Sarai
Saraid
Scholastica
Scientia
Septima
Seraphina
Seraphita
Shireen
Sidonia
Sidony
Sigismunda
Sigrid
Sissot
Sophonisba
Sophronia
Swanhild

Thalia
Theophania
Theophila
Thyra [1]
Tiffany
Tiphania
Tryphosa

Unity
Urania
Ursel

Victriola
Vittoria

Welburgha
Williamina

Yolande

Zenobia
Zilia
Ziliola

[1] *Thyra* has recently (ca. 1940 onwards) been showing signs of a return to grace.